Project Management

FOR

DUMMIES®

3RD EDITION

by Stanley E. Portny

Certified Project Management Professional (PMP)

WILEY

Wiley Publishing, Inc.

Project Management For Dummies®, 3rd Edition

Published by
Wiley Publishing, Inc.
111 River St.
Hoboken, NJ 07030-5774
www.wiley.com

Copyright © 2010 by Wiley Publishing, Inc., Indianapolis, Indiana

Published simultaneously in Canada

Library of Congress Control Number: 2010924586

ISBN: 978-0-470-57452-2

Manufactured in the United States of America

10 9 8 7 6 5 4 3 2 1

About the Author

 **Stan Portny,** president of Stanley E. Portny and Associates, LLC, is an internationally recognized expert in project management and project leadership. During the past 30 years, he's provided training and consultation to more than 150 public and private organizations in consumer products, insurance, pharmaceuticals, finance, information technology, telecommunications, defense, and healthcare. He has developed and conducted training programs for more than 50,000 management and staff personnel in engineering, sales and marketing, research and development, information systems, manufacturing, operations, and support areas.

Stan combines an analyst's eye with an innate sense of order and balance and a deep respect for personal potential. He helps people understand how to control chaotic environments and produce dramatic results while still achieving personal and professional satisfaction. Widely acclaimed for his dynamic presentations and unusual ability to establish a close rapport with seminar participants, Stan specializes in tailoring his training programs to meet the unique needs of individual organizations. His clients have included ADP, ADT, American International Group, Burlington Northern Railroad, Hewlett Packard, Nabisco, Novartis Pharmaceuticals, Pitney Bowes, UPS, Vanguard Investment Companies, and the United States Navy and Air Force.

A Project Management Institute–certified Project Management Professional (PMP), Stan received his bachelor's degree in electrical engineering from the Polytechnic Institute of Brooklyn. He holds a master's degree in electrical engineering and the degree of electrical engineer from the Massachusetts Institute of Technology. Stan has also studied at the Alfred P. Sloan School of Management and the George Washington University National Law Center.

Stan provides on-site training in all aspects of project management, project team building, and project leadership. He can work with you to assess your organization's current project-management practices, develop planning and control systems and procedures, and review the progress of ongoing projects. In addition, Stan can serve as the keynote speaker at your organization's or professional association's meetings.

To discuss this book or understand how Stan can work with you to enhance your organization's project-management skills and practices, please contact him at Stanley E. Portny and Associates, LLC, 20 Helene Drive, Randolph, New Jersey 07869; phone 973-366-8500; e-mail Stan@StanPortny.com; Web site www.StanPortny.com.

DATE DUE

JUN 1 4 2012

Dedication

To my wife, Donna; my son, Brian; and my son and daughter-in-law, Jonathan and Marci. May we continue to share life's joys together.

Author's Acknowledgments

Writing and publishing this book was a team effort, and I would like to thank the many people who helped to make it possible. First, I want to thank Tracy Boggier, my acquisitions editor, who first contacted me to discuss the possibility of my writing this third edition of my book. Thanks to her for making that phone call, for helping me prepare the proposal, for helping to get the project off to a smooth and timely start, for coordinating the publicity and sales, and for helping to bring all the pieces to a successful conclusion.

Thanks to Georgette Beatty, my project editor, and Amanda Langferman, my copy editor, for their guidance, support, and the many hours they spent polishing the text into a smooth, finished product. And thanks to Anita Griner, my technical reviewer, for her many insightful observations and suggestions.

Finally, thanks to my family for their continued help and inspiration. Thanks to Donna, who never doubted that this book would become a reality and who shared personal and stylistic comments as she reviewed the text countless times while always making it seem like she found it enjoyable and enlightening. Thanks to Brian, Jonathan, and Marci, whose interest and excitement helped motivate me to see the third edition of this book through to completion.

Publisher's Acknowledgments

We're proud of this book; please send us your comments at http://dummies.custhelp.com. For other comments, please contact our Customer Care Department within the U.S. at 877-762-2974, outside the U.S. at 317-572-3993, or fax 317-572-4002.

Some of the people who helped bring this book to market include the following:

Acquisitions, Editorial, and Media Development

Senior Project Editor: Georgette Beatty
(*Previous Edition: Chad R. Sievers*)

Acquisitions Editor: Tracy Boggier

Copy Editor: Amanda M. Langferman
(*Previous Edition: Pam Ruble*)

Assistant Editor: Erin Calligan Mooney

Editorial Program Coordinator: Joe Niesen

Technical Editor: Anita E. Griner, MBA, PMP

Editorial Manager: Michelle Hacker

Editorial Assistant: Jennette ElNaggar

Cover Photo: iStock

Cartoons: Rich Tennant
(www.the5thwave.com)

Composition Services

Project Coordinator: Katherine Crocker

Layout and Graphics: Ashley Chamberlain, Samantha K. Cherolis, Joyce Haughey

Proofreaders: John Greenough, Sossity R. Smith

Indexer: Cheryl Duksta

Publishing and Editorial for Consumer Dummies

    Diane Graves Steele, Vice President and Publisher, Consumer Dummies

    Kristin Ferguson-Wagstaffe, Product Development Director, Consumer Dummies

    Ensley Eikenburg, Associate Publisher, Travel

    Kelly Regan, Editorial Director, Travel

Publishing for Technology Dummies

    Andy Cummings, Vice President and Publisher, Dummies Technology/General User

Composition Services

    Debbie Stailey, Director of Composition Services

Contents at a Glance

Table of Contents

Introduction

*P*rojects have been around since ancient times. Noah building the ark, Leonardo da Vinci painting the *Mona Lisa,* Edward Gibbon writing *The Decline and Fall of the Roman Empire,* Jonas Salk developing the polio vaccine — all projects. And, as you know, these were all masterful successes. (Well, the products were a spectacular success, even if schedules and resource budgets were drastically overrun!)

Why, then, is the topic of project management of such great interest today? The answer is simple: The audience has changed and the stakes are higher.

Historically, projects were large, complex undertakings. The first project to use modern project-management techniques — the Polaris weapons system in the early 1950s — was a technical and administrative nightmare. Teams of specialists planned and tracked the myriad of research, development, and production activities. They produced mountains of paper to document the intricate work. As a result, people started to view project management as a highly technical discipline with confusing charts and graphs; they saw it as inordinately time-consuming, specialist-driven, and definitely off-limits for the common man or woman!

Because of the ever-growing array of huge, complex, and technically challenging projects in today's world, people who want to devote their careers to planning and managing them are still vital to their successes. Over the past 25 to 30 years, however, the number of projects in the regular workplace has skyrocketed. Projects of all types and sizes are now *the* way that organizations accomplish their work.

At the same time, a new breed of project manager has emerged. This new breed may not have set career goals to become project managers — many among them don't even consider themselves to be project managers. But they do know they must successfully manage projects to move ahead in their careers. Clearly, project management has become a critical skill, not a career choice.

Even though these people realize they need special tools, techniques, and knowledge to handle their new types of assignments, they may not be able or willing to devote large amounts of time to acquiring them, which is where this book comes in. I devote this book to that silent majority of project managers.

About This Book

This book helps you recognize that the basic tenets of successful project management are simple. The most complex analytical technique takes less than ten minutes to master! In this book, I introduce information that's necessary to plan and manage projects, and I provide important guidelines for developing and using this information. Here, you discover that the real challenge to a successful project is dealing with the multitude of people whom a project may affect or need for support. I present plenty of tips, hints, and guidelines for identifying key players and then involving them.

But knowledge alone won't make you a successful project manager — you need to apply it. This book's theme is that project-management skills and techniques aren't burdensome tasks you perform because some process requires it. Rather, they're a way of thinking, communicating, and behaving. They're an integral part of how we approach all aspects of our work every day.

So I've written the book to be direct and (relatively) easy to understand. But don't be misled — the simple text still navigates all the critical tools and techniques you'll need to support your project planning, scheduling, budgeting, organizing, and controlling. So buckle up!

I present this information in a logical and modular progression. Examples and illustrations are plentiful — so are the tips and hints. And I inject humor from time to time to keep it all doable. My goal is that you finish this book feeling that good project management is a necessity and that you're determined to practice it!

Conventions Used in This Book

To help you navigate through this book, I use the following conventions to help you find your way:

- ✔ I use *italics* to point out new words and to alert you to their definitions, which are always close by. On occasion, I also use italics for added emphasis.

- ✔ I use **bold** text to indicate keywords in bulleted lists or to highlight action parts in numbered lists.

- ✔ I put all Web sites in `monofont`.

When this book was printed, some Web addresses may have needed to break across two lines of text. If that happened, rest assured that I haven't put in any extra characters (such as hyphens) to indicate the break. So, when using one of these Web addresses, just type in exactly what you see in this book, pretending as though the line break doesn't exist.

What You're Not to Read

Of course, I want you to read every single word, but I understand your life is busy and you may have time to read only what's relevant to your experience. In that case, feel free to skip the sidebars. Although the sidebars offer interesting and real-life stories of my own experiences, they're not vital to grasping the concepts.

Foolish Assumptions

When writing this book, I assumed that a widely diverse group of people will read it, including the following:

- Senior managers and junior assistants (tomorrow's senior managers)
- Experienced project managers and people who've never been on a project team
- People who've had significant project-management training and people who've had none
- People who've had years of real-world business and government experience and people who've just entered the workforce

I assume that you have a desire to take control of your environment. After reading this book, I hope you wonder (and rightfully so) why all projects aren't well managed — because you'll think these techniques are so logical, straightforward, and easy to use. But I also assume you recognize there's a big difference between *knowing* what to do and *doing* it. And I assume you realize you'll have to work hard to overcome the forces that conspire to prevent you from using these tools and techniques.

Finally, I assume you'll realize that you can read this book repeatedly and learn something new and different each time. Think of this book as a comfortable resource that has more to share as you experience new situations.

How This Book Is Organized

Each chapter is self-contained, so you can read the chapters that interest you the most first — without feeling lost because you haven't read the book from front to back. The book is divided into the following six parts.

Part I: Understanding Expectations (The Who, What, and Why of Your Project)

In this part, I discuss the unique characteristics of projects and the key issues you may encounter in a project-oriented organization. I also show you how to clearly define your project's proposed results, how to identify the people who will play a role, and how to determine your project's work.

Part II: Planning Time: Determining When and How Much

In this part, I cover how to develop the project schedule and estimate the resources (both personnel and nonpersonnel) you need. I also show you how to identify and manage project risks.

Part III: Group Work: Putting Your Team Together

In this part, I show you how to identify, organize, and deal with people who play a part in your project's success. I explain how to define team members' roles and get your project off to a positive start.

Part IV: Steering the Ship: Managing Your Project to Success

In this part, I explain how to monitor, track, analyze, and report on your project's activities. I also show you how to establish and maintain effective communications between you and all your project audiences and how to demonstrate leadership that energizes your project team. Then I discuss how to bring your project to a successful closure.

Part V: Taking Your Project Management to the Next Level

Here, I discuss how to use available technology to help you plan, organize, and control your project. I also discuss a technique for evaluating activity performance and resource expenditures on larger projects.

Part VI: The Part of Tens

Every *For Dummies* book has this fun part that gives you tidbits of information in an easy-to-chew format. In this part, I share tips on how to plan a project and how to be a better project manager. I also include one additional nugget of information: The appendix illustrates systematic processes for planning your project and for using the essential controls that I discuss throughout this book.

Icons Used in This Book

I include small icons in the left margins of the book to alert you to special information in the text. Here's what they mean:

This icon leads into hypothetical situations illustrating techniques and issues.

I use this icon to point out terms or issues that are a bit more technical.

I use this icon to point out important information you want to keep in mind as you apply the techniques and approaches.

This icon highlights techniques or approaches you can use to improve your project-management practices.

This icon highlights potential pitfalls and danger spots.

Where to Go from Here

You can read this book in many ways, depending on your own project-management knowledge and experience and your current needs. However, I suggest you first take a minute to scan the table of contents and thumb through the sections of the book to get a feeling for the topics I address.

If you're new to project management and are just beginning to form a plan for a project, first read Parts I and II, which explain how to plan outcomes, activities, schedules, and resources. If you want to find out how to identify and organize your project's team and other key people, start with Chapter 4 and Part III. If you're ready to begin work or you're already in the midst of your project, you may want to start with Part IV. Or, feel free to jump back and forth, hitting the chapters with topics that interest you the most.

The most widely recognized reference of project-management best practices is *A Guide to the Project Management Body of Knowledge* (*PMBOK*), published by the Project Management Institute (PMI). The fourth and most recent edition of *PMBOK* (*PMBOK 4*) was published in 2008. The Project Management Professional (PMP) certification — the most recognized project-management credential throughout the world — includes an examination (administered by PMI) with questions based on *PMBOK 4*.

Because I base my book on best practices for project-management activities, the tools and techniques I offer are in accordance with *PMBOK 4*. However, if you're preparing to take the PMP examination, use my book as a companion to *PMBOK 4*, not as a substitute for it.

As you read this book, keep the following points in mind:

- ✔ *PMBOK 4* identifies *what* best practices are but doesn't address in detail *how* to perform them or deal with difficulties you may encounter as you try to perform them. In contrast, my book focuses heavily on *how* to perform the project-management techniques and processes.

- ✔ I've revised and updated my book so that all the tools and techniques discussed and all the terminology used to describe those tools and techniques are in agreement with those used in *PMBOK 4*.

- ✔ Where appropriate, I include a section at the end of each chapter that specifies where the topics in the chapter are addressed in *PMBOK 4*.

- ✔ *PMBOK 4* often contains highly technical language and detailed processes, which people mistakenly dismiss as being relevant only for larger projects. My book, however, deliberately frames terms and discussions to be user-friendly. As a result, people who work on projects of all sizes can understand how to apply the tools and techniques presented.

No matter how you make your way through this book, plan on reading all the chapters more than once — the more you read a chapter, the more sense its approaches and techniques will make. And who knows? A change in your job responsibilities may create a need for certain techniques you've never used before. Have fun and good luck!

Part I

Understanding Expectations (The Who, What, and Why of Your Project)

The 5th Wave   By Rich Tennant

"Hey! Who's project managing this?"

In this part . . .

The most difficult part of a new project is often deciding where to begin. Expectations are high, while time and resources are frequently low.

In this part, I identify how a project differs from other activities you perform in your organization, and I present a snapshot of the steps you need to take to plan, organize, and control your project. I offer you specific techniques and approaches to define clearly what you want your project to accomplish and who needs to be involved. Finally, I show you how to determine the work you have to do to meet the expectations for your project.

Chapter 1

Project Management: The Key to Achieving Results

Successful organizations create projects that produce desired results in established time frames with assigned resources. As a result, businesses are increasingly driven to find individuals who can excel in this project-oriented environment.

Because you're reading this book, chances are good that you've been asked to manage a project. So, hang on tight — you're going to need a new set of skills and techniques to steer that project to successful completion. But not to worry! This chapter gets you off to a smooth start by showing you what projects and project management really are and by helping you separate projects from nonproject assignments. This chapter also offers the rationale for why projects succeed or fail and gets you into the project-management mindset.

Determining What Makes a Project a Project

No matter what your job is, you handle a myriad of assignments every day: prepare a memo, hold a meeting, design a sales campaign, or move to new offices. Or maybe your day sounds more like this: make the information systems more user-friendly, develop a research compound in the laboratory, or improve the organization's public image. Not all these assignments are projects. How can you tell which ones are and which ones aren't? This section is here to help.

Understanding the three main components that define a project

A *project* is a temporary undertaking performed to produce a unique product, service, or result. Large or small, a project always has the following three components:

- ✔ **Specific scope:** Desired results or products (Check out Chapter 2 for more on describing desired results.)
- ✔ **Schedule:** Established dates when project work starts and ends (See Chapter 5 for how to develop responsive and feasible project schedules.)
- ✔ **Required resources:** Necessary amounts of people, funds, and other resources (See Chapter 6 for how to establish whom you need for your project and Chapter 7 for how to set up your budget and determine any other resources needs.)

As illustrated in Figure 1-1, each component affects the other two. For example: Expanding the type and characteristics of desired outcomes may require more time (a later end date) or more resources. Moving up the end date may necessitate paring down the results or increasing project expenditures (for instance, by paying overtime to project staff). Within this three-part project definition, you perform work to achieve your desired results.

Figure 1-1: The relationship between the three main components of a project.

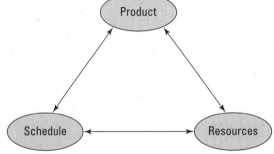

Although many other considerations may affect a project's performance (see the discussions in the "Defining Project Management" section later in this chapter for more), these three components are the basis of a project's definition for the following three reasons:

- ✔ The only reason a project exists is to produce the results specified in its scope.

- ✔ The project's end date is an essential part of defining what constitutes successful performance — the desired result must be provided by a certain time to meet its intended need.

- ✔ The availability of resources shapes the nature of the products the project can produce.

A Guide to the Project Management Body of Knowledge, 4th Edition (*PMBOK 4*), elaborates on these components by

- ✔ Emphasizing that *product* includes the basic nature of what is to be produced (for example, a new training program or a new prescription drug), as well as its required characteristics (for example, the topics that the training program must address), which are defined as its *quality*

- ✔ Noting that *resources* refers to funds, as well as to other, nonmonetary resources, such as people, equipment, raw materials, and facilities

PMBOK 4 also emphasizes that *risk* (the likelihood that not everything will go exactly according to plan) is an important consideration when defining a project and that guiding a project to success involves continually managing tradeoffs among all these factors.

Recognizing the diversity of projects

Projects come in a wide assortment of shapes and sizes. For example, projects can

- ✔ **Be large or small**

    - Installing a new subway system, which may cost more than $1 billion and take 10 to 15 years to complete, is a project.

    - Preparing an ad hoc report of monthly sales figures, which may take you one day to complete, is also a project.

- ✔ **Involve many people or just you**

    - Training all 10,000 of your organization's staff in a new affirmative-action policy is a project.

    - Rearranging the furniture and equipment in your office is also a project.

✓ **Be defined by a legal contract or by an informal agreement**

- A signed contract between you and a customer that requires you to build a house defines a project.

- An informal promise you make to install a new software package on your colleague's computer also defines a project.

✓ **Be business-related or personal**

- Conducting your organization's annual blood drive is a project.

- Having a dinner party for 15 people is also a project.

No matter what the individual characteristics of your project are, you define it by the same three components I describe in the previous section: results (or scope), start and end dates, and resources. The information you need to plan and manage your project is the same for any project you manage, although the ease and the time to develop it may differ. The more thoroughly you plan and manage your projects, the more likely you are to succeed.

Describing the four stages of a project

Every project, whether large or small, passes through the following four stages:

✓ **Starting the project:** This stage involves generating, evaluating, and framing the business need for the project and the general approach to performing it and agreeing to prepare a detailed project plan. Outputs from this stage may include approval to proceed to the next stage, documentation of the need for the project and rough estimates of time and resources to perform it (often included in a project charter), and an initial list of people who may be interested in, involved with, or affected by the project.

✓ **Organizing and preparing:** This stage involves developing a plan that specifies the desired results; the work to do; the time, the cost, and other resources required; and a plan for how to address key project risks. Outputs from this stage may include a project plan documenting the intended project results and the time, resources, and supporting processes to help create them.

✓ **Carrying out the work:** This stage involves establishing the project team and the project support systems, performing the planned work, and monitoring and controlling performance to ensure adherence to the current plan. Outputs from this stage may include project results, project progress reports, and other communications.

✓ **Closing the project:** This stage involves assessing the project results, obtaining customer approvals, transitioning project team members to new assignments, closing financial accounts, and conducting a post-project evaluation. Outputs from this stage may include final, accepted and approved project results and recommendations and suggestions for applying lessons learned from this project to similar efforts in the future.

A project by any other name — just isn't a project

People often confuse the following two terms with *project:*

✔ **Process:** A *process* is a series of routine steps to perform a particular function, such as a procurement process or a budget process. A process isn't a one-time activity that achieves a specific result; instead, it defines *how* a particular function is to be done every time. Processes like the activities that go into buying materials are often parts of projects.

✔ **Program:** This term can describe two different situations. First, a *program* can be a set of goals that gives rise to specific projects, but, unlike a project, a program can never be completely accomplished. For example, a health-awareness program can never completely achieve its goal (the public will never be totally aware of all health issues as a result of a health-awareness program), but one or more projects may accomplish specific results related to the program's goal (such as a workshop on minimizing the risk of heart disease). Second, a program sometimes refers to a group of specified projects that achieve a common goal.

For small projects, this entire life cycle can take a few days. For larger projects, it can take many years! In fact, to allow for greater focus on key aspects and to make it easier to monitor and control the work, project managers often subdivide larger projects into separate phases, each of which is treated as a mini-project and passes through these four life cycle stages. No matter how simple or complex the project is, however, these four stages are the same.

In a perfect world, you complete one stage of your project before you move on to the next one; and after you complete a stage, you never return to it again. But the world isn't perfect, and project success often requires a flexible approach that responds to real situations that you may face, such as the following:

✔ **You may have to work on two (or more) project stages at the same time to meet tight deadlines.** Working on the next stage before you complete the current one increases the risk that you may have to redo tasks, which may cause you to miss deadlines and spend more resources than you originally planned. If you choose this strategy, be sure people understand the potential risks and costs associated with it (see Chapter 8 for how to assess and manage risks).

✔ **Sometimes you learn by doing.** Despite doing your best to assess feasibility and develop detailed plans, you may realize you can't achieve what you thought you could. When this situation happens, you need to return to the earlier project stages and rethink them in light of the new information you've acquired.

✔ **Sometimes things change unexpectedly.** Your initial feasibility and benefits assessments are sound and your plan is detailed and realistic. However, certain key project team members leave the organization without warning during the project. Or a new technology emerges, and it's more appropriate to use than the one in your original plans. Because ignoring these occurrences may seriously jeopardize your project's success, you need to return to the earlier project stages and rethink them in light of these new realities.

Defining Project Management

Project management is the process of guiding a project from its beginning through its performance to its closure. Project management includes five sets of processes, which I describe in more detail in the following sections:

✔ **Initiating processes:** Clarifying the business need, defining high-level expectations and resource budgets, and beginning to identify audiences that may play a role in your project

✔ **Planning processes:** Detailing the project scope, time frames, resources, and risks, as well as intended approaches to project communications, quality, and management of external purchases of goods and services

✔ **Executing processes:** Establishing and managing the project team, communicating with and managing project audiences, and implementing the project plans

✔ **Monitoring and controlling processes:** Tracking performance and taking actions necessary to help ensure project plans are successfully implemented and the desired results are achieved

✔ **Closing processes:** Ending all project activity

As illustrated in Figure 1-2, these five process groups help support the project through the four stages of its life cycle. Initiating processes support the work to be done when starting the project, and planning processes support the organizing and preparing stage. Executing processes guide the project tasks performed when carrying out the work, and closing processes are used to perform the tasks that bring the project to an end. The figure highlights how you may cycle back from executing processes to planning processes when you have to return to the organizing and preparing stage to modify existing plans to address problems you encounter or new information you acquire while carrying out the project work. Finally, monitoring and controlling processes are used in each of the four stages to help ensure that work is being performed according to plans.

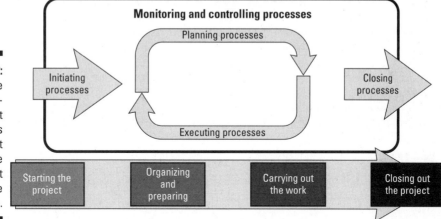

Figure 1-2:
The five project-management process groups that support the four project life cycle stages.

Successfully performing these processes requires the following:

- **Information:** Accurate, timely, and complete data for the planning, performance monitoring, and final assessment of the project
- **Communication:** Clear, open, and timely sharing of information with appropriate individuals and groups throughout the project's duration
- **Commitment:** Team members' personal promises to produce the agreed-upon results on time and within budget

Examining the initiating processes

All projects begin with an idea. Perhaps your organization's client identifies a need; or maybe your boss thinks of a new market to explore; or maybe you think of a way to refine your organization's procurement process.

Sometimes the initiating process is informal. For a small project, it may consist of just a discussion and a verbal agreement. In other instances, especially for larger projects, a project requires a formal review and decision by your boss and/or other members of your organization's senior management team.

Decision makers consider the following two questions when deciding whether to move ahead with a project:

- ***Should* we do it?** Are the benefits we expect to achieve worth the costs we'll have to pay? Are there better ways to approach the issue?
- ***Can* we do it?** Is the project technically feasible? Are the required resources available?

If the answer to both questions is "Yes," the project can proceed to the organizing and preparing stage (see the following section), during which a project plan is developed. If the answer to either question is a definite, iron-clad "No," under no circumstances should the project go any further. If nothing can be done to make it desirable and feasible, the decision makers should cancel the project immediately. Doing anything else guarantees wasted resources, lost opportunities, and a frustrated staff. (Check out the later sidebar "Performing a benefit-cost analysis" if you need extra help determining the answer to the first question.)

Suppose you're in charge of the publications department in your organization. You've just received a request to have a 20,000-page document printed in ten minutes, which requires equipment that can reproduce at the rate of 2,000 pages per minute.

You check with your staff and confirm that your document-reproducing equipment has a top speed of 500 pages per minute. You check with your suppliers and find out that the fastest document-reproducing equipment available today has a top speed of 1,000 pages per minute. Do you agree to plan and perform this project when you know you can't possibly meet the request? Of course not.

Rather than promising something you know you can't achieve, consider asking your customer whether she can change the request. For example, can she accept the document in 20 minutes? Can you reproduce certain parts of the document in the first ten minutes and the rest later?

During some projects, you may be convinced that you can't meet a particular request or that the benefits of the project aren't worth the costs involved. Be sure to check with the people who developed or approved the project. They may have information you don't, or you may have additional information that they weren't aware of when they approved the request.

Performing a benefit-cost analysis

A *benefit-cost analysis* is a comparative assessment of all the benefits you anticipate from your project and all the costs to introduce the project, perform it, and support the changes resulting from it. Benefit-cost analyses help you to

✔ Decide whether to undertake a project or decide which of several projects to undertake.

✔ Frame appropriate project objectives.

✔ Develop appropriate *before* and *after* measures of project success.

✔ Prepare estimates of the resources required to perform the project work.

You can express some anticipated benefits in monetary equivalents (such as reduced operating costs or increased revenue). For other benefits, numerical measures can approximate some, but not all, aspects. If your project is to improve staff morale, for example, you may consider associated benefits to include reduced turnover, increased productivity, fewer absences, and fewer formal grievances. Whenever possible, express benefits and costs in monetary terms to facilitate the assessment of a project's net value.

Consider costs for all phases of the project. Such costs may be nonrecurring (such as labor, capital investment, and certain operations and services) or recurring (such as changes in personnel, supplies, and materials or maintenance and repair). In addition, consider the following:

✔ Potential costs of not doing the project

✔ Potential costs if the project fails

✔ Opportunity costs (in other words, the potential benefits if you had spent your funds successfully performing a different project)

The farther into the future you look when performing your analysis, the more important it is to convert your estimates of benefits over costs into today's dollars. Unfortunately, the farther you look, the less confident you can be of your estimates. For example, you may expect to reap benefits for years from a new computer system, but changing technology may make your new system obsolete after only one year.

Thus, the following two key factors influence the results of a benefit-cost analysis:

✔ How far into the future you look to identify benefits

✔ On which assumptions you base your analysis

Although you may not want to go out and design a benefit-cost analysis by yourself, you definitely want to see whether your project already has one and, if it does, what the specific results of that analysis were.

The excess of a project's expected benefits over its estimated costs in today's dollars is its *net present value (NPV)*. The net present value is based on the following two premises:

✔ **Inflation:** The purchasing power of a dollar will be less one year from now than it is today. If the rate of inflation is 3 percent for the next 12 months, $1 today will be worth $0.97 12 months from today. In other words, 12 months from now, you'll pay $1 to buy what you paid $0.97 for today.

✔ **Lost return on investment:** If you spend money to perform the project being considered, you'll forego the future income you could earn by investing it conservatively today. For example, if you put $1 in a bank and receive simple interest at the rate of 3 percent compounded annually, 12 months from today you'll have $1.03 (assuming zero-percent inflation).

To address these considerations when determining the NPV, you specify the following numbers:

✔ **Discount rate:** The factor that reflects the future value of $1 in today's dollars, considering the effects of both inflation and lost return on investment

✔ **Allowable payback period:** The length of time for anticipated benefits and estimated costs

In addition to determining the NPV for different discount rates and payback periods, figure the project's *internal rate of return* (the value of discount rate that would yield an NPV of zero) for each payback period.

Beware of assumptions that you or other people make when assessing your project's potential value, cost, and feasibility. For example, just because your requests for overtime have been turned down in the past doesn't guarantee they'll be turned down again this time.

Considering the planning processes

When you know what you hope to accomplish and you believe it's possible, you need a detailed plan that describes how you and your team will make it happen. Include the following in your project-management plan:

- An overview of the reasons for your project (Chapter 2 tells you what to include.)

- A detailed description of intended results (Chapter 2 explains how to describe desired results.)

- A list of all constraints the project must address (Chapter 2 explores the different types of constraints a project may face.)

- A list of all assumptions related to the project (Chapter 2 discusses how to frame assumptions.)

- A list of all required work (Chapter 4 discusses how to identify all required project work.)

- A breakdown of the roles you and your team members will play (Chapter 10 explains how to describe roles and responsibilities.)

- A detailed project schedule (Chapter 5 explains how to develop your schedule.)

- Needs for personnel, funds, and nonpersonnel resources (such as equipment, facilities, and information) (Chapter 6 illustrates how to estimate resource personnel needs, and Chapter 7 takes a close look at estimating nonpersonnel needs and developing your project's budget.)

- A description of how you plan to manage any significant risks and uncertainties (Chapter 8 explains how to identify and plan for risks.)

- Plans for project communications (Chapter 13 discusses how to keep everyone who's involved in your project up-to-date.)

- Plans for ensuring project quality (Chapter 12 covers how to track progress and maintain control of your project throughout its life cycle so as to achieve success.)

Always put your project plans in writing; doing so helps you clarify details and reduces the chances that you'll forget something. Plans for large projects can take hundreds of pages, but a plan for a small project can take only a few lines on a piece of paper (or a tablecloth!).

The success of your project depends on the clarity and accuracy of your plan and on whether people believe they can achieve it. Considering past experience in your project plan makes your plan more realistic; involving people in the plan's development encourages their commitment to achieving it.

Often the pressure to get fast results encourages people to skip the planning and get right to the tasks. Although this strategy can create a lot of immediate activity, it also creates significant chances for waste and mistakes.

Be sure your project's drivers and supporters review and approve the plan in writing before you begin your project (see Chapter 3). For a small project, you may need only a brief e-mail or someone's initials on the plans. For a larger project, though, you may need a formal review and signoff by one or more levels of your organization's management.

Examining the executing processes

After you've developed your project-management plan and set your appropriate project baselines, it's time to get to work and start executing your plan. This is often the phase when management gets more engaged and excited to see things being produced.

Preparing

Preparing to begin the project work involves the following tasks (see Chapter 11 for details):

- **Assigning people to all project roles:** Confirm the individuals who'll perform the project work, and negotiate agreements with them and their managers to assure they'll be available to work on the project team.

- **Introducing team members to each other and to the project:** Help people begin developing interpersonal relationships with each other. Help them appreciate the overall purpose of the project and how the different parts will interact and support each other.

- **Giving and explaining tasks to all team members:** Describe to all team members what work they're responsible for producing and how the team members will coordinate their efforts.

- **Defining how the team will perform its essential functions:** Decide how the team will handle routine communications, make different project decisions, and resolve conflicts. Develop any procedures that may be required to guide performance of these functions.

- **Setting up necessary tracking systems:** Decide which system(s) and accounts you'll use to track schedules, work effort, and expenditures, and set them up.

✔ **Announcing the project to the organization:** Let the project audiences know that your project exists, what it will produce, and when it will begin and end.

Suppose you don't join your project team until the actual work is getting underway. Your first task is to understand how people decided initially that the project was possible and desirable. If the people who participated in the start of the project and the organizing and preparing stages overlooked important issues, you need to raise them now. When searching for the project's history, check minutes from meetings, memos, letters, e-mails, and technical reports. Then consult with all the people involved in the initial project decisions.

Performing

Finally, you get to perform the project work! The performing subgroup of the executing processes includes the following tasks (see Chapters 13 and 14 for more details):

✔ **Doing the tasks:** Perform the work that's in your plan.

✔ **Assuring quality:** Continually confirm that work and results conform to requirements and applicable standards and guidelines.

✔ **Managing the team:** Assign tasks, review results, and resolve problems.

✔ **Developing the team:** Provide needed training and mentoring to improve team members' skills.

✔ **Sharing information:** Distribute information to appropriate project audiences.

Examining the monitoring and controlling processes

As the project progresses, you need to ensure that plans are being followed and desired results are being achieved. The monitoring and controlling processes include the following tasks (see Chapter 12 for specific activities):

✔ **Comparing performance with plans:** Collect information on outcomes, schedule achievements, and resource expenditures; identify deviations from your plan; and develop corrective actions.

✔ **Fixing problems that arise:** Change tasks, schedules, or resources to bring project performance back on track with the existing plan, or negotiate agreed-upon changes to the plan itself.

✔ **Keeping everyone informed:** Tell project audiences about the team's achievements, project problems, and necessary revisions to the established plan.

Acknowledging the closing processes

Finishing your assigned tasks is only part of bringing your project to a close. In addition, you must do the following (see Chapter 15 for a discussion of each of these points):

- ✔ Get your clients' approvals of the final results.

- ✔ Close all project accounts (if you've been charging time and money to special project accounts).

- ✔ Help team members move on to their next assignments.

- ✔ Hold a post-project evaluation with the project team to recognize project achievements and to discuss lessons you can apply to the next project. (At the very least, make informal notes about these lessons and how you'll use them in the future.)

Knowing the Project Manager's Role

The project manager's job is challenging. For instance, she often coordinates technically specialized professionals — who may have limited experience working together — to achieve a common goal. Although the project manager's own work experience is often technical in nature, her success requires a keen ability to identify and resolve sensitive organizational and interpersonal issues. In this section, I describe the main tasks that a project manager handles and note potential challenges she may encounter.

Looking at the project manager's tasks

Historically, the performance rules in traditional organizations were simple: Your boss made assignments; you carried them out. Questioning your assignments was a sign of insubordination or incompetence.

But these rules have changed. Today your boss may generate ideas, but you assess how to implement them. You confirm that a project meets your boss's (and your organization's) real need and then determine the work, schedules, and resources you require to implement it.

Handling a project any other way simply doesn't make sense. The project manager must be involved in developing the plans because she needs the opportunity to clarify expectations and proposed approaches and then to raise any questions she may have *before* the project work begins.

The key to project success is being proactive. Instead of waiting for others to tell you what to do,

✔ Seek out information because you know you need it.

✔ Follow the plan because you believe it's the best way.

✔ Involve people whom you know are important for the project.

✔ Raise issues and risks, analyze them, and elicit support to address them.

✔ Share information with the people you know need to have it.

✔ Put all important information in writing.

✔ Ask questions and encourage other people to do the same.

✔ Commit to your project's success.

Staving off potential excuses for not following a structured project-management approach

Be prepared for other people to fight your attempts to use proven project-management approaches. And trust me: You need to be prepared for everything! The following list provides a few examples of excuses you may encounter as a project manager and the appropriate responses you can give.

✔ **Excuse:** Our projects are all crises; we have no time to plan.

Response: Unfortunately for the excuse giver, this logic is illogical! In a crisis, you have limited time and resources to address the critical issues, and you definitely can't afford to make mistakes. Because acting under pressure and emotion (the two characteristics of crises) practically guarantees that mistakes will occur, you can't afford not to plan.

✔ **Excuse:** Structured project management is only for large projects.

Response: No matter what size the project is, the information you need to perform it is the same. What do you need to produce? What work has to be done? Who's going to do it? When will it end? Have you met expectations?

Large projects may require many weeks or months to develop satisfactory answers to these questions. Small projects that last a few days or less may take only 15 minutes, but, either way, you still have to answer the questions.

✔ **Excuse:** These projects require creativity and new development. They can't be predicted with any certainty.

Response: Some projects are more predictable than others. However, people awaiting the outcomes of any project still have expectations for what they'll get and when. Therefore, a project with many uncertainties needs a manager to develop and share initial plans and then to assess and communicate the effects of unexpected occurrences.

Even if you don't encounter these specific excuses, you can adapt these response examples to address your own situations.

Avoiding "shortcuts"

The short-term pressures of your job as a project manager may encourage you to act today in ways that cause you, your team, or your organization to pay a price tomorrow. Especially with smaller, less formal projects, you may feel no need for organized planning and control.

Don't be seduced into the following, seemingly easier shortcuts:

- **Jumping directly from starting the project to carrying out the work:** You have an idea and your project's on a short schedule. Why not just start doing the work? Sounds good, but you haven't defined the work to be done!

  Other variations on this shortcut include the following:

  - **"This project's been done many times before, so why do I have to plan it out again?"** Even though projects can be similar to past ones, some elements are always different. Perhaps you're working with some new people, using a new piece of equipment, and so on. Take a moment now to be sure your plan addresses the current situation.

  - **"Our project's different than it was before, so what good is trying to plan?"** Taking this attitude is like saying you're traveling in an unknown area, so why try to lay out your route on a road map? Planning for a new project is important because no one's taken this particular path before. Although your initial plan may have to be revised during the project, you and your team need to have a clear statement of your intended plan from the outset.

- **Failing to prepare in your carrying out the work stage:** Time pressure is often the apparent justification for this shortcut. However, the real reason is that people don't appreciate the need to define procedures and relationships before jumping into the actual project work. See Chapter 11 for a discussion of why this preparation step is so important — and get tips on how to complete it.

- **Jumping right into the work when you join the project in the carrying out the work stage:** The plan has already been developed, so why go back and revisit the starting the project and the organizing and preparing stages? Actually, you need to do so for two reasons:

  - To identify any issues that the developers may have overlooked

  - To understand the reasoning behind the plan and decide whether you feel the plan is achievable

- **Only partially completing the closing stage:** At the end of one project, you often move right on to the next. Scarce resources and short deadlines encourage this rapid movement, and starting a new project is always more challenging than wrapping up an old one.

However, you never really know how successful your project is if you don't take the time to ensure that all tasks are complete and that you've satisfied your clients. If you don't take positive steps to apply the lessons this project has taught you, you're likely to make the same mistakes you made in this project again or fail to repeat this project's successful approaches.

Staying aware of other potential challenges

Projects are temporary; they're created to achieve particular results. Ideally, when the results are achieved, the project ends. Unfortunately, this transitory nature of projects may create some project-management challenges, including the following:

✔ **Additional assignments:** People may be asked to accept an assignment to a new project in addition to — not in lieu of — existing assignments. And they may not be asked how the new work may affect their existing projects. (Higher management may just assume the project manager can handle everything.) When conflicts arise over a person's time, the organization may not have adequate guidelines or procedures to resolve those conflicts (or they may not have any guidelines at all).

✔ **New people on new teams:** People who haven't worked together before and who may not even know each other may be assigned to the same project team. This lack of familiarity with each other may slow the project down because team members may

- Have different operating and communicating styles

- Use different procedures for performing the same type of activity

- Not have the time to develop mutual respect and trust

Flip to Part III for guidance on how to put together a successful team and get off on the right foot.

✔ **No direct authority:** For most projects, the project manager and team members have no direct authority over each other. Therefore, the rewards that usually encourage top performance (such as salary increases, superior performance appraisals, and job promotions) aren't available. In addition, conflicts over time commitments or technical direction may require input from a number of sources. As a result, they can't be settled with one, unilateral decision. (See Chapter 10 for suggestions on how to work effectively with people when you have no direct authority over them.)

Do You Have What It Takes to Be an Effective Project Manager?

You're reading this book because you want to be a better project manager, right? Well, before you really jump in, I suggest you do a quick self-evaluation to see what your strengths and weaknesses are. By answering the following ten questions, you can get an idea of what subjects you need to spend more time on so you can be as effective as possible. Good luck!

Questions

1. Are you more concerned about being everyone's friend or getting a job done right?

2. Do you prefer to do technical work or manage other people doing technical work?

3. Do you think the best way to get a tough task done is to do it yourself?

4. Do you prefer your work to be predictable or constantly changing?

5. Do you prefer to spend your time developing ideas instead of explaining those ideas to other people?

6. Do you handle crises well?

7. Do you prefer to work by yourself or with others?

8. Do you think you shouldn't have to monitor people after they've promised to do a task for you?

9. Do you believe people should be self-motivated to perform their jobs?

10. Are you comfortable dealing with people at all organizational levels?

Answers

1. Although maintaining good working relations is important, the project manager often must make decisions for the good of the project that some people don't agree with.

2. Most project managers achieve their positions because of their strong performance on technical tasks. However, after you become a project manager, your job is to encourage other people to produce high-quality technical work rather than to do it all yourself.

3. Believing in yourself is important. However, the project manager's task is to help other people develop to the point where they can perform tasks with the highest quality.

4. The project manager tries to minimize unexpected problems and situations through responsive planning and timely control. However, when problems do occur, the project manager must deal with them promptly to minimize their impact on the project.

5. Though coming up with ideas can help your project, the project manager's main responsibility is to ensure that every team member correctly understands all ideas that are developed.

6. The project manager's job is to provide a cool head to size up the situation, choose the best action, and encourage all members to do their parts in implementing the solution.

7. Self-reliance and self-motivation are important characteristics for a project manager. However, the key to any project manager's success is to facilitate interaction among a diverse group of technical specialists.

8. Although you may feel that honoring one's commitments is a fundamental element of professional behavior, the project manager needs both to ensure that people maintain their focus and to model how to work with others cooperatively.

9. People should be self-motivated, but the project manager has to encourage them to remain motivated by their job assignments and related opportunities.

10. The project manager deals with people at all levels — from upper management to support staff — who perform project-related activities.

Check out the table of contents to find out where I discuss these different aspects of the project manager's job in more depth.

Relating This Chapter to the PMP Exam and PMBOK 4

Pay special attention to Table 1-1, which notes topics in this chapter that may be addressed on the Project Management Professional (PMP) certification exam and that are included in *A Guide to the Project Management Body of Knowledge,* 4th Edition (*PMBOK 4*).

Table 1-1	Chapter 1 Topics in Relation to the PMP Exam and *PMBOK 4*	
Topic	*Location in PMBOK 4*	*Comments*
Definition of a project (see the section "Determining What Makes a Project a Project")	1.2. What is a Project?	The two definitions are essentially the same.
The stages in a project's life cycle (see the section "Describing the four stages of a project")	2.1.1. Characteristics of the Project Life Cycle	The two sets of four project life cycle stages are the same.
Definition of project management (see the section "Defining Project Management")	1.3. What is Project Management?	The two definitions are the same.
The five project-management process groups (see the section "Defining Project Management")	1.3. What is Project Management?	The two sets of five process groups are the same.
The initiating processes (see the section "Examining the initiating processes")	3.3. Initiating Process Group	The processes listed in both sources are essentially the same.
The planning processes (see the section "Considering the planning processes")	3.4. Planning Process Group	The processes listed in both sources are essentially the same.
The executing processes (see the section "Examining the executing processes")	3.5. Executing Process Group	The processes listed in both sources are essentially the same.
The monitoring and controlling processes (see the section "Examining the monitoring and controlling processes")	3.6. Monitoring and Controlling Process Group	The processes listed in both sources are essentially the same.
The closing processes (see the section "Acknowledging the closing processes")	3.7. Closing Process Group	The processes listed in both sources are essentially the same.
The project manager's role (see the section "Knowing the project manager's role")	1.6. Role of a Project Manager	The listings of roles in the two sources are essentially the same.

Chapter 2

Clarifying What You're Trying to Accomplish — and Why

In This Chapter

▶ Understanding your project's Scope Statement

▶ Figuring out how your project fits into the big picture

▶ Identifying project constraints — and working with them

▶ Handling the unknowns of project planning

*A*ll projects are created for a reason — someone identifies a need and devises a project to address that need. How well the project ultimately addresses that need defines the project's success or failure.

This chapter helps you develop a mutual agreement between the project's requesters and the project team about your project's goals and expectations. It also helps you establish the conditions necessary to perform the project work.

Defining Your Project with a Scope Statement

A *Scope Statement* is a written confirmation of the results your project will produce and the terms and conditions under which you'll perform your work. Both the people who requested the project and the project team should agree to all terms in the Scope Statement before actual project work begins.

Your Scope Statement should include the following information:

✔ **Justification:** How and why your project came to be, the business need(s) it addresses, the scope of work to be performed, and how it will affect and be affected by other related activities

✔ **Objectives:** The products, services, and/or results your project will produce (also referred to as *deliverables*)

✔ **Product scope description:** The features and functions of the products, services, and/or results your project will produce

✔ **Product acceptance criteria**: The process and criteria for accepting completed products, services, or results

✔ **Constraints:** Restrictions that limit what you can achieve, how and when you can achieve it, and how much achieving it can cost

✔ **Assumptions:** Statements about how you will address uncertain information as you conceive, plan, and perform your project

Think of your Scope Statement, when viewed together with the other components of your project plan, as a binding agreement in which

✔ You and your team commit to producing certain results.

Your project's requesters commit that they'll consider your project 100 percent successful if you produce these results.

✔ You and your team identify all restrictions regarding your approach to the work and what you need to support your work.

Your project's requesters agree that there are no restrictions other than the ones you've identified and that they'll provide you the support you declare you need.

✔ You and your team identify all assumptions you made when agreeing to the terms of your Scope Statement.

Your project's requesters agree that, if any of these assumptions prove to be invalid, you may have to modify some or all of your project plans.

Of course, predicting the future is impossible. In fact, the farther into the future you try to look, the less certain your predictions can be. However, your Scope Statement represents your project commitments based on what you know today and expect to be true in the future. If and when situations change, you have to assess the effect of the changes on all aspects of your project and propose the necessary changes to your Scope Statement. Your project's requesters always have the option of either accepting your proposed changes (allowing the project to continue) or canceling your project.

Documents closely related to a Scope Statement

Your organization may use a number of other documents that address issues similar to those included in the Scope Statement. When you use these other documents as sources of information to prepare or describe your project plan, be careful to note how they differ from the Scope Statement. Here's a list of some of the more common documents that contain information similar to that in a Scope Statement:

- **Market requirements document:** A formal request to develop or modify a product. This document (typically prepared by a member of your organization's sales and marketing group) may lead to the creation of a project. However, in its original form, this document reflects only the *desires* of the person who wrote it. It doesn't reflect an assessment of whether meeting the request is possible or in the company's best interest, nor is it a commitment to meet the request.

- **Business requirements document:** A description of the business needs that a requested product, service, or system must address.

- **Technical requirements or specifications document:** A description of the characteristics that the products and services produced must have.

- **Project request:** A written request for a project by a group within the organization. The project request indicates a desire for a project rather than a mutual agreement and commitment to perform it.

- **Statement of work:** A narrative description of products, services, or results to be supplied by a project.

- **Project profile:** A document that highlights the key information about a project (sometimes also called a *project summary* or a *project abstract*).

- **Project charter:** A document issued by upper management that formally establishes a project and authorizes the project manager to use organizational resources to perform project activities.

- **Work order:** A written description of work that people or groups within your organization will perform in support of your project. The signed work order focuses on work performance rather than overall project outcomes.

- **Contract:** A legal agreement for providing specified goods or services.

Looking at the Big Picture: How Your Project Fits In

Understanding the situation and thought processes that led to your project's creation helps ensure that you and your project successfully meet people's expectations. This section helps you clarify the first two elements of your Scope Statement: your project's justification and objectives.

Figuring out why you're doing the project

When you take on a project, *why* you're doing it may seem obvious — because your boss told you to. The real question, though, isn't why you choose to accept the assignment but why the project must be done (by you or anyone else) in the first place.

The following sections help you identify people who may benefit from your project so you can then determine how their expectations and needs helped to justify the project.

Identifying the initiator

Your first task in discovering your project's underlying justification is to determine who had the original idea that led to your project (this person is called the *project's initiator*). Project success requires that, at a minimum, you meet this person's needs and expectations.

Identifying your project's initiator is easy when he's the person who directly assigns it to you. More likely, however, the person who gives you the project is passing along an assignment he received from someone else. If your project has passed through several people before it reaches you, you may have difficulty determining who really had the initial idea. Further, the original intent may have become blurred if people in the chain purposely or inadvertently changed the assignment a little as they passed it on.

To determine who came up with the original idea for your project, take the following steps:

1. **Ask the person who assigns you the project whether he originated the idea.**

2. **If that person didn't initiate the idea, ask the following questions:**

   • Who gave him the assignment?

   • Who else, if anyone, was involved in passing the assignment to him?

   • Who had the original idea for the project?

3. **Check with all the people you identified in Step 2 and ask them the same questions.**

4. **Check the following written records that may confirm who originally had the idea:**

   • Minutes from division-, department-, and organization-wide planning and budget sessions

   • Correspondence and e-mail referring to the project

   • Reports of planning or feasibility studies

A *feasibility study* is a formal investigation to determine the likely success of performing certain work or achieving certain results.

In addition to helping you identify the people who initiated your project, these written sources may shed light on what these people hope to get from it.

5. **Consult with people who may be affected by or are needed to support your project; they may know who originated the idea.**

Be as specific as possible when specifying your project initiator. In other words, don't write "The sales department requested promotional literature for product Alpha." Instead, write "Mary Smith, the sales representative for the northeast region, requested promotional literature for product Alpha."

Be sure to distinguish between drivers and supporters as you seek to find your project's initiator (see Chapter 3 for more information about drivers and supporters):

- ✔ *Drivers* have some say when defining the results of the project. They tell you what you *should* do.

- ✔ *Supporters* help you perform your project. They tell you what you *can* do.

For example, the vice president of finance who requests a project to upgrade the organization's financial information systems is a project driver. The manager of the computer center who must provide staff and resources to upgrade the organization's information systems is a project supporter.

Sometimes supporters claim to be drivers. For example, when the manager of the computer center is asked, he may say he initiated the project. In reality, however, the manager authorized the people and funds to perform the project, but the vice president of finance initiated the project.

Recognizing other people who may benefit from your project

Although they may not have initiated the idea, other people may benefit from your completed project. They may be people who work with, support, or are clients of your project's drivers, or they may have performed similar projects in the past. They may have expressed interests or needs in areas addressed by your project in meetings, correspondence, or informal conversations.

Identify these other people as soon as possible to determine what their particular needs and interests are and how you can appropriately address them. These additional audiences may include people who

- ✔ Know the project exists and have expressed an interest in it

- ✔ Know it exists but don't realize it can benefit them

- ✔ Are unaware of your project

Identify these additional audiences by doing the following:

- ✔ Review all written materials related to your project.
- ✔ Consult with your project's drivers and supporters
- ✔ Encourage everyone you speak to about the project to identify others who may benefit from it.

As you identify people who can benefit from your project, also identify people who strongly oppose it. Figure out why they oppose your project and whether you can address their concerns. Take the time to determine whether they may be able to derive any benefits from your project, and, if they can, explain these benefits to them. If they continue to oppose your project, make a note in your risk-management plan about their opposition and how you plan to deal with it (see Chapter 8 for how to analyze and plan for project risks and uncertainties).

Distinguishing the project champion

A *project champion* is a person in a high position in the organization who strongly supports your project; advocates for your project in disputes, planning meetings, and review sessions; and takes necessary actions to help ensure that your project is successful.

Sometimes the best champion is one whose support you never have to use. Just knowing that this person supports your project helps other people appreciate its importance and encourages them to work diligently to ensure its success.

Check with your project's drivers and supporters to find out whether your project already has a champion. If it doesn't, work hard to recruit one by looking for people who can reap benefits from your project and who have sufficient power and influence to encourage serious, ongoing organizational commitment to your project. Explain to these people why the success of your project is in their best interest and how you may need their specific help as your project progresses. Assess how interested they are in your project and how much help they're willing to provide.

Considering people who'll implement the results of your project

Most projects create a product or service to achieve a desired result. Often, however, the person who asks you to create the product or service isn't the one who'll actually use it.

Suppose your organization's director of sales and marketing wants to increase annual sales by 10 percent in the next fiscal year. She decides that developing and introducing a new product, XYZ, will allow her to achieve this goal. However, she won't actually go to all your organization's customers and sell them XYZ; her sales staff will. Even though they didn't come up with the idea to develop XYZ, the sales staff may have strong opinions about the characteristics XYZ should have — and so will the customers who ultimately buy (or don't buy!) the product.

To identify the real users of project products and services, try to do the following early in your project planning:

✔ Clarify the products and services that you anticipate producing.

✔ Identify exactly who will use these products and services and how they'll use them.

After you identify these people, consult with them to determine any additional interests or needs they may have that your project should also address.

Determining your project drivers' real expectations and needs

The needs that your project addresses may not always be obvious. Suppose, for example, that your organization decides to sponsor a blood drive. Is the real reason for your project to address the shortage of blood in the local hospital or to improve your organization's image in the local community?

The needs your project must satisfy to successfully achieve its purpose are termed your project's *requirements*.

When you clearly understand your project's requirements, you can

✔ Choose project activities that enable you to accomplish the true desired results (see Chapter 4 for information on identifying project activities).

✔ Monitor performance during and at the end of the project to ensure that you're meeting the real needs (see Chapter 12 for more information on how to track a project during performance).

✔ Realize when the project isn't meeting the real needs so that you can suggest modifying or canceling it.

When you're initially assigned a project, you hope you're told the products you're supposed to produce and the needs you're supposed to address. However, often you're told what to produce (the outcomes), but you have to figure out the needs yourself.

Consider the following questions as you work to define your project's requirements:

✔ **What needs do people want your project to address?** Don't worry at this point whether your project actually can address these needs or whether it's the best way to address the needs. You're just trying to identify the hopes and expectations that led to this project in the first place.

✔ **How do you know that the needs you identify are the real hopes and expectations that people have for your project?** Determining people's real thoughts and feelings can be difficult. Sometimes they don't want to share them; sometimes they don't know how to express them clearly.

When speaking with people to determine the needs your project should address, try the following techniques:

- ✔ Encourage them to speak at length about their needs and expectations.
- ✔ Listen carefully for any contradictions.
- ✔ Encourage them to clarify vague ideas.
- ✔ Try to confirm your information from two or more independent sources.
- ✔ Ask them to indicate the relative importance of addressing each of their needs.

The following scheme is useful for prioritizing a person's needs:

- ✔ **Must:** The project must address these needs, at the very least.
- ✔ **Should:** The project should address these needs, if at all possible.
- ✔ **Nice to:** It would be nice for the project to address these needs, if doing so doesn't affect anything else.

See whether your organization performed a formal benefit-cost analysis for your project. A *benefit-cost analysis* is a formal identification and assessment of the following (see Chapter 1 for further details):

- ✔ The benefits anticipated from your project
- ✔ The costs of
  - • Performing your project
  - • Using and supporting the products or services produced by your project

The benefit-cost analysis documents the results that people were counting on when they decided to proceed with your project. Therefore, the analysis is an important source for the real needs that your project should address.

Confirming that your project can address people's needs

Although needs may be thoroughly documented (see the preceding section), you may have difficulty determining whether your project can successfully address those needs. On occasion, companies fund formal feasibility studies to determine whether a project can successfully address a particular need.

Other times, however, your project may be the result of a brainstorming session or someone's creative vision. In this case, you may have less confidence that your project can accomplish its expected results. Don't automatically reject a project at this point, but do aggressively determine the chances for success and the actions you can take to increase these chances. If you can't find sufficient information to support your analysis, consider asking for a formal feasibility study.

If you feel the risk of project failure is too great, share your concerns with the key decision makers and explain why you recommend not proceeding with your project. See the discussion of risk management in Chapter 8 for more information.

Uncovering other activities that relate to your project

Your project doesn't exist in a vacuum. It may require results from other projects, it may generate products that other projects will use, and it may address needs that other projects also address. For these reasons, you need to identify projects related to yours as soon as possible so you can coordinate the use of shared personnel and resources and minimize unintended overlap in project activities and results.

Check the following sources to identify projects that may be related to yours:

- ✔ Your project's audiences
- ✔ Centrally maintained lists of projects planned or being performed by your organization
- ✔ Organization-wide information-sharing vehicles, such as newsletters or your organization's intranet
- ✔ Your organization's project management office (PMO)
- ✔ Upper-management committees responsible for approving and overseeing your organization's projects
- ✔ Your organization's finance department, which may have established labor or cost accounts for such projects
- ✔ Your organization's procurement department, which may have purchased goods or services for such projects
- ✔ Your organization's information technology department, which may be storing, analyzing, or preparing progress reports for such projects
- ✔ Functional managers whose people may be working on such projects

Emphasizing your project's importance to your organization

How much importance your organization places on your project directly influences the chances for your project's success. When conflicting demands for scarce resources arise, resources usually go to those projects that can produce the greatest benefits for the organization.

Your project's perceived value depends on its intended benefits and people's awareness of those benefits. Take the following steps to help people understand how your project will support the organization's priorities:

✔ **Look for existing statements or documents that confirm your project's support of your organization's priorities.** Consult the following sources to find out more about your organization's priorities:

- **Long-range plan:** A formal report that identifies your organization's overall direction, specific performance targets, and individual initiatives for the next one to five years

- **Annual budget:** The detailed list of categories and individual initiatives that your organization will financially support during the year

- **Capital appropriations plan:** The itemized list of all planned expenditures (over an established minimum amount) for facilities and equipment purchases, renovations, and repairs during the year

- **Your organization's Key Performance Indicators (KPIs):** Performance measures that describe your organization's progress toward its goals

When you review these documents, note whether your project or its intended outcome is specifically mentioned.

In addition, determine whether your organization has made specific commitments to external customers or upper management related to your project's completion.

✔ **Describe in the justification portion of your Scope Statement how your project relates to the organization's priorities.** Include existing discussions of your project from the information sources mentioned in the preceding step. If your project isn't specifically referenced in these sources, prepare a written explanation of how your project and its results will impact the organization's priorities.

Occasionally, you may find it difficult to identify specific results that people expect your project to generate. Perhaps the person who initiated the project has assumed different responsibilities and no longer has any interest in it, or maybe the original need the project was designed to address has changed. If people have trouble telling you how your project will help your organization, ask them what would happen if you didn't perform your project. If they conclude that it wouldn't make a difference, ask them how you can modify your project to benefit the organization. If they don't think your project can be changed to produce useful results, consider suggesting that the project be canceled.

Organizations are consistently overworked and understaffed. Spending precious time and resources on a project that everyone agrees will make no difference is the last thing your organization needs or wants. More likely, people do realize that your project can have a positive impact on the organization. Your job, then, is to help these people consistently focus on these valuable results.

Being exhaustive in your search for information

In your quest to find out what your project is supposed to accomplish and how it fits into your organization's overall plans, you have to seek information that's sensitive, sometimes contradictory, and often unwritten. Getting this information isn't always easy, but following these tips can help make your search more productive:

✓ **Try to find several sources for the same piece of information.** The greater the number of independent sources that contain the same information, the more likely the information is correct.

✓ **Whenever possible, get information from primary sources.** A *primary source* contains the original information. A *secondary source* is someone else's report of the information from the primary source.

Suppose you need information from a recently completed study. You can get the information from the primary source (which is the actual report of the study written by the scientists who performed it), or you can get it from secondary sources (such as articles in magazines or scientific journals by authors who paraphrased and summarized the original report).

The farther your source is from the primary source, the more likely the secondary information differs from the real information.

✓ **Look for written sources because they're the best.** Check relevant minutes from meetings, correspondence, e-mail, reports from other projects, long-range plans, budgets, capital improvement plans, market requirement documents, and benefit-cost analyses.

✓ **Speak with two or more people from the same area to confirm information.** Different people have different styles of communication as well as different perceptions of the same situation. Speak with more than one person, and compare their messages to determine any contradictions.

If you get different stories, speak with the people again to verify their initial information. Determine whether the people you consulted are primary or secondary sources (primary sources tend to be more accurate than secondary ones). Ask the people you consulted to explain or reconcile any remaining differences.

✓ **When speaking with people about important information, arrange to have at least one other person present.** Doing so allows two different people to interpret what they hear from the same individual.

✓ **Write down all information you obtain from personal meetings.** Share your written notes and summaries with other people who were present at the meeting to ensure that your interpretation is correct and to serve as a reminder of agreements made during the meeting.

✓ **Plan to meet at least two times with your project's key audiences.** Your first meeting starts them thinking about issues. Allow some time for them to think over your initial discussions and to think of new ideas related to those issues. A second meeting gives you a chance to clarify any ambiguities or inconsistencies from the first session. (See Chapter 3 for more information on project audiences.)

✔ **Practice active listening skills in all your meetings and conversations.** See Chapter 13 for information on how to practice active listening.

✔ **Wherever possible, confirm what you heard in personal meetings with written sources.** When you talk with people, they share their perceptions and opinions. Compare those perceptions and opinions with written, factual data (from primary sources, if possible). Discuss any discrepancies with those same people.

Drawing the line: Where your project starts and stops

Sometimes your project stands alone, but more often it's one part of related efforts to achieve a common result. You want to avoid duplicating the work of these other related projects, and, where appropriate, you want to coordinate your efforts with theirs.

Your description of your project's scope of work should specify clearly where your project starts and where it ends. Suppose your project is to develop a new product for your organization. You may frame your project's scope description as follows:

This project entails designing, developing, and testing a new product.

If you feel your statement is in any way ambiguous, you may clarify your scope further by stating what you will not do:

This project won't include finalizing the market requirements or launching the new product.

To make sure your project's scope of work description is clear, do the following:

✔ **Check for hidden inferences.** Suppose your boss has asked you to design and develop a new product. Check to be sure she doesn't assume you'll also perform the market research to determine the new product's characteristics.

✔ **Use words that clearly describe intended activities.** Suppose your project entails *the implementation of a new information system.* Are you sure that everyone defines *implementation* in the same way? For instance, do people expect it to include installing the new software, training people to use it, evaluating its performance, fixing problems with it, or something else?

✔ **Confirm your understanding of your project's scope with your project's drivers and supporters.**

A colleague of mine had an assignment to prepare for the competitive acquisition of certain equipment. She developed a plan to include the selection of the vendor, award of the contract, and production and delivery of the equipment. Her boss was stunned with my colleague's project estimate of six months and $500,000. He thought it would take less than two months and cost less than $25,000.

After a brief discussion with her boss, my colleague realized her only job was to select the potential vendor, not actually place the order and have the equipment manufactured and delivered. Although she clarified her misunderstanding, she still wondered aloud, "But why would we select a vendor if we didn't want to actually buy the equipment?"

Of course, she missed the point. The question wasn't whether the company planned to buy the equipment. (Certainly the intention to buy the equipment was the reason for her project.) The real question was whether her project or a different project in the future would purchase the equipment.

Stating your project's objectives

As I mention earlier in this chapter, *objectives* are outcomes your project will produce (they're also referred to as *deliverables*). Your project's outcomes may be products or services you develop or the results of using these products and services. The more clearly you define your project's objectives, the more likely you are to achieve them. Include the following elements in your objectives:

✔ **Statement:** A brief narrative description of what you want to achieve

✔ **Measures:** Indicators you'll use to assess your achievement

✔ **Performance specifications:** The value(s) of each measure that define success

Suppose you take on a project to reformat a report that summarizes monthly sales activity. You may frame your project's objective as shown in Table 2-1.

Table 2-1	An Illustration of a Project Objective	
Statement	*Measures*	*Performance Specifications*
A revised report that summarizes monthly sales activity	Content	Report must include total number of items sold, total sales revenue, and total number of returns for each product line.
	Schedule	Report must be operational by August 31.
	Budget	Development expenditures are not to exceed $40,000.
	Approvals	New report format must be approved by the vice president of sales, regional sales manager, district sales manager, and sales representatives.

Sometimes people try to avoid setting a specific target by establishing a range of values that defines successful performance. But setting a range is the same as avoiding the issue. Suppose you're a sales representative and your boss says you'll be successful if you achieve $20 million to $25 million in sales for the year. As far as you're concerned, you'll be 100 percent successful as soon as you reach $20 million. Most likely, however, your boss will consider you 100 percent successful only when you reach $25 million. Although you and your boss appeared to reach an agreement, you didn't.

In the following sections, I explain how to create clear and specific objectives, identify all types of objectives, and respond to resistance to objectives.

Making your objectives clear and specific

You need to be crystal clear when stating your project's objectives. The more specific your project objectives are, the greater your chances are of achieving them. Here are some tips for developing clear objectives:

- ✔ **Be brief when describing each objective.** If you take an entire page to describe a single objective, most people won't read it. Even if they do read it, your objective probably won't be clear and may have multiple interpretations.

- ✔ **Don't use technical jargon or acronyms.** Each industry (such as pharmaceuticals, telecommunications, finance, and insurance) has its own vocabulary, and so does each company within that industry. Within companies, different departments (such as accounting, legal, and information services) also have their own jargons. Because of this proliferation of specialized languages, the same three-letter acronym (TLA) can have two or more meanings in the same organization! To reduce the chances for misunderstandings, express your objectives in language that people of all backgrounds and experiences are familiar with.

✔ **Make your objectives SMART, as follows:**

- **S**pecific: Define your objectives clearly, in detail, with no room for misinterpretation.

- **M**easurable: State the measures and performance specifications you'll use to determine whether you've met your objectives.

- **A**ggressive: Set challenging objectives that encourage people to stretch beyond their comfort zones.

- **R**ealistic: Set objectives the project team believes it can achieve.

- **T**ime sensitive: Include the date by which you'll achieve the objectives.

✔ **Make your objectives controllable.** Make sure that you and your team believe you can influence the success of each objective. If you don't believe you can, you may not commit 100 percent to achieving it (and most likely you won't even try). In that case, it becomes a wish, not an objective.

✔ **Identify all objectives.** Time and resources are always scarce, so if you don't specify an objective, you won't (and shouldn't) work to achieve it.

✔ **Be sure drivers and supporters agree on your project's objectives.** When drivers buy into your objectives, you feel confident that achieving the objectives constitutes true project success. When supporters buy into your objectives, you have the greatest chance that people will work their hardest to achieve them.

If drivers don't agree with your objectives, revise them until they do agree. After all, your drivers' needs are the whole reason for your project! If supporters don't buy into your objectives, work with them to identify their concerns and develop approaches they think can work.

Probing for all types of objectives

When you start a project, the person who makes the initial project request often tells you the major results she wants to achieve. However, she may want the project to address other items that she forgot to mention to you. And other (as yet unidentified) people may also want your project to accomplish certain results.

You need to identify *all* project objectives as early as possible so you can plan for and devote the necessary time and resources to accomplishing each one. When you probe to identify all possible objectives, consider that projects may have objectives in the following three categories:

✔ Physical products or services

✔ The effects of these products or services

✔ General organizational benefits that weren't the original reason for the project

Suppose that your information technology (IT) department is about to purchase and install a new software package for searching and analyzing information in the company's parts-inventory database. The following are examples of objectives this project may have in each category:

- ✔ **Physical product or service:** The completed installation and integration of the new software package with the parts-inventory database

- ✔ **The effect of a product or service:** Reduced inventory-storage costs due to timelier ordering facilitated by the new software

- ✔ **A general organizational benefit:** Use of the new software with other company databases

An objective is different from a *serendipity* (a chance occurrence or coincidence). In the previous example of the new software package, consider that one project driver won't be completely satisfied unless the software for the parts-inventory database is also installed and integrated with the company's product-inventory database. In this case, installing the system on the company's product-inventory database must be an objective of your project so you must devote specific time and resources to accomplish it. On the other hand, if your audience will be happy whether you do or don't install the software on the second database, being able to use the software on that database is a serendipity — so you shouldn't devote any time or resources specifically to accomplishing it.

Determining all project objectives requires you to identify all drivers who may have specific expectations for your project. See Chapter 3 for a discussion of the different types of audiences and tips on how to identify them all.

Anticipating resistance to clearly defined objectives

Some people are uncomfortable committing to specific objectives because they're concerned they may not achieve them. Unfortunately, no matter what the reason, not having specific objectives makes it more difficult to know whether you're addressing your drivers' true expectations and whether you're meeting those expectations. In other words, when your objectives aren't specific, you increase the chances that your project won't succeed.

Here are some excuses people give for not defining their objectives too specifically, along with suggestions for addressing those excuses:

- ✔ **Excuse 1: Too much specificity stifles creativity.**

   Response: Creativity should be encouraged — the question is where and when. You want your project's drivers to be clear and precise when stating their objectives; you want your project's supporters to be creative when figuring out ways to meet these objectives. You want to understand what people *do* expect from your project, not what they *may* expect. The more clearly you can describe their actual objectives, the easier it is to determine whether (and how) you can meet them.

✔ **Excuse 2: Your project entails research and new development, and you can't tell today what you'll be able to accomplish.**

Response: Objectives are targets, not guarantees. Certain projects have more risks than others. When you haven't done a task before, you don't know whether it's possible. And, if it is possible, you don't know how long it'll take and how much it'll cost. But you must state at the outset exactly what you want to achieve and what you think is possible, even though you may have to change your objectives as the project progresses.

✔ **Excuse 3: What if interests or needs change?**

Response: Objectives are targets based on what you know and expect today. If conditions change in the future, you may have to revisit one or more of your objectives to see whether they're still relevant and feasible or whether they, too, must change.

✔ **Excuse 4: The project's requestor doesn't know what she specifically wants her project to achieve.**

Response: Ask her to come back when she does. If you begin working on this project now, you have a greater chance of wasting time and resources to produce results that the requestor later decides she doesn't want.

✔ **Excuse 5: Even though specific objectives help determine when you've succeeded, they also make it easier to determine when you haven't.**

Response: Yep. That's true. However, because your project was framed to accomplish certain results, you need to know if those results were achieved. If they weren't, you may have to perform additional work to accomplish them. In addition, you want to determine the benefits the organization is realizing from the money it's spending.

Marking Boundaries: Project Constraints

Naturally, you'd like to operate in a world where everything is possible — that is, where you can do anything necessary to achieve your desired results. Your clients and your organization, on the other hand, would like to believe that you can achieve everything they want with minimal or no cost to them. Of course, neither situation is true.

Defining the constraints you must work within introduces reality into your plans and helps clarify expectations. As you plan and implement your project, think in terms of the following two types of constraints:

✔ **Limitations:** Restrictions other people place on the results you have to achieve, the time frames you have to meet, the resources you can use, and the way you can approach your tasks

✔ **Needs:** Requirements you stipulate must be met so you can achieve project success

The following sections help you determine your project's limitations and needs.

Working within limitations

Project limitations may influence how you perform your project and may even determine whether or not you (and your project's drivers and supporters) decide to proceed with your project. Consult with your project's drivers and supporters to identify limitations as early as possible so you can design your plan to accommodate them.

Understanding the types of limitations

Project limitations typically fall into several categories. By recognizing these categories, you can focus your investigations and thereby increase the chances that you'll discover all limitations affecting your project. Your project's drivers and supporters may have preset expectations or requirements in one or more of the following categories:

- **Results:** The products and effect of your project. For example, the new product must cost no more than $300 per item to manufacture, or the new book must be fewer than 384 pages in length.

- **Time frames:** When you must produce certain results. For example, your project must be done by June 30. You don't know whether it's possible to finish by June 30; you just know that someone expects the product to be produced by then.

- **Resources:** The type, amount, and availability of resources to perform your project work. Resources can include people, funds, equipment, raw materials, facilities, information, and so on. For example, you have a budget of $100,000; you can have two people full time for three months; or you can't use the test laboratory during the first week in June.

- **Activity performance:** The strategies for performing different tasks. For example, you're told that you must use your organization's printing department to reproduce the new users' manuals for the system you're developing. You don't know what the manual will look like, how many pages it'll be, the number of copies you'll need, or when you'll need them. Therefore, you can't know whether your organization's printing department is up to the task. But at this point, you do know that someone expects you to have the printing department do the work.

Be careful of vague limitations; they provide poor guidance for what you can or can't do, and they can demoralize people who have to deal with them. Here are some examples of vague limitations and how you can improve them:

✔ **Time frame limitation:**

  - **Vague:** "Finish this project as soon as possible." This statement tells you nothing. With this limitation, your audience may suddenly demand your project's final results — with no advance warning.

  - **Specific:** "Finish this project by close of business June 30."

✔ **Resource limitation:**

  - **Vague:** "You can have Laura Webster on your project part time in May." How heavily can you count on her? From Laura's point of view, how can she juggle all her assignments in that period if she has no idea how long each one will take?

  - **Specific:** "You can have Laura Webster on your project four hours per day for the first two weeks in May."

When people aren't specific about their constraints, you can't be sure whether you can honor their requests. The longer people wait to be specific, the less likely you are to adhere to the limitation and successfully complete your project.

Looking for project limitations

Determining limitations is a fact-finding mission, so your job is to identify and examine all possible sources of information. You don't want to miss anything, and you want to clarify any conflicting information. After you know what people expect, you can determine how (or whether) you can meet those expectations. Try the following approaches:

✔ **Consult your audiences.** Check with drivers about limitations regarding desired results; check with supporters about limitations concerning activity performance and resources.

✔ **Review relevant written materials.** These materials may include long-range plans, annual budgets and capital appropriations plans, benefit-cost analyses, feasibility studies, reports of related projects, minutes of meetings, and individuals' performance objectives.

✔ **When you identify a limitation, be sure to note its source.** Confirming a limitation from different sources increases your confidence in its accuracy. Resolve conflicting opinions about a limitation as soon as possible.

Addressing limitations in your Scope Statement

List all project limitations in your Scope Statement. If you have to explore ways to modify your project plan in the future, this list of limitations can help define alternatives that you can and cannot consider.

You can reflect limitations in your project in two ways:

- ✔ **Incorporate limitations directly into your plan.** For example, if a key driver says you have to finish your project by September 30, you may choose to set September 30 as your project's completion date. Of course, because September 30 is the outside limit, you may choose to set a completion date of August 31. In this case, the limitation influences your target completion date but isn't equivalent to it.

- ✔ **Identify any project risks that result from a limitation.** For example, if you feel the target completion date is unusually aggressive, the risk of missing that date may be significant. You want to develop plans to minimize and manage that risk throughout your project. (See Chapter 8 for more information on how to assess and plan for risks and uncertainties.)

Dealing with needs

As soon as possible, decide on the situations or conditions necessary for your project's success. Most of these needs relate to project resources. Here are a few examples of resource-related needs:

- ✔ **Personnel:** "I need a technical editor for a total of 40 hours in August."

- ✔ **Budget:** "I need a budget of $10,000 for computer peripherals."

- ✔ **Other resources:** "I need access to the test laboratory during June."

Be as clear as possible when describing your project's needs. The more specific you are, the more likely other people are to understand and meet those needs.

Sometimes you can identify needs very early in your project planning. More often, however, particular needs surface as you create a plan that addresses the drivers' expectations. As your list of needs grows, check with your project's supporters to decide how the new needs can be met and at what cost. Check with your project's drivers to confirm that the estimated additional cost is justified, and modify your project documentation to reflect any changes in planned results, activities, schedules, or resources.

Facing the Unknowns When Planning

As you proceed through your planning process, you can identify issues or questions that may affect your project's performance. Unfortunately, just identifying these issues or questions doesn't help you address them.

For every potential issue you identify, make assumptions regarding unknowns associated with it. Then use these assumptions as you plan your project. Consider the following examples:

✔ **Issue:** You don't have a final, approved budget for your project.

Approach: *Assume* you'll get $50,000 for your project. *Plan* for your project to spend up to, but no more than, $50,000. Develop detailed information to demonstrate why your project budget must be $50,000, and share that information with key decision makers.

✔ **Issue:** You don't know when you'll get authorization to start work on your project.

Approach: *Assume* you'll receive authorization to start work on August 1. *Plan* your project work so that no activities start before August 1. Explain to key decision makers why your project must start on August 1, and work with them to facilitate your project's approval by that date.

Note: Don't forget to consider all project assumptions when you develop your project's risk-management plan. See Chapter 8 for more info.

Relating This Chapter to the PMP Exam and PMBOK 4

Table 2-2 notes topics in this chapter that may be addressed on the Project Management Professional (PMP) certification exam and that are also included in *A Guide to the Project Management Body of Knowledge,* 4th Edition (*PMBOK 4*).

Table 2-2	Chapter 2 Topics in Relation to the PMP Exam and *PMBOK 4*	
Topic	*Location in PMBOK 4*	*Comments*
Contents of a Scope Statement (see the section "Defining Your Project with a Scope Statement")	5.2.3.1. Project Scope Statement 5.1. Collect Requirements	The Scope Statement contents addressed in this book agree with those stated in *PMBOK 4*.
Definition and examples of project audiences (see the section "Figuring Out Why You're Doing the Project")	2.3. Stakeholders	Project audiences are composed of drivers, supporters, and observers (see Chapter 3). Drivers and supporters together are called stakeholders. *PMBOK 4* only considers stakeholders when discussing people to consider involving in your project.
Defining and determining project requirements (see the section "Determining your project drivers' real expectations and needs")	5.1. Collect Requirements	In addition to what this book covers, *PMBOK 4* distinguishes between project requirements and product requirements.
Framing project objectives (see the section "Stating your project's objectives")	5.1. Collect Requirements	*PMBOK 4* uses the term *product acceptance criteria* to encompass measures and specifications.
Definition and examples of project constraints (see the section "Marking Boundaries: Project Constraints")	1.3. What is Project Management? 6.4.1.5. Project Scope Statement	The definition of a constraint in both books is the same. *PMBOK 4* doesn't specifically distinguish between limitations and needs.
Definition and examples of project assumptions (see the section "Facing the Unknowns When Planning")	6.4.1.5. Project Scope Statement	The definition of an assumption in both books is the same.

Chapter 3

Knowing Your Project's Audience: Involving the Right People

In This Chapter

▶ Identifying your project's diverse audiences and building an audience list

▶ Considering your drivers, supporters, and observers

▶ Determining who has authority in your project

▶ Prioritizing your audiences by their levels of power and interest

*O*ften a project is like an iceberg: Nine-tenths of it lurks below the surface. You receive an assignment and you think you know what it entails and who needs to be involved. Then, as the project unfolds, new people emerge who may affect your goals and your approach to the project.

You risk compromising your project in the following two ways when you don't involve key people or groups in your project in a timely manner:

✔ First, you may miss important information that can affect the project's performance and ultimate success.

✔ Second, and sometimes more painful, you may insult someone. And you can be sure that, when someone feels you have slighted or insulted him, he'll take steps to make sure you don't do it again!

As soon as you begin to think about a new project, start to identify people who may play a role. This chapter shows you how to identify these candidates; how to decide whether, when, and how to involve them; and how to determine who has the authority, power, and interest to make critical decisions.

Understanding Your Project's Audiences

A *project audience* is any person or group that supports, is affected by, or is interested in your project. Your project's audiences can be inside or outside your organization, and knowing who they are helps you

✓ Plan whether, when, and how to involve them.

✓ Determine whether the scope of the project is bigger or smaller than you originally anticipated.

You may hear other terms used in the business world to describe project audiences, but these terms address only some of the people from your complete project audience list. Here are some examples:

✓ A *stakeholder* list identifies people and groups who support or are affected by your project. The stakeholder list doesn't usually include people who are merely interested in your project.

✓ A *distribution* list identifies people who receive copies of written project communications. These lists are often out-of-date for a couple of reasons. Some people remain on the list simply because no one removes them; other people are on the list because no one wants to run the risk of insulting them by removing them. In either case, having their names on this list doesn't ensure that these people actually support, are affected by, or are interested in your project.

✓ *Team members* are people whom the project manager directs. All team members are stakeholders, and, as such, they're part of the project audience, but the audience list includes more than just team members.

Developing an Audience List

As you identify the different audiences for your project, record them in an audience list. Check out the following sections for information on how to develop this list.

Starting your audience list

A project audience list is a living document. You need to start developing your list as soon as you begin thinking about your project. Write down any names that occur to you; when you discuss your project with other people, ask them who they think may be affected by or interested in your project. Then select a small group of the audiences you identify and conduct a formal brainstorming session. Continue to add and subtract names to your audience list until you can't think of anyone else.

In the following sections, I explain how to refine your audience list by using specific categories and recognizing important potential audiences; I wrap up with a sample to show you how to put your own list together.

Using specific categories

To increase your chances of identifying all appropriate people, develop your audience list in categories. You're less likely to overlook people when you consider them department by department or group by group instead of trying to identify everyone from the organization individually at the same time.

Start your audience list by developing a hierarchical grouping of categories that covers the universe of people who may be affected by, needed to support, or interested in your project. I often start with the following groups:

✔ **Internal:** People and groups inside your organization

- **Upper management:** Executive-level management responsible for the general oversight of all organization operations

- **Requesters:** The person who came up with the idea for your project and all the people through whom the request passed before you received it

- **Project manager:** The person with overall responsibility for successfully completing the project

- **End users:** People who will use the goods or services the project will produce

- **Team members:** People assigned to the project whose work the project manager directs

- **Groups normally involved:** Groups typically involved in most projects in the organization, such as the human resources, finance, contracts, and legal departments

- **Groups needed just for this project:** Groups or people with special knowledge related to this project

✔ **External:** People and groups outside your organization

- **Clients or customers:** People or groups that buy or use your organization's products or services

- **Collaborators:** Groups or organizations with whom you may pursue joint ventures related to your project

- **Vendors, suppliers, and contractors:** Organizations that provide personnel, raw materials, equipment, or other resources required to perform your project's work

- **Regulators:** Government agencies that establish regulations and guidelines that govern some aspect of your project work

- **Professional societies:** Groups of professionals that may influence or be interested in your project

- **The public:** The local, national, and international community of people who may be affected by or interested in your project

Dealing with reality rather than ignoring it

A number of years ago, I ran into a woman who had attended one of my project-management training sessions. She said she was using several of the techniques discussed in the course and found them to be very helpful. However, she also said that, after making a serious attempt to create an audience list, she found this tool to be impractical and of little value.

She explained that her boss had assigned her a project that she had to finish in two months. She immediately developed an audience list, but, much to her horror, the list included more than 150 names! How, she wondered, was she supposed to involve more than 150 people in a two-month project? She concluded that the audience list was clearly of no help.

In fact, her audience list had served its purpose perfectly. Identifying the people at the outset who would affect the success of her project gave her three options:

- ✔ She could plan how and when to involve each person during the project.

- ✔ She could assess the potential consequences of not involving one or more of her audiences.

- ✔ She could discuss extending the project deadline or reducing its scope with her boss if she felt she couldn't ignore any of the audiences.

The audience list itself doesn't decide whom you should involve in your project. Instead, it specifies those people who may affect the success of your project so you can weigh the benefits and the costs of including or omitting them.

Continue to subdivide these categories further until you arrive at position descriptions and the names of the people who occupy them.

Considering audiences that are often overlooked

As you develop your audience list, be sure not to overlook the following potential audiences:

- ✔ **Support groups:** These people don't tell you what you should do; instead, they help you accomplish the project's goals. If support groups know about your project early, they can fit you into their work schedules more readily. They can also tell you information about their capabilities and processes that may influence what your project can accomplish and by when you can do so. Such groups include

  - Facilities

  - Finance

  - Human resources

  - Information services

  - Legal services

  - Procurement or contracting

Discovering the real end users

A major international bank based in the United States had spent millions of dollars revising and upgrading its information system. Project personnel had worked closely with special liaisons in Europe who represented the interests of the local bank personnel who would actually be entering and retrieving data from the new system. When the bank introduced the upgraded system, they discovered a fatal problem: More than 90 percent of the local bank personnel in Europe were non-English speaking, but the system documentation was all written in English. The enhanced systems were unusable!

The system designers had spent substantial time and money working with the liaisons to identify and address the interests and needs of the end users. However, the liaisons had raised only issues from their own experience instead of identifying and sharing the needs and concerns of the local bank personnel. Because English was the primary language of all the liaisons, they failed to consider the possible need to prepare system instructions in multiple languages. Putting the local bank personnel on the audience list along with the liaisons would've reminded the project personnel not to overlook their special needs.

- Quality

- Security

- Project management office

✔ **End users of your project's products:** People or groups who will use the goods and services your project produces. Involving end users at the beginning and throughout your project helps ensure that the goods and services produced are as easy as possible to implement and use and are most responsive to their true needs. It also confirms that you appreciate the fact that the people who will use a product may have important insights into what it should look like and do, which increases the chances that they will work to implement the products successfully.

In some cases, you may omit end users on your audience list because you don't know who they are. In other situations, you may think you have taken them into account through *liaisons* — people who represent the interests of the end users. (Check out the nearby sidebar "Discovering the real end users" for a costly example of what can happen when you depend solely on liaisons.)

✔ **People who will maintain or support the final product:** People who will service your project's final products affect the continuing success of these products. Involving these people throughout your project gives them a chance to make your project's products easier to maintain and support. It also allows them to become familiar with the products and effectively build their maintenance into existing procedures.

Examining a sample audience list

Suppose you're asked to coordinate your organization's annual blood drive. Table 3-1 illustrates some of the groups and people you may include in your project's audience list as you prepare for your new project.

Table 3-1	A Portion of an Audience List	
Category	**Subcategory**	**Audiences**
Internal	Upper management	Executive oversight committee, vice president of sales and marketing, vice president of operations, vice president of administration
	Requester	Vice president of sales, manager of community relations
	Project manager	Senior events coordinator
	Team members	Customer service representative, community relations representative, administrative assistant
	Groups normally involved	Finance, facilities, legal, and human resources departments
	Groups needed just for this project	Project manager and team from last year's blood drive, public relations
External	Clients, customers	Prior donors, potential donors, hospitals and medical centers receiving the blood from the drive
	Vendors, contractors	Attending nurses, food-service provider, facility's landlord, local blood center
	Regulatory agencies	Local board of health
	Professional societies	American Medical Association, American Association of Blood Banks
	Public	Local community, local newspapers, local television and radio stations

Ensuring your audience list is complete and up-to-date

Many different groups of people may influence the success of or have an interest in your project. Knowing who these people are allows you to plan to involve them at the appropriate times during your project. Therefore, identifying all project audiences as soon as possible and reflecting any changes in those audiences as soon as you find out about them are important steps to take as you manage your project.

To ensure your audience list is complete and up-to-date, consider the following guidelines:

✔ **Eventually identify each audience by position description and name.** You may, for example, initially identify people from *sales and marketing* as an audience. Eventually, however, you want to specify the particular people from that group, such as *brand manager for XYZ product, Sharon Wilson,* and their contact information.

✔ **Speak with a wide range of people.** Check with people in different organizational units, from different disciplines, and with different tenures in the organization. Ask every person whether she can think of anyone else you should speak with. The more people you speak with, the less likely you are to overlook someone important.

✔ **Allow sufficient time to develop your audience list.** Start to develop your list as soon as you become project manager. The longer you think about your project, the more potential audiences you can identify. Throughout the project, continue to check with people to identify additional audiences.

✔ **Include audiences who may play a role at any time during your project.** Your only job at this stage is to identify names so you don't forget them. At a later point, you can decide whether, when, and how to involve these people (see the "Considering the Drivers, Supporters, and Observers in Your Audience" section later in this chapter).

✔ **Include team members' functional managers.** Include the people to whom the project manager and team members directly report. Even though functional managers usually don't perform project tasks themselves, they can help ensure that the project manager and team members devote the time they originally promised to the project and that they have the resources necessary to perform their project assignments.

✔ **Include a person's name on the audience list for every role she plays.** Suppose your boss plans to provide expert technical advice to your project team. Include your boss's name twice — once as your direct supervisor and once as the technical expert. If your boss is promoted but continues to serve as a technical advisor to your project, the separate listings remind you that a new person now occupies your direct supervisor's slot.

✔ **Continue to add and remove names from your audience list throughout your project.** Your audience list evolves as you understand more about your project and as your project changes. Plan to review your list at regular intervals throughout the project to identify names that should be added or deleted. Encourage people involved in your project to continually identify new audiences as they think of them.

✔ **When in doubt, write down a person's name.** Your goal is to avoid overlooking someone who may play an important part in your project. Identifying a potential audience member doesn't mean you have to involve that person; it simply means you have to consider her. Eliminating the name of someone who won't be involved is a lot easier than trying to add the name of someone who should be.

Using an audience list template

An *audience list template* is a predesigned audience list that contains typical categories and audiences for a particular type of project. You may develop and maintain your own audience list templates for tasks you perform, functional groups may develop and maintain audience list templates for tasks they typically conduct, or your organization's project management office may develop and maintain templates for the entire organization.

Regardless of who maintains the template, it reflects people's cumulative experiences. As the organization continues to perform projects of this type, audiences that were overlooked in earlier efforts may be added and audiences that proved unnecessary may be removed. Using these templates can save you time and improve your accuracy.

Suppose you prepare the budget for your department each quarter. After doing a number of these budgets, you know most of the people who give you the necessary information, who draft and print the document, and who have to approve the final budget. Each time you finish another budget, you revise your audience list template to include new information from that project. The next time you prepare your quarterly budget, you begin your audience list with your template. You then add and subtract names as appropriate for that particular budget preparation.

When using audience list templates, keep the following guidelines in mind:

✔ **Develop templates for frequently performed tasks and for entire projects.** Audience list templates for kicking off the annual blood drive or submitting a newly developed drug to the Food and Drug Administration are valuable. But so are templates for individual tasks that are part of these projects, such as awarding a competitive contract or printing a document. Many times projects that appear totally new contain some tasks that you've done before. You can still reap the benefits of your prior experience by including the audience list templates for these tasks in your overall project audience list.

✔ **Focus on position descriptions rather than the names of prior audiences.** Identify an audience as *accounts payable manager* rather than *Bill Miller*. People come and go, but functions endure. For each specific project, you can fill in the appropriate names.

✔ **Develop and modify your audience list template from previous projects that actually worked, not from initial plans that looked good but lacked key information.** Often you develop a detailed audience list at the start of your project but don't revise the list during the project or add audiences that you overlooked in your initial planning. If you only update your template with information from an initial list, your template can't reflect the discoveries you made throughout the project.

✔ **Encourage your team to brainstorm possible audiences before you show them an existing audience list template.** Encouraging people to identify audiences without guidance or restrictions increases the chances that they'll think of audiences that were overlooked on previous projects.

✔ **Use templates as starting points, not ending points.** Make clear to your team that the template isn't the final list. Every project differs in some ways from similar ones. If you don't critically examine the template, you may miss people who weren't involved in previous projects but whom you need to consider for this one.

✔ **Reflect your different project experiences in your audience list templates.** The post-project evaluation is an excellent time to review, critique, and modify your audience list for a particular project (see Chapter 15 for details on the post-project evaluation).

Templates can save time and improve accuracy. However, starting with a template that's too polished can suggest you've already made up your mind about the contents of your final list, which may discourage people from freely sharing their thoughts about other potential audiences. In addition, their lack of involvement in the development of the project's audience list may lead to their lack of commitment to the project's success.

Considering the Drivers, Supporters, and Observers in Your Audience

After identifying everyone in your project audience, it's time to determine which of the following groups they fall into. Then you can decide whether to involve them and, if so, how and when.

✔ **Drivers:** People who have some say in defining the results of your project. You're performing your project for these people.

✔ **Supporters:** The people who help you perform your project. Supporters include individuals who authorize or provide the resources for your project, as well as those who actually work on it.

Including a project champion

A *project champion* is a person in a high position in the organization who strongly supports your project; advocates for your project in disputes, planning meetings, and review sessions; and takes whatever actions are necessary to help ensure the successful completion of your project.

As soon as you start planning, find out whether your project has a champion. If it doesn't, try to recruit one. An effective project champion has the following characteristics:

✔ Sufficient power and authority to resolve conflicts over resources, schedules, and technical issues

✔ A keen interest in the results of your project

✔ A willingness to have his or her name cited as a strong supporter of your project

---

✔ **Observers:** People who are neither drivers nor supporters, but who are interested in the activities and results of your project. Observers have no say in your project, and they're not actively involved in it. However, your project may affect them at some point in the future.

Separating audiences into these three categories helps you decide what information to seek from them and what to share with them, as well as to clarify the project decisions in which to involve them.

Suppose an information technology group has the job of modifying the layout and content of a monthly sales report for all sales representatives. The vice president of sales requested the project, and the chief information officer (CIO — the boss of the head of the information technology group) approved it. As the project manager for this project, consider categorizing your project's audiences as follows:

✔ **Drivers:** The vice president of sales is a driver because he has specific reasons for revising the report. The CIO is a potential driver because she may hope to develop certain new capabilities for her group through this project. Individual sales representatives are all drivers for this project because they'll use the redesigned report to support their work.

✔ **Supporters:** The systems analyst who designs the revised report, the training specialist who trains the users, and the vice president of finance who authorizes the funds for changing the manual are all supporters.

✔ **Observers:** The head of the customer service department is a potential observer because he hopes your project will lead to an improved problem-tracking system this year.

Beware of supporters who try to act like drivers. In the preceding example, the analyst who finalizes the content and format of the report may try to include certain items that she thinks are helpful. However, only the real drivers should determine the specific data that go into the report. The analyst just determines whether it's possible to include the desired data and what doing so will cost.

Keep in mind that one person can be both a driver and a supporter. For example, the vice president of sales is a driver for the project to develop a revised monthly sales report, but he's also a supporter if he has to transfer funds from the sales department budget to pay for developing the report.

The following sections help you identify when you need to involve drivers, supporters, and observers, and the best ways to keep them involved.

Deciding when to involve your audiences

Projects pass through the following four stages as they progress from an idea to completion (see Chapter 1 for detailed explanations of these stages):

- ✔ Starting the project
- ✔ Organizing and preparing
- ✔ Carrying out the work
- ✔ Closing the project

Plan to involve drivers, supporters, and observers in each stage of your project's life cycle. The following sections tell you how you can do so.

Drivers

Involve drivers from the start to the finish of your project. Keeping them involved is critical because they define what your project should produce, and they evaluate your project's success when it's finished. Check out Table 3-2 to see how to keep drivers involved during the four stages of your project.

Table 3-2	Involving Drivers in the Different Project Stages	
Stage	**Involvement Level**	**Rationale**
Starting the project	Heavy	Identify and speak with as many drivers as possible. Their desires and your assessment of feasibility can influence whether you should pursue the project. If you uncover additional drivers later, explore with them the issues that led to the project; ask them to identify and assess any special expectations they may have.

(continued)

Table 3-2 *(continued)*

Stage	Involvement Level	Rationale
Organizing and preparing	Moderate to heavy	Consult with drivers to ensure your project plan addresses their needs and expectations. Have them formally approve the plan before you start the actual project work.
Carrying out the work	Moderate	As the project gets under way, announce and introduce the drivers to the project team. Having the drivers talk about their needs and interests reinforces the importance of the project and helps team members form a more accurate picture of project goals. Also, having the drivers meet team members increases the drivers' confidence that the members can successfully complete the project. While performing the project work, keep drivers apprised of project accomplishments and progress to sustain their ongoing interest and enthusiasm. Involving drivers in this way also allows you to confirm that the results are meeting their needs.
Closing the project	Heavy	Have drivers assess the project's results and determine whether their needs and expectations were met. Identify their recommendations for improving performance on similar projects in the future.

Supporters

Just as with drivers, involve supporters from start to finish. Because they perform and support the project work, they need to know about changing requirements so they can promptly identify and address problems. Keeping them actively involved also sustains their ongoing motivation and commitment to the project. Check out Table 3-3 to see how to keep supporters involved during your project's four stages.

Table 3-3   Involving Supporters in the Different Project Stages

Stage	Involvement Level	Rationale
Starting the project	Moderate	Wherever possible, have key supporters assess the feasibility of meeting driver expectations. If you identify key supporters later in the project, have them confirm the feasibility of previously set expectations.

Stage	Involvement Level	Rationale
Organizing and preparing	Heavy	Supporters are the major contributors to the project plan. Because they facilitate or do all the work, have them determine necessary technical approaches, schedules, and resources. Also have them formally commit to all aspects of the plan.
Carrying out the work	Heavy	Familiarize all supporters with the planned work. Clarify how the supporters will work together to achieve the results. Have supporters decide how they'll communicate, resolve conflicts, and make decisions throughout the project. Throughout the project, keep supporters informed of project progress, encourage them to identify performance problems they encounter or anticipate, and work with them to develop and implement solutions to these problems.
Closing the project	Heavy	Have supporters conclude their different tasks. Inform them of project accomplishments and recognize their roles in project achievements. Elicit their suggestions for handling similar projects more effectively in the future.

Observers

After you choose the observers with whom you want to actively share project information, involve them minimally throughout the project because they neither tell you what should be done nor help you do it. Table 3-4 shows how you may keep observers involved.

Because observers don't directly influence or affect your project, be sure to carefully manage the time and effort you spend sharing information with them. When deciding whom to involve and how to share information with them, consider the following:

- ✔ Their level of interest in your project
- ✔ The likelihood that your project will affect them at some point in the future
- ✔ The need to maintain a good working relationship with them

See the section "Assessing Your Audience's Power and Interest" later in this chapter for information on what to consider when deciding how to involve different audiences.

Table 3-4	Involving Observers in the Different Project Stages	
Stage	*Involvement Level*	*Rationale*
Starting the project	Minimal	Inform observers of your project's existence and its main goals.
Organizing and preparing	Minimal	Inform observers about the project's planned outcomes and time frames.
Carrying out the work	Minimal	Tell observers that the project has started, and confirm the dates for planned milestones. Inform observers of key project achievements.
Closing the project	Minimal	When the project is done, inform observers about the project's products and results.

Using different methods to keep your audiences involved

Keeping drivers, supporters, and observers informed as you progress in your project is critical to the project's success. Choosing the right method for involving each audience group can stimulate that group's continued interest and encourage its members to actively support your work. Consider the following approaches for keeping your project audiences involved throughout your project:

- ✔ **One-on-one meetings:** One-on-one meetings (formal or informal discussions with one or two other people about project issues) are particularly useful for interactively exploring and clarifying special issues of interest with a small number of people.

- ✔ **Group meetings:** These meetings are planned sessions for some or all team members or audiences. Smaller meetings are useful to brainstorm project issues, reinforce team member roles, and develop mutual trust and respect among team members. Larger meetings are useful to present information of general interest.

- ✔ **Informal written correspondence:** Informal written correspondence (notes, memos, letters, and e-mails) helps you document informal discussions and share important project information.

- ✔ **More formal information-sharing vehicles:** Information resources, such as project newsletters or sites on the organization's intranet, may be useful for sharing nonconfidential and noncontroversial information with larger audiences.

> ✓ **Written approvals:** Written approvals (such as a technical approach to project work or formal agreements about a product, schedule, or resource commitment) serve as records of project decisions and achievements.

See Chapter 13 for additional information on sharing information about your project's ongoing performance.

Making the most of your audience's involvement

To maximize your audiences' involvement and contributions, consider the following guidelines throughout your project:

- ✓ **Involve audiences early in the project planning if they have a role later on.** Give your audiences the option to participate in planning even if they don't perform until later in the project. Sometimes they can share information that'll make their tasks easier. At the least, they can reserve time to provide their services when you need them.

- ✓ **If you're concerned with the legality of involving a specific audience, check with your legal department or contracts office.** Suppose you're planning to award a competitive contract to buy certain equipment. You want to know whether prospective bidders typically have this equipment on hand and how long it'll take to receive it after you award the contract. However, you're concerned that speaking to potential contractors in the planning stage may tip them off about the procurement and lead to charges of favoritism by unsuccessful bidders who didn't know about the procurement in advance.

    Instead of ignoring this important audience, check with your contracts office or legal department to determine how you can get the information you want and still maintain the integrity of the bidding process.

- ✓ **Develop a plan with all key audiences to meet their information needs and interests as well as yours.** Determine the information they want and the information you believe they need. Also decide when to provide that information and in what format. Finally, clarify what you want from them and how and when they can provide it.

- ✓ **Always be sure you understand each audience's *What's In It For Me* (WIIFM).** Clarify why it's in each audience's interest to see your project succeed. Throughout your project, keep reminding your audiences of the benefits they'll realize when your project's complete and the progress your project has made toward achieving those benefits. Find out more about identifying project benefits for different audiences in Chapter 14.

Confirming Your Audience's Authority

In project terms, *authority* refers to the overall right to make project decisions that others must follow, including the right to apply project resources, expend funds, or give approvals. Having opinions about how an aspect *should be* addressed is different from having the authority to decide how it *will be* addressed. Mistaking a person's level of authority can lead to frustration, as well as wasted time and money.

Confirm that the people you've identified as audiences have the authority to make the decisions they need to make to perform their tasks. If they don't have that authority, find out who does and how to bring those people into the process.

At the beginning of the carrying out the work stage in your projects, take the following steps to define each audience member's authority:

1. **Clarify each audience member's tasks and decisions.**

   Define with each person his tasks and his role in those tasks. For example, will he just work on the task, or will he also approve the schedules, resource expenditures, and work approaches?

2. **Ask each audience member what his authority is regarding each decision and task.**

   Ask about individual tasks rather than all issues in a particular area. For example, a person can be more confident about his authority to approve supply purchases up to $5,000 than about his authority to approve all equipment purchases, no matter the type or amount.

   Clarify decisions that the audience member can make himself. For decisions needing someone else's approval, find out whose approval he needs. (Ask, never assume!)

3. **Ask each audience member how he knows what authority he has.**

   Does a written policy, procedure, or guideline confirm the authority? Did the person's boss tell him in conversation? Is the person just assuming? If the person has no specific confirming information, encourage him to get it.

4. **Check out each audience member's history of exercising authority.**

   Have you or other people worked with this person in the past? Has he been overruled on decisions that he said he was authorized to make? If so, ask him why he believes he won't be similarly overruled this time.

5. **Verify whether anything has recently changed regarding each audience member's authority.**

Is there any reason to believe that this person's authority has changed? Is the person new to his current group? To his current position? Has the person recently started working for a new boss? If any of these situations exists, encourage the person to find specific documentation to confirm his authority for his benefit as well as yours.

Reconfirm the information in these steps when a particular audience's decision-making assignments change. Suppose, for example, that you initially expect all individual purchases on your project to be at or under $2,500. Bill, the team representative from the finance group, assures you that he has the authority to approve such purchases for your project without checking with his boss. Midway through the project, you find that you have to purchase a piece of equipment for $5,000. Be sure to verify with Bill that he can personally authorize this larger expenditure. If he can't, find out whose approval you need and plan how to get it.

Assessing Your Audience's Power and Interest

An audience's potential impact on a project depends on the power it has to exercise and the interest it has in exercising that power. Assessing the relative levels of each helps you decide with whom you should spend your time and effort to realize the greatest benefits.

Power is a person's ability to influence the actions of others. This ability can derive either from the direct authority the person has to require people to respond to her requests (*ascribed power;* see the previous section and Chapter 10 for more about authority) or the ability she has to induce others to do what she asks because of the respect they have for her professionally or their affinity for her as a person (*achieved power*). (See Chapter 14 for more information.) In either case, the more power a person has, the better able she is to marshal people and resources to support your project.

On the other hand, a person's *interest* in something is how much she cares or is curious about it or how much she pays attention to it. The more interested a person is in your project, the more likely she is to want to use her power to help the project succeed.

You can define an audience's relative levels of power and interest related to your project as being either *high* or *low*. You then have four possible combinations for each audience's relative levels of power and interest. The particular values of an audience's power and interest ratings suggest the chances that the audience may have a significant impact on your project and, therefore, the relative importance of keeping that audience interested and involved in your project.

Most often you base the assessments of an audience's power over and interest in your project on the aggregated individual, subjective opinions of you, your team members, members of your project's other audiences, people who have worked with the audience on other projects, subject matter experts, and/or members of the audience themselves. If you assign a value of *1* to each individual rating of *high* and *0* to each individual rating of *low,* you'd rate an audience's power or interest as *high* if the resulting average of the individual assessments were 0.5 or greater and *low* if it were below 0.5.

Typically, drivers and supporters have higher levels of power over your project than observers.

Figure 3-1 depicts a Power-Interest Grid, which represents these four possible power-interest combinations as distinct quadrants on a two-dimensional graph. As the project manager, you should spend a minimal amount of time and effort with audiences who have low levels of both power and interest (Quadrant I), increasingly greater amounts of time and effort with audiences that have a low level of power and a high level of interest (Quadrant II) and a low level of interest and a high level of power (Quadrant III), respectively. You should spend the most time and effort keeping audiences with high degrees of both power and interest (Quadrant IV) informed and involved. (Check out Chapter 13 for different ways to communicate with your project's audiences.)

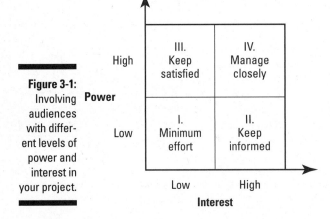

Figure 3-1:
Involving audiences with different levels of power and interest in your project.

Relating This Chapter to the PMP Exam and PMBOK 4

Table 3-5 notes topics in this chapter that may be addressed on the Project Management Professional (PMP) certification exam and that are also included in *A Guide to the Project Management Body of Knowledge,* 4th Edition (*PMBOK 4*).

Table 3-5	Chapter 3 Topics in Relation to the PMP Exam and *PMBOK 4*	
Topic	*Location in PMBOK 4*	*Comments*
Definition of project audience (see the section "Understanding Your Project's Audiences")	2.3. Stakeholders 10.1. Identify Stakeholders	Project drivers and supporters are the project stakeholders. *PMBOK 4* addresses stakeholders only when discussing people to consider involving in your project.
Developing an audience list (see the section "Developing an Audience List")	3.3.2. Identify Stakeholders 10.1.3.1. Stakeholder Register	*PMBOK 4* discusses how to develop a stakeholder register rather than an audience list.
Examples of project audiences (see the section "Developing an Audience List")	2.3. Stakeholders 10.1. Identify Stakeholders	The examples of stakeholders (drivers and supporters in this book) are similar.
Classifying audiences as drivers, supporters, or observers (see the section "Considering the Drivers, Supporters, and Observers in Your Audience")	2.3. Stakeholders	*PMBOK 4* considers drivers and supporters (although it doesn't refer to them by those names) only when discussing people who may affect your project.
Keeping audiences involved (see the section "Considering the Drivers, Supporters, and Observers in Your Audience")	2.3. Stakeholders 10.3. Distribute Information 10.4. Manage Stakeholder Expectations	The two discussions of how and when to involve stakeholders address similar approaches and alternatives.
Conducting a stakeholder analysis (see the section "Assessing Your Audience's Power and Interest")	10.1.2.1. Stakeholder Analysis	The two discussions of why and how to conduct a stakeholder analysis address similar points.

Chapter 4

Developing Your Game Plan: Getting from Here to There

. . . .

In This Chapter

▶ Dividing your work into manageable pieces

▶ Developing and displaying a Work Breakdown Structure

▶ Dealing with unknown circumstances and documenting what you need to know

. . . .

*T*he keys to successful project planning and performance are completeness and continuity. You want to identify all important information in your project plan and address all aspects of your plan during project performance.

Describing in detail all the work required to complete your project helps you accomplish these tasks. Your description of project work provides the basis for scheduling and resource planning, defining roles and responsibilities, assigning work to team members, capturing key project performance data, and reporting on completed project work. This chapter helps you break down your project work into manageable pieces.

Divide and Conquer: Working on Your Project in Manageable Chunks

Two of my major concerns when I start a new project are remembering to plan for all important pieces of work and accurately estimating the time and resources required to perform that work. To address both issues, I develop a logical framework to define all work that's necessary to complete the project.

A while back, a friend who loves jigsaw puzzles told me about an acquaintance who had asked him to assemble a 5,000-piece puzzle of the United States. When his acquaintance suggested that, before he start, he determine whether any pieces were missing and, if so, which ones, my friend laughed.

He always found out this information by trying to assemble the puzzle and noting any holes that remained after he'd used all the available pieces. How else could he do it?

You've probably had a similar puzzle-like experience with your project assignments. Suppose you're asked to design and present a training program. You and a colleague work intensely for a couple of months developing the content and materials, arranging for the facilities, and inviting the participants. A week before the session, you ask your colleague whether he's made arrangements to print the training manuals. He says that he thought you were dealing with it, and you say that you thought he was dealing with it. Unfortunately, neither of you arranged to have the manuals printed because you each thought the other person was handling it. Now you have a training session in a week, and you don't have the time or money to print the needed training notebooks.

How can you avoid situations like this one in the future? By using a structured approach in the organizing and preparing stage of your project to identify all required project work. The following sections explain how to accomplish this task by subdividing project intermediate and final products into finer levels of detail and specifying the work required to produce them.

Thinking in detail

The most important guideline to remember when identifying and describing project work is this: Think in detail! In my experience, people consistently underestimate the time and resources they need for their project work because they just don't recognize everything they have to do to complete it.

Suppose you have to prepare a report of your team's most recent meeting. Based on your past experience with preparing many similar reports, you quickly figure it'll take a few days to do this one. But how confident are you that this estimate is correct? Are you sure you've considered all the different work that writing this particular report will entail? Will the differences between this report and others you've worked on mean more time and more work for you? How can you tell?

The best way to determine how long and how much work a project will take to complete is to break down the required project work into its component deliverables, a process called *decomposition*. (A *deliverable* is an intermediate or final product, service, and/or result your project will produce. See Chapter 2 for more information on project deliverables, or objectives as they're often called.)

The greater the detail in which you decompose a project, the less likely you are to overlook anything significant. For example, creating the report in the preceding illustration actually entails producing three separate deliverables: a draft, reviews of the draft, and the final version. Completing the final version of the report, in turn, entails producing two deliverables: the handwritten version and the printed version. By decomposing the project into the deliverables necessary to generate the final report, you're more likely to identify all the work you need to do to complete the project.

Observe the following two guidelines when decomposing your project:

- ✔ **Allow no gaps:** Identify all components of the deliverable you're decomposing. In the example of creating a meeting report, if you have *allowed no gaps*, you'll have the desired final product in hand after you've produced the draft, the reviews of the draft, and the final version. However, if you feel that you'll have to do additional work to transform these three subproducts into a final product, you need to define the subproduct(s) that this additional work will produce.

- ✔ **Allow no overlaps:** Don't include the same subproduct in your decomposition of two or more different deliverables. For example, don't include completed reviews of the draft by your boss and the vice president of your department as parts of the draft (the first deliverable) if you've already included them with all other reviews under reviews of the draft (the second deliverable).

The first guideline — allow no gaps — is also referred to as the *100% rule.* This rule states that the components of a project include 100% of the work and all the deliverables required by the project scope and do not include any work or deliverables that fall outside of the project scope. This rule applies at all levels within the hierarchy.

Specifying the parts and subparts of your project in this way decreases the chance that you'll overlook something significant, which will help you develop more accurate estimates of the time and resources needed to do the project.

Thinking of hierarchy with the help of a Work Breakdown Structure

Thinking in detail is critical when you're planning your project, but you also need to consider the big picture. If you fail to identify a major part of your project's work, you won't have the chance to detail it! Thus, you must be both comprehensive and specific.

My friend's jigsaw puzzle dilemma (refer to this section's intro) suggests an approach that can help you achieve your goal. He can count the pieces before assembling the puzzle to determine whether any piece is missing. However, knowing that he has only 4,999 pieces can't help him determine which piece is missing. He needs to divide the 5,000 pieces into smaller groups that he can examine and understand. Consider that he divides the puzzle of the United States into 50 separate 100-piece puzzles, one for each of the 50 states. Because he knows the United States has 50 states, he's confident that each piece of the puzzle should be in one and only one box.

Suppose he takes it a step further and divides each state into four quadrants each comprised of 25 pieces. Again, he can count the pieces in each box to see whether any are missing. However, determining which one of 25 pieces is missing from the northeast sector of New Jersey is easier than figuring out which piece is missing from the 5,000-piece puzzle of the entire United States.

Figure 4-1 shows how you can depict necessary project work in a *Work Breakdown Structure* (WBS), a deliverable-oriented, hierarchical decomposition of the work required to achieve a project's objectives and produce the required project products.

The different WBS levels have had many different names. The top element is typically called a *project* and the lowest level of detail is typically called a *work package.* However, the levels in between have been called *phases, subprojects, work assignments, tasks, subtasks,* and *deliverables.* In this book, the top-level box (the Level 1 component) is a *project,* the lowest-level of detail is a *work package,* and the elements in between are *Level 2 components, Level 3 components,* and so forth. A work package is comprised of activities that must be performed to produce the deliverable it represents.

Specifically, Figure 4-1 shows that the entire project, represented as a Level 1 component, can be subdivided into Level 2 components, and some or all Level 2 components can be subdivided into Level 3 components. You can continue to subdivide all the components you create in the same manner until you reach a point at which you think the components you defined are sufficiently detailed for planning and management purposes. These Level "n" components, where *n* is the number of the lowest-level component in a particular WBS branch, are called *work packages.*

Level 1	Level 2	Level 3	Level "n"
Project	Components	Components	Work packages

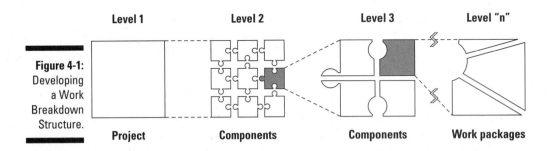

Figure 4-1: Developing a Work Breakdown Structure.

Suppose you're responsible for creating and presenting a new training program for your organization. To get started, you'd develop a WBS for this project as follows:

1. Determine the major deliverables or products to be produced.

Ask yourself, "What major intermediate or final products or deliverables must be produced to achieve the project's objectives?"

You may identify the following items:

- Training program needs statement

- Training program design

- Participant notebooks

- Trained instructor

- Program testing

- Training program presentation

2. **Divide each of these major deliverables into its component deliverables in the same manner.**

   Choose any one of these deliverables to begin with. Suppose you choose *Training program needs statement.*

   Ask, "What intermediate deliverables must I have so I can create the needs statement?"

   You may determine that you require the following:

   - Interviews of potential participants

   - A review of materials discussing the needs for the program

   - A report summarizing the needs this program will address

3. **Divide each of these work pieces into its component parts.**

   Suppose you choose to start with *Interviews of potential participants.*

   Ask, "What deliverables must I have to complete these interviews?"

   You may decide that you have to produce the following deliverables:

   - Selected interviewees

   - Interview questionnaire

   - Interview schedule

   - Completed interviews

   - Report of interview findings

   But why stop here? You can break each of these five items into finer detail and then break those pieces into even finer detail. How far should you go? The following sections can help you answer that question.

Asking four key questions

Determining how much detail you need isn't a trivial task. You want to describe your work in sufficient detail to support accurate planning and meaningful tracking. But the benefits of this detail must justify the additional time you spend developing and maintaining your plans and reporting your progress. Asking the following four questions about each WBS component can help you decide whether you've defined it in enough detail:

✔ Do you require two or more intermediate deliverables to produce this deliverable?

✔ Can you accurately estimate the resources you'll need to perform the work to produce this deliverable? (Resources include personnel, equipment, raw materials, money, facilities, information, and so on.)

✔ Can you accurately estimate how long it will take to produce this deliverable?

✔ If you have to assign the work to produce this deliverable to someone else, are you confident that person will understand exactly what to do?

If you answer yes to the first question or no to any one of the other three, break down the deliverable into the components necessary to produce it.

Your answers to these questions depend on how familiar you are with the work, how critical the activity is to the success of your project, what happens if something goes wrong, whom you may assign to perform the activity, how well you know that person, and so on. In other words, the correct level of detail for your WBS depends on your judgment.

If you're a little uneasy about answering these four questions, try this even simpler test: Subdivide your WBS component into additional deliverables if you think either of the following situations applies:

✔ The component will take much longer than two calendar weeks to complete.

✔ The component will require much more than 80 person-hours to complete.

Remember that these estimates are just guidelines. For example, if you estimate it'll take two weeks and two days to prepare a report — you've probably provided sufficient detail. But if you figure it'll take two to three months to finalize requirements for your new product, you need to break the deliverable *finalized requirements* into more detail because

✔ Experience has shown that there can be so many different interpretations of what is supposed to occur during these two to three months that you can't be sure your time and resource estimates are correct, and you can't confidently assign the task to someone to perform.

✔ You don't want to wait two or three months to confirm that work is on schedule by verifying that a desired product has been produced on time.

Making assumptions to clarify planned work

Sometimes you haven't defined the work in sufficient detail, but certain unknowns stop you from defining it further. How do you resolve this dilemma? You make assumptions regarding the unknowns. If, during the course of your project, you find that any of your assumptions are wrong, you can change your plan to reflect the correct information.

For example, suppose you decide that the *Completed interviews* deliverable from Step 3 in the example to develop and present a new training program introduced earlier in this section needs more detail so you can estimate its required time and resources. However, you don't know how to break it down further because you don't know how many people you'll interview or how many separate sets of interviews you'll conduct. If you assume you'll interview five groups of seven people each, you can then develop specific plans for arranging and conducting each of these sessions. In most situations, it's best to consider a guess in the middle of the possible range. To determine how sensitive your results are to the different values, you may want to analyze several different assumptions.

Be sure to write your assumption down so you remember to change your plan if you conduct more or less than five interview sessions. See the discussion in Chapter 2 for more information about detailing assumptions.

Using action verbs to describe activities

Use action verbs when framing the titles of the activities that comprise a work package to clarify the nature of the work they entail. Action verbs can improve your time and resource estimates, your work assignments to team members, and your tracking and reporting because they provide a clear picture of what an activity entails.

Consider the assignment to prepare a report after a team meeting. Suppose you choose *Draft Report* to be one of its work packages. If you don't break down *Draft Report* further, you haven't indicated clearly whether it includes any or all of the following actions:

- ✔ Collecting information for the draft
- ✔ Determining length and format expectations and restrictions
- ✔ Handwriting the draft
- ✔ Reviewing the draft yourself before officially circulating it to others

But, if you simply word the work package *Design and handwrite the draft report — voilà!* Your scope of work is instantly clearer. A few well-chosen words at this level go a long way.

Using a WBS for large and small projects

You need to develop a WBS for very large projects, very small projects, and everything in between. Building a skyscraper, designing a new airplane, researching and developing a new drug, and revamping your organization's information systems all need a WBS. So, too, do writing a report, scheduling and conducting a meeting, coordinating your organization's annual blood drive, and moving into your new office. The size of the WBS may vary immensely depending on the project, but the hierarchical scheme used to develop each one is the same.

Conducting a survey: Using the Work Breakdown Structure

Suppose your boss asks you to estimate how long it'll take to survey people regarding the characteristics a new product your company may develop should have. Based on your experience with doing similar types of assessments in the past, you figure you'll need to contact people at the company headquarters, at two regional activity centers, and from a sampling of current clients. You tell your boss the project will take you between one and six months to complete.

Have you ever noticed that bosses aren't happy when you respond to their question of "How long will it take?" with an answer of "Between one and six months"? You figure that finishing anytime before six months meets your promise, but your boss expects you can be done in one month, given some (okay, a lot of) hard work. The truth is, though, you don't have a clue how long the survey will take because you have no idea how much work you'll have to do to complete it.

Developing a WBS encourages you to define exactly what you have to do and, correspondingly, improves your estimate of how long each step will take. In this example, you decide to conduct three different surveys: personal interviews with people at your headquarters, phone conference calls with people at the two regional activity centers, and a mail survey of a sample of your company's clients. Realizing you need to describe each survey in more detail, you begin by considering the mail survey and decide it includes five deliverables:

✔ **A sample of clients to survey:** You figure you need one week to select your sample of clients if the sales department has a current record of all company clients. You check with that department, and, thankfully, it does.

✔ **A survey questionnaire:** As far as this deliverable is concerned, you get lucky. A colleague tells you she thinks that the company conducted a similar survey of a different target population a year ago and that extra questionnaires from that effort may still be around. You find that a local warehouse has 1,000 of these questionnaires and —yes!— they're perfect for your survey. How much time do you need to allow for designing and printing the questionnaires? Zero!

✔ **Survey responses:** You determine you'll need a response rate of at least 70 percent for the results to be valid. You consult with people who've done these types of surveys before and find out that, to have an acceptable chance of achieving a minimum response rate of 70 percent, you have to use the following three-phased approach:

1. Initial mailing out and receiving of questionnaires (estimated time = four weeks)

2. Second mailing out and receiving of questionnaires to nonrespondents (estimated time = four weeks)

3. Phone follow-ups with people who still haven't responded, encouraging them to complete and return their surveys (estimated time = two weeks)

✔ **Data analyses:** You figure you'll need about two weeks to enter and analyze the data you expect to receive.

✔ **A final report:** You estimate it'll take two weeks to prepare the final report.

Now, instead of one to six months, you can estimate the time you need to complete your mail survey to be 15 weeks. Because you've clarified the work you have to do and how you'll do it, you're more confident you can reach your goal, and you've increased the chances that you will!

Note: To develop the most accurate estimates of your project's duration, in addition to the nature of the work you do, you need to consider the types and amounts of resources you require, together with their capacities and availabilities (see Chapter 5 for more on how to estimate durations). However, this example illustrates that using just a WBS to refine the definition of your project's work components significantly improves your estimates.

Occasionally your detailed WBS may seem to make your project more complex than it really is. I agree that 100 tasks (not to mention 10,000) written out can be a little unnerving! However, the WBS doesn't create a project's complexity; the WBS just displays it. In fact, by clearly portraying all aspects of your project work, the WBS actually simplifies your project.

Check out the sidebar "Conducting a survey: Using the Work Breakdown Structure" for an illustration of how a WBS helps you develop a more accurate estimate of the time you need to complete your work.

Dealing with special situations

With a little bit of thought, you can break most WBS elements into components. However, this section looks a little more closely at several special situations that require some creativity.

Representing conditionally repeating work

Suppose your project contains a deliverable that requires an unknown number of repetitive cycles to produce, such as getting a report approved. In reality, you write the report and submit it for review and approval. If the reviewers approve the report, you proceed to the next phase of your project (such as distributing the report). But if the reviewers don't approve the report, you have to revise it to incorporate their comments and then resubmit it for a second review and approval. If they approve the second draft, you proceed to the next phase of your project. But if they still don't approve that draft, you have to repeat the process (or try to catch them in a better mood).

Revising the draft is *conditional work;* it will only be done if a certain condition (in the report example, not receiving the reviewers' approval) comes to pass. Unfortunately, a WBS doesn't include conditional work — you plan to perform every piece of work you detail in your WBS. However, you can represent conditional work in the following two ways:

✔ **You can define a single deliverable as *Approved report* and assign it a duration.** In effect, you're saying that you can create as many *Reviewed but not approved versions of the report* as necessary (each of which is an intermediate deliverable) to obtain the final reviewed and approved version within the established time period.

✔ **You can assume that you'll need a certain number of revisions and include the intermediate deliverable created after each one (a different *Reviewed but not approved version of the report*) in your WBS.** This approach allows more meaningful tracking.

Whichever approach you choose, be sure to document it in your project plan.

Assuming that your project needs three reviews and two revisions doesn't guarantee that your draft will be good to go only after the third review. If your draft is approved after the first review, congratulations! You can move on to the next piece of work immediately (that is, you don't perform two revisions just because the plan assumed you would have to!).

However, if you still haven't received approval after the third review, you continue to revise it and submit it for further review until you do get the seal of approval you need. Of course, then you have to reexamine your plan to determine the impact of the additional reviews and revisions on the schedule and budget of future project activities.

A plan isn't a guarantee of the future; it's your statement of what you'll work to achieve. If you're unable to accomplish any part of your plan, you must revise it accordingly (and promptly).

Handling work with no obvious break points

Sometimes you can't see how to break a piece of work into two-week intervals. Other times that detail just doesn't seem necessary. Even in these situations, however, you want to divide the work into smaller chunks to remind yourself to periodically verify that your current schedule and resource estimates are still valid.

Check out the sidebar "Keeping a close eye on your project" for an illustration of why it's important to have frequent milestones to support project tracking and how to deal with WBS components that have no obvious break points.

No matter how carefully you plan, something unanticipated can always occur. The sooner you find out about such an occurrence, the more time you have to minimize any negative impact on your project.

Keeping a close eye on your project

A number of years back, I met a young engineer at one of my training sessions. Soon after he joined his organization, he was asked to design and build a piece of equipment for a client. He submitted a purchase request to his procurement department for the raw materials he needed and was told that, if they didn't arrive by the promised delivery date in six months, he should notify the procurement specialist he was working with so she could investigate the situation. He was uneasy about waiting six months without checking periodically to see whether everything was still on schedule, but being young, inexperienced, and new to the organization, he wasn't comfortable trying to fight this established procedure. So he waited six months.

When he didn't receive his raw materials by the promised delivery date, he notified the procurement specialist, who, in turn, checked with the vendor. It turned out that there had been a major fire in the vendor's facilities five months earlier and that production had just resumed the previous week. The vendor estimated his materials would be shipped in about five months!

I suggested that he could've divided the waiting time into one-month intervals and called the vendor at the end of each month to see whether anything had occurred that changed the projected delivery date. Although checking periodically wouldn't have prevented the fire, he would've known about it five months sooner and could've made other plans immediately. (See Chapter 8 for more information on how to deal with risk and uncertainty in your projects.)

Planning a long-term project

A long-term project presents an entirely different challenge. Often the work you perform a year or more in the future depends on the results of the work you do between now and then. Even if you can accurately predict the work you'll perform later, the farther into the future you plan, the more likely it is that something will change and require you to modify your plans.

When developing a WBS for a long-term project, use a *rolling-wave approach,* in which you continually refine your plans throughout the life of your project as you discover more about the project and its environment. This approach acknowledges that uncertainties may limit your plan's initial detail and accuracy, and it encourages you to reflect more accurate information in your plans as soon as you discover it. Apply the rolling-wave approach to your long-term project by taking the following steps:

1. **Break down the first three months' work into components that take two weeks or less to complete.**

2. **Plan the remainder of the project in less detail, perhaps describing the work in packages you estimate to take between one and two months to complete.**

3. **Revise your initial plan at the end of the first three months to detail your work for the next three months in components that take two weeks or less to complete.**

4. **Modify any future work as necessary, based on the results of your first three months' work.**

5. **Continue revising your plan in this way throughout the project.**

Creating and Displaying Your Work Breakdown Structure

You can use several different schemes to develop and display your project's WBS, and each one can be effective under different circumstances. This section looks at a few of those different schemes and provides some examples and advice on how and when to apply them.

Considering different schemes for organizing your WBS

You can use many different schemes to subdivide project work into WBS components; the following are five possible ones with examples of each:

- ✔ **Product components:** Floor plan, training manuals, or screen design
- ✔ **Functions:** Design, launch, review, or test
- ✔ **Project phases:** Initiation, design, or construction
- ✔ **Geographical areas:** Region 1 or the northwest
- ✔ **Organizational units:** Marketing, operations, or facilities

Project phases, product components, and functions are the most often used.

 When you choose a scheme to organize the subelements of a WBS component, continue to use that same scheme to define all subelements under that WBS component to prevent possible overlap in categories. For example, consider that you want to develop finer detail for the WBS component titled *Report.* You may choose to break out the detail according to function, such as *Draft report, Reviews of draft report,* and *Final report.* Or you may choose to break it out by product component, such as *Section 1, Section 2,* and *Section 3.*

Don't define *Report's* subelements by using some items from both schemes, such as *Section 1, Section 2, Reviews of draft report,* and *Final report.* Combining schemes in this way increases the chances of either including work twice or overlooking it completely. For example, the work to prepare the final version of Section 2 could be included in either of two subelements: *Section 2* or *Final report.*

Consider the following questions when choosing a scheme:

- ✔ **What higher-level milestones will be most meaningful when reporting progress?** For example, is it more helpful to report that *Section 1* is completed or that the entire *Draft report* is done?

- ✔ **How will you assign responsibility?** For example, is one person responsible for the draft, reviews, and final report of Section 1, or is one person responsible for the drafts of Sections 1, 2, and 3?

- ✔ **How will you and your team members actually do the work?** For example, is the drafting, reviewing, and finalizing of Section 1 separate from the same activities for Section 2, or are all chapters drafted together, reviewed together, and finalized together?

Using different approaches to develop your WBS

How you develop your WBS depends on how familiar you and your team are with your project, whether similar projects have been successfully performed in the past, and how many new methods and approaches you'll use. Choose one of the following two approaches for developing your WBS depending on your project's characteristics:

- ✔ **Top-down:** Start at the top level in the hierarchy and systematically break WBS elements into their component parts.

  This approach is useful when you have a good idea of the project work involved before the actual work begins. The top-down approach ensures that you thoroughly consider each category at each level, and it reduces the chances that you overlook work in any of your categories.

- ✔ **Brainstorming:** Generate all possible work and deliverables for this project and then group them into categories.

  Brainstorming is helpful when you don't have a clear sense of a project's required work at the outset. This approach encourages you to generate any and all possible pieces of work that may have to be done, without worrying about how to organize them in the final WBS. After you decide that a proposed piece of work is a necessary part of the project, you can identify any related work that is also required.

Whichever approach you decide to use, consider using stick-on notes to support your WBS development. As you identify pieces of work, write them on the notes and put them on the wall. Add, remove, and regroup the notes as you continue to think through your work. This approach encourages open sharing of ideas and helps all people appreciate — in detail — the nature of the work that needs to be done.

The top-down approach

Use the following top-down approach for projects that you or others are familiar with:

1. **Specify all Level 2 components for the entire project.**

2. **Determine all necessary Level 3 components for each Level 2 component.**

3. **Specify the Level 4 components for each Level 3 component as necessary.**

4. **Continue in this way until you've detailed all project deliverables and work components completely. The lowest-level components in each WBS chain are your project's work packages.**

The brainstorming approach

Use the following brainstorming approach for projects involving untested methods or for projects you and your team members aren't familiar with:

1. **Write down all deliverables and components of work that you think your project entails.**

   Don't worry about overlap or level of detail.

   Don't discuss wording or other details of the work items.

   Don't make any judgments about the appropriateness of the work.

2. **Group these items into a few major categories with common characteristics and eliminate any deliverables or work components that aren't required.**

   These groups are your *Level 2* categories.

3. **Divide the deliverables and work components under each Level 2 category into groups with common characteristics.**

   These groups are your *Level 3* categories.

4. **Now use the top-down method to identify any additional deliverables or work components that you overlooked in the categories you created.**

5. **Continue in this manner until you've described all project deliverables and work components completely. The lowest-level components in each WBS chain are your project's work packages.**

Considering different ways to categorize your project's work

Although you eventually want to use only one WBS for your project, early in the development of your WBS, you can look at two or more different hierarchical schemes. Considering your project from two or more perspectives helps you identify work you may have overlooked.

Suppose a local community wants to open a halfway house for substance abusers. Figures 4-2 and 4-3 depict two different schemes to categorize the work for this community-based treatment facility. The first scheme classifies the work by product component, and the second classifies the work by function:

✔ Figure 4-2 defines the following components as Level 2 categories: staff, facility, residents (people who'll be living at the facility and receiving services), and community training.

✔ Figure 4-3 defines the following functions as Level 2 categories: planning, recruiting, buying, and training.

Figure 4-2:
A product component scheme for a WBS for preparing to open a community-based treatment facility.

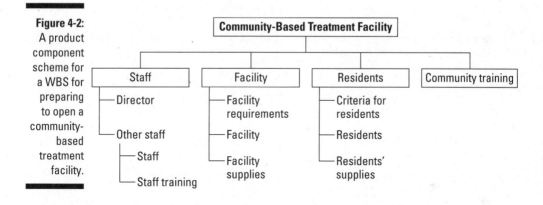

Figure 4-3:
A functional scheme for a WBS for preparing to open a community-based treatment facility.

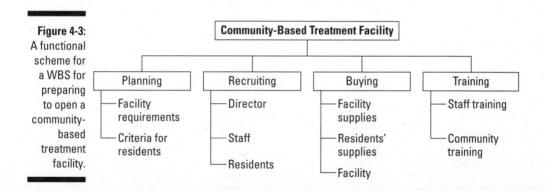

Both WBSs contain the same lowest-level components or work packages.

When you think about your project in terms of major functions (rather than final product components), you realize that you forgot the following work:

✔ Planning for staff recruiting

✔ Buying staff supplies

✔ Planning for your community training

After you identify the work components you overlooked, you can include them in either of the two WBSs.

Be sure you choose only one WBS before you leave your project's planning phase. Nothing confuses people faster than trying to use two or more different WBSs to describe the same project.

Labeling your WBS entries

As the size of a project grows, its WBS becomes increasingly complex. Losing sight of how a particular piece of work relates to other parts of the project is easy to do. Unfortunately, this problem can lead to poor coordination between related work efforts and a lack of urgency on the part of people who must perform the work.

Figure 4-4 illustrates a scheme for labeling your WBS components so you can easily see their relationships with each other and their relative positions in the overall project WBS:

✔ The first digit *(1)*, the Level 1 identifier, indicates the project in which the item is located.

✔ The second digit *(5)* indicates the Level 2 component of the project in which the item is located.

✔ The third digit *(7)* refers to the Level 3 component under the Level 2 component *1.5.* in which the item is located.

Figure 4-4:
A useful scheme for identifying your WBS components.

1.5.7.3. Order Materials

→ Level 4 (Work package)
→ Level 3
→ Level 2
→ Level 1 (Project)

> ✔ The fourth and last digit *(3)* is a unique identifier assigned to distinguish this item from the other Level 4 components under the Level 3 component *1.5.7*. If *1.5.7.3. Order Materials* isn't subdivided further, it's a work package.

Displaying your WBS in different formats

You can display your WBS in several different formats. This section looks at three of the most common ones.

The organization-chart format

Figure 4-5 shows a WBS in the *organization-chart format* (also referred to as a *hierarchy diagram* or *graphical view*). This format effectively portrays an overview of your project and the hierarchical relationships of different categories at the highest levels. However, because this format generally requires a lot of space, it's less effective for displaying large WBSs.

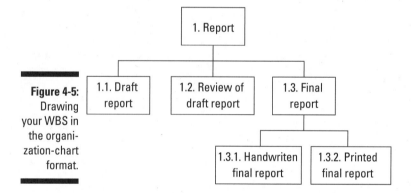

Figure 4-5: Drawing your WBS in the organization-chart format.

The indented-outline format

The *indented-outline format* in Figure 4-6 is another way to display your WBS. This format allows you to read and understand a complex WBS with many components. However, you can easily get lost in the details of a large project with this format and forget how the different pieces all fit together.

Both the organization-chart format and the indented-outline format can be helpful for displaying the WBS for a small project. For a large project, however, consider using a combination of the organization-chart and the indented-outline formats to explain your WBS. You can display the Level 1 and Level 2 components in the organization-chart format and portray the detailed breakout for each Level 2 component in the indented-outline format.

1.   Report

   1.1.   Draft report

   1.2.   Reviews of draft report

   1.3.   Final report

      1.3.1.   Handwritten final report

      1.3.2.   Printed final report

Figure 4-6:
Depicting
your WBS
in the
indented-
outline
format.

The bubble-chart format

The *bubble-chart format* in Figure 4-7 is particularly effective for supporting brainstorming to develop your WBS for both small and large projects. You interpret the bubble-chart format as follows:

- ✔ The bubble in the center represents your entire project (in this case, *Report*).

- ✔ Lines from the center bubble lead to Level 2 breakouts (in this case, *Draft report, Reviews of draft,* and *Final report*).

- ✔ Lines from each Level 2 component lead to Level 3 components related to the Level 2 component. (In this case, the Level 2 element *Final report* consists of the two Level 3 elements *Handwritten final report* and *Printed final report.*)

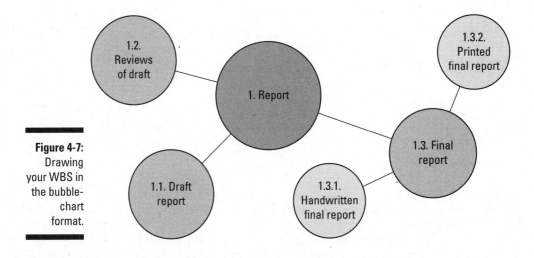

Figure 4-7:
Drawing
your WBS in
the bubble-
chart
format.

The freeform nature of the bubble-chart format makes it effective for easily recording thoughts generated during a brainstorming session. You can also easily rearrange components as you proceed with your analysis.

The bubble-chart format isn't effective for displaying your WBS to audiences who aren't familiar with your project. Use this format to develop your WBS with your team, but transpose it into an organization-chart or indented-outline format when you present it to people outside your team.

Improving the quality of your WBS

You increase the chances for project success when your WBS is accurate and complete *and* when people who will be performing the work understand and agree with it. The following guidelines suggest some ways to improve your WBS's accuracy and acceptance:

- ✔ **Involve the people who'll be doing the work.** When possible, involve them during the initial development of the WBS. If they join the project after the initial planning, have them review and critique the WBS before they begin work.

- ✔ **Review and include information from WBSs from similar projects.** Review plans and consult people who've worked on projects similar to yours that were successful. Incorporate your findings into your WBS.

- ✔ **Keep your WBS current.** When you add, delete, or change WBS elements during your project, be sure to reflect these changes in your WBS. (See "Documenting What You Need to Know about Your Planned Project Work" later in this chapter for more about sharing the updated WBS with the team.)

- ✔ **Make assumptions regarding uncertain activities.** If you're not sure whether you'll do a particular activity, make an assumption and prepare your WBS based on that assumption. Be sure to document that assumption. If your assumption proves to be wrong during the project, change your plan to reflect the true situation. (See the sections "Making assumptions to clarify planned work" and "Representing conditionally repeating work" for more about assumptions.)

- ✔ **Remember that your WBS identifies only your project's deliverables; it doesn't depict their chronological order.** Nothing is wrong with including activities from left to right or top to bottom in the approximate order that you'll perform them. However, in complex projects, you may have difficulty showing detailed interrelationships among activities in the WBS format. The purpose of the WBS is to ensure that you identify all project deliverables. Check out Chapter 5 for more on developing your project schedule.

Using templates

A *WBS template* is an existing WBS that contains deliverables typical for a particular type of project. This template reflects people's cumulative experience from performing many projects of the same type. As people perform more projects, they add deliverables to the template that were overlooked and remove deliverables that weren't needed. Using templates can save you time and improve your accuracy.

Although templates can save time and improve accuracy, don't inhibit people's active involvement in the development of the WBS by using a template that's too polished. Lack of people's involvement can lead to missed activities and lack of commitment to project success.

This section looks at how you can develop a WBS template and improve its accuracy and completeness.

Drawing on previous experience

By drawing on previous experience, you can prepare your WBS in less time than it takes to develop a whole new WBS and be more confident that you've included all essential pieces of work.

Suppose you prepare your department's quarterly budget. After doing a number of these budgets, you know most of the work you have to perform. Each time you finish another budget, you revise your WBS template to include new information you gleaned from the recently completed project.

The next time you start to plan a quarterly budget–preparation project, begin with the WBS template you've developed from your past projects. Then add and subtract elements as appropriate for this particular budget preparation.

Improving your WBS templates

The more accurate and complete your WBS templates are, the more time they can save on future projects. This section offers several suggestions for continually improving the quality of your WBS templates.

When using templates, keep the following in mind:

- ✔ **Develop templates for frequently performed tasks as well as for entire projects.** Templates for the annual organization blood drive or the submission of a newly developed drug to the Food and Drug Administration are valuable. So are templates for individual tasks that are part of these projects, such as awarding a competitive contract or having a document printed. You can always incorporate templates for individual pieces of work into a larger WBS for an entire project.

✔ **Develop and modify your WBS template from previous projects that worked, not from initial plans that looked good.** Often you develop a detailed WBS at the start of your project, but you may forget to add intermediate or final deliverables that you overlooked in your initial planning. If you update your template from a WBS that you prepared at the *start* of your project, it won't reflect what you discovered *during* the actual performance of the project.

✔ **Use templates as starting points, not ending points.** Make it clear to your team members and others involved in the project that the template is only the start for your WBS, not the final version. Every project differs in some ways from similar ones performed in the past. If you don't critically examine the template, you may miss work that wasn't done in previous projects but that needs to be done in this one.

✔ **Continually update your templates to reflect your experiences from different projects.** The post-project evaluation is a great opportunity to review and critique your original WBS. (See Chapter 15 for information on how to plan and conduct this evaluation.) At the end of your project, take a moment to revise your WBS template to reflect what you found.

Identifying Risks While Detailing Your Work

In addition to helping you identify work you need to complete, a WBS helps you identify unknowns that may cause problems when you attempt to perform that work. As you think through the work you have to do to complete your project, you often identify considerations that may affect how or whether you can perform particular project activities. Sometimes you have the information you need to assess and address a consideration and sometimes you don't. Identifying and dealing effectively with information you need but don't have can dramatically increase your chances for project success.

Unknown information falls into one of two categories:

✔ **A known unknown:** Information you know you need that someone else has but you don't.

✔ **An unknown unknown:** Information you know you need that neither you nor anyone else has because it doesn't yet exist.

You deal with known unknowns by finding out who has the information you need and then getting it. You deal with unknown unknowns by using one or more of the following strategies:

 ✔ Buying insurance to minimize damage that occurs if something doesn't turn out the way you expected

 ✔ Developing contingency plans to follow if something doesn't turn out the way you expected

 ✔ Trying to influence what the information eventually turns out to be

In the project *Conducting a survey* discussed in the "Conducting a survey: Using the Work Breakdown Structure" sidebar earlier in this chapter, you figure you'll need a week to select a sample of clients to survey if the sales department has a current data tape listing all the company's clients. At this point, whether the data tape exists is a *known unknown* — it's unknown to you, but, if it exists, someone else knows about it. You deal with this unknown by calling people to find someone who knows whether such a data tape does or does not exist.

You experience a different situation when you become aware that twice in the past month computer operators at your company accidentally destroyed a data tape when they spilled coffee on it as they were preparing to mount it on a tape drive. As part of your current project *(Conducting a survey),* you need to have a computer operator mount a tape on a tape drive. Not surprisingly, you're now concerned that the operator may spill coffee on your tape and destroy it, too.

Whether or not the operator will spill coffee on your tape is an unknown unknown when you prepare the WBS for your project plan. You can't determine beforehand whether the operator will spill coffee on your tape because it's an unintended, unplanned act (at least you hope so!).

Because you can't find out for certain whether or not this occurrence will happen, you can consider taking one or more of the following approaches to address this risk:

 ✔ **Develop a contingency plan.** For example, in addition to developing a scheme for the computerized selection of names directly from the data tape, have the statistician who guides the selection of the sample develop a scheme for selecting names randomly by hand from the hard copy of the data tape.

 ✔ **Take steps to reduce the likelihood that coffee is spilled on your data tape.** For example, on the morning that your data tape is to be run, check beforehand for open cups of coffee in the computer room.

Of course, if you feel the chances the operator will spill coffee on your data tape are sufficiently small, you can always choose to do nothing beforehand and just deal with the situation if and when it actually occurs.

Developing the WBS helps you identify a situation that may compromise your project's success. You then must decide how to deal with that situation. See Chapter 8 for more detailed information on how to identify and manage project risks and uncertainties.

Documenting What You Need to Know about Your Planned Project Work

After preparing your project WBS, take some time to gather essential information about all work packages (lowest-level WBS components), and keep it in a *WBS dictionary* that's available to all project team members. You and your team will use this information to develop the remaining parts of your plan, as well as to support the tracking, controlling, and replanning of activities during the project. The project manager (or her designee) should approve all changes to information in this dictionary.

At a minimum, the WBS dictionary contains but isn't limited to the following information for all WBS components:

- ✔ **WBS component title and WBS identification code:** Descriptors that uniquely identify the WBS component

- ✔ **Activities included:** List of all the activities that must be performed to create the deliverable identified in the work package

- ✔ **Work detail:** Narrative description of work processes and procedures

- ✔ **Schedule milestones:** Significant events in the component's schedule

- ✔ **Quality requirements:** Desired characteristics of the deliverables produced in the WBS component

- ✔ **Acceptance criteria:** Criteria that must be met before project deliverables are accepted

- ✔ **Required resources:** People, funds, equipment, facilities, raw materials, information, and so on that these activities need

For larger projects, you maintain the WBS — including all its components from Level 1 down to and including the work packages — together in the same hierarchical representation, and you keep all the activities that comprise the work packages in an activity list and/or the WBS dictionary. Separating the WBS components in this way helps you more easily see and understand the important interrelationships and aspects of the project deliverables and work.

On smaller projects, however, you may combine the deliverable-oriented WBS components and the activities that comprise each work package in the same hierarchical display.

Relating This Chapter to the PMP Exam and PMBOK 4

Table 4-1 notes topics in this chapter that may be addressed on the Project Management Professional (PMP) certification exam and that are also included in *A Guide to the Project Management Body of Knowledge,* 4th Edition (*PMBOK 4*).

Table 4-1	Chapter 4 Topics in Relation to the PMP Exam and *PMBOK 4*	
Topic	*Location in PMBOK 4*	*Comments*
Definition of a WBS (see the section "Divide and Conquer: Working on Your Project in Manageable Chunks")	5.3. Create WBS	The definitions of WBS used by the two sources are equivalent.
Creating your WBS (see the sections "Using different approaches to develop your WBS," "Considering different ways to categorize your project's work," "Labeling your WBS entries," "Improving the quality of your WBS," and "Using templates")	5.3.2.1. Decomposition	Both sources mention the same techniques and approaches.
Different WBS display formats (see the section "Displaying your WBS in different formats")	5.3.2.1. Decomposition	Both sources address the same display formats.
WBS dictionary (see the section "Documenting What You Need to Know about Your Planned Project Work")	5.3.3.2. WBS Dictionary	The definitions of the WBS dictionary used by the two sources are equivalent.

Part II
Planning Time: Determining When and How Much

The 5th Wave   By Rich Tennant

"Sorry, Cedric the King cut my budget for additional fools. He said the project already had enough fools on it."

In this part . . .

You have the greatest chance of achieving project success when you have a plan that meets your client's needs and that you believe is possible to accomplish.

In this part, I show you how to develop a feasible and responsive initial project schedule and how to respond when you need to complete your project earlier than planned. I discuss how to estimate the people, funds, and other resources you need to perform the project work. And last, but definitely not least, I discuss how you can identify and deal with potential project risks.

Chapter 5

You Want This Project Done When?

*P*roject assignments always have deadlines. So even though you're not sure what your new project is supposed to accomplish, you want to know when it has to be finished. Unfortunately, when you find out the desired end date, your immediate reaction is often one of panic: "But I don't have enough time!"

The truth is, when you first receive your project assignment, you usually have no idea how long it'll take to complete. Initial reactions tend to be based more on fear and anxiety than on facts, especially when you're trying to juggle multiple responsibilities and the project sounds complex.

To help you develop a more realistic estimate of how long your project will take, you need an organized approach that clarifies how you plan to perform your project's activities, what schedules are possible, and how you'll meet deadlines that initially appear unrealistic. This chapter describes a technique that helps you proactively develop an achievable schedule (while keeping your anxiety in check).

The discussion in this chapter on using network diagrams to develop project schedules is the most technically detailed presentation in this book. Even though the technique takes about ten minutes to master, the explanations and illustrations can appear overwhelming at first glance. If this is your first contact with flowcharts, I suggest you initially scan this chapter for the main points and then read the different sections several times. The more you read the text, the more logical the explanations become. However, if you get frustrated with the technical details, put the book away and come back to it later. You'll be surprised how much clearer the details are the second or third time around!

Picture This: Illustrating a Work Plan with a Network Diagram

To determine the amount of time you need for any project, you have to determine the following two pieces of information:

- ✔ **Sequence:** The order in which you perform the activities
- ✔ **Duration:** How long each individual activity takes

For example, suppose you have a project consisting of ten activities, each of which takes one week to complete. How long will it take you to complete your project? The truth is, you can't tell. You may finish the project in one week if you can perform all ten activities at the same time and have the resources to do so. You may take ten weeks if you have to do the activities one at a time in sequential order. Or you may take between one and ten weeks if you have to do some, but not all, activities in sequence.

To develop a schedule for a small project, you can probably consider the durations and sequential interdependencies in your head. But projects with 15 to 20 activities or more — many of which you can perform at the same time — require an organized method to guide your analysis.

This section helps you develop feasible schedules by showing you how to draw network diagrams and then how to choose the best one for your project.

Defining a network diagram's elements

A *network diagram* is a flowchart that illustrates the order in which you perform project activities. It's your project's test laboratory — it gives you a chance to try out different strategies before performing the work.

No matter how complex your project is, its network diagram has the following three elements: milestones, activities, and durations.

Milestone

A *milestone*, sometimes called an *event*, is a significant occurrence in the life of a project. Milestones take no time and consume no resources; they occur instantaneously. Think of them as signposts that signify a point in your trip to project completion. Milestones mark the start or end of one or more activities. Examples of milestones are *draft report approved* and *design begun*.

Activity

An *activity* is a component of work performed during the course of a project. Activities take time and consume resources; you describe them using action verbs. Examples of activities are *design report* and *conduct survey*.

Make sure you define activities and milestones clearly. The more clearly you define them, the more accurately you can estimate the time and resources needed to perform them, the more easily you can assign them to someone else, and the more meaningful your reporting of schedule progress becomes.

Duration

Duration is the total number of work periods it takes to complete an activity. The amount of work effort required to complete the activity, people's availability, and whether people can work on the activity at the same time all affect the activity's duration. Capacity of nonpersonnel resources (for example, a computer's processing speed and the pages per minute that a copier can print) and availability of those resources also affect duration. In addition, delay can add to an activity's duration. For example, if your boss spends one hour reading your memo after it sat in her inbox for four days and seven hours, the activity's duration is five days, even though your boss spends only one hour reading it.

Understanding the basis of a duration estimate helps you figure out ways to reduce it. For example, suppose you estimate that testing a software package requires that it run for 24 hours on a computer. If you can use the computer only 6 hours in any one day, the duration for your software test is four days. Doubling the number of people working on the test won't reduce the duration to two days, but getting approval to use the computer for 12 hours a day will.

The units of time describe two related, but different, activity characteristics. *Duration* is the number of work periods required to perform an activity; *work effort* is the amount of time a person needs to work full time on the activity to complete it. (See Chapter 6 for more details on work effort.) For example, suppose 4 people had to work together full time for 5 days to complete an activity. The activity's duration is 5 days. The work effort is 20 person-days (4 people multiplied by 5 days).

Drawing a network diagram

Determining your project's end date requires you to choose the dates that each project activity starts and ends and the dates that each milestone is reached. You can determine these dates with the help of a network diagram.

The *activity-on-node* technique (also called *activity-in-box* or *precedence diagramming method*) for drawing a network diagram uses the following three symbols to describe the diagram's three elements:

- ✔ **Boxes:** Boxes represent activities and milestones. If the duration is *0*, it's a milestone; if it's greater than *0*, it's an activity. Note that milestone boxes are sometimes highlighted with lines that are bold, double, or otherwise more noticeable.

- ✔ **Letter *t*:** The letter *t* represents duration.

- ✔ **Arrows:** Arrows represent the direction work flows from one activity or milestone to the next. Upon completion of an activity or reaching of a milestone, you can proceed either to a milestone or directly to another activity as indicated by the arrow(s) leaving that activity or milestone.

Figure 5-1 presents a simple example of an activity-on-node network diagram. When you reach Milestone A (the box on the left), you can perform Activity 1 (the box in the middle), which you estimated will take two weeks to complete. Upon completing Activity 1, you reach Milestone B (the box on the right). The arrows indicate the direction of workflow.

Figure 5-1:
The three symbols in an activity-on-node network diagram, with *t* representing duration.

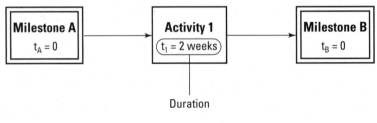

Milestone A
$t_A = 0$

Activity 1
$t_1 = 2\ weeks$

Milestone B
$t_B = 0$

Duration

Those of you who have worked with network diagrams in the past may have seen them drawn in another format called *activity-on-arrow,* also called the *classical approach,* an *arrow diagram,* or a *PERT chart* (see the section "Improving activity duration estimates" later in this chapter for an explanation of PERT analysis). This format represents milestones with circles and activities with arrows. However, because the activity-on-node technique is the one most used today, I draw all network diagrams in this book in this format.

Analyzing a Network Diagram

Think of your project as a trip you and several friends are planning to take. Each of you has a car and will travel a different route to the final destination. During the trip, two or more of your routes will cross at certain places. You agree that all people who pass through a common point must arrive at that point before anyone can proceed on the next leg of the journey. The trip is over when all of you reach the final destination.

You certainly don't want to undertake a trip this complex without planning it out on a road map. After all, planning your trip allows you to

✔ Determine how long the entire trip will take.

✔ Identify potential difficulties along the way.

✔ Consider alternate routes to get to your final destination more quickly.

This section helps you plan your project schedule by telling you how to read and interpret a road map (your network diagram) so you can determine the likely consequences of your possible approaches.

Reading a network diagram

Use the following two rules as you draw and interpret your network diagram. After you understand these rules, analyzing the diagram is a snap:

✔ **Rule 1:** After you finish an activity or reach a milestone, you can proceed to the next activity or milestone, as indicated by the arrow(s).

✔ **Rule 2:** Before you can start an activity or reach a milestone, you must first complete all activities and reach all milestones with arrows pointing to the activity you want to start or milestone you want to reach.

Figure 5-2 illustrates a network diagram. According to Rule 1, from *Start,* you can proceed to work on either Activity 1 or 3, which means you can do either Activity 1 or Activity 3 by itself or both Activities 1 and 3 at the same time. In other words, these two activities are independent of each other.

You may also choose to do neither of the activities. Rule 1 is an *allowing* relationship, not a *forcing* relationship. In other words, you can work on any of the activities that the arrows from *Start* lead to, but you don't have to work on any of them. For example, suppose a part of your plan includes two activities to build a device: *receive parts* and *assemble parts.* As soon as you receive the parts, you can start to assemble them; in fact, you can't start to assemble them until you receive them. But after you receive all the parts you ordered, neither rule says you must start to assemble them immediately; you can assemble them if you want to, or you can wait.

Of course, if you wait, the completion of the assembly will be delayed. But that's your choice.

According to Rule 2, you can start working on Activity 2 in Figure 5-2 as soon as you complete Activity 1 because the arrow from Activity 1 is the only one leading to Activity 2. Rule 2, therefore, is a *forcing* (or requiring) relationship. If arrows from three activities led to Activity 2, you'd have to complete all three activities before starting Activity 2. (The diagram doesn't indicate that you can start working on Activity 2 by completing only one or two of the three activities that lead to it.)

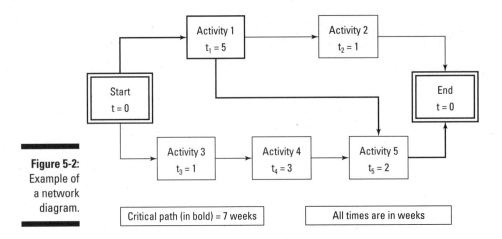

Figure 5-2:
Example of
a network
diagram.

Critical path (in bold) = 7 weeks

All times are in weeks

Interpreting a network diagram

You can use your network diagram to figure out when to start and end activities and when you'll finish the entire project if you perform the activities in this way. To find out the schedule that your approach will allow, you need the following information:

- ✔ **Critical path:** A sequence of activities that takes the longest time to complete

- ✔ **Noncritical path:** A sequence of activities in which you can delay activities and still finish your project in the shortest possible time

- ✔ **Slack time (also called *float*):** The maximum amount of time you can delay an activity and still finish your project in the shortest possible time

- ✔ **Earliest start date:** The earliest date you can start an activity

- ✔ **Earliest finish date:** The earliest date you can finish an activity

- ✔ **Latest start date:** The latest date you can start an activity and still finish your project in the shortest possible time

- ✔ **Latest finish date:** The latest date you can finish an activity and still finish your project in the shortest possible time

You can use the *Critical Path Method (CPM)* to determine this information and to build your project's overall schedule. The following sections illustrate how this method works.

The importance of the critical path

The length of your project's *critical path(s)* in your network diagram defines your project's length (hence, the *Critical Path* Method for determining your project's schedule). If you want to finish your project in less time, consider ways to shorten its critical path.

Monitor critical-path activities closely during performance because *any* delay in critical-path activities will delay your project's completion. Also closely monitor any activities on paths that are close to being critical because any minor delay on those paths can also delay your project's completion.

Your project can have two or more critical paths at the same time. In fact, every path in your project can be critical if every one of them takes the same amount of time. However, when every path is critical, you have a high-risk situation; a delay in any activity immediately causes a delay in the completion of the project.

Critical paths can change as your project unfolds. Sometimes activities on a critical path finish so early that the path becomes shorter than one or more other paths that were initially considered noncritical. Other times, activities on an initially noncritical path are delayed to the point where the sum of their completion times becomes greater than the length of the current critical path (which turns the initially noncritical path into a critical one).

The forward pass — determining critical paths, noncritical paths, and earliest start and finish dates

Your first step in analyzing your project's network diagram is to start at the beginning and see how quickly you can complete the activities along each path. This start-to-finish analysis is called the *forward pass*.

To help you understand what a forward pass is, you can perform one through the diagram in Figure 5-2. According to Rule 1, you can consider working on either Activity 1 or Activity 3 (or both together) as soon as the project starts (check out the section "Reading a network diagram" earlier in this chapter for more info on the two rules of network diagram analysis). First, consider Activities 1 and 2 on the upper path:

- ✔ The earliest you can start Activity 1 is the moment the project starts (the beginning of week 1).

- ✔ The earliest you can finish Activity 1 is the end of week 5 (add Activity 1's estimated duration of five weeks to its earliest start time, which is the start of the project).

- ✔ According to Rule 2, the earliest you can start Activity 2 is the beginning of week 6 because the arrow from Activity 1 is the only one leading to Activity 2.

- ✔ The earliest you can finish Activity 2 is the end of week 6 (add Activity 2's estimated duration of one week to its earliest start time at the beginning of week 6).

So far, so good. Now consider Activities 3, 4, and 5 on the lower path of the diagram:

- ✓ The earliest you can start Activity 3 is the moment the project starts (the beginning of week 1).
- ✓ The earliest you can finish Activity 3 is the end of week 1.
- ✓ The earliest you can start Activity 4 is the beginning of week 2.
- ✓ The earliest you can finish Activity 4 is the end of week 4.

You have to be careful when you try to determine the earliest you can start Activity 5. According to Rule 2, the two arrows entering Activity 5 indicate you must finish both Activity 1 and Activity 4 before you begin Activity 5. Even though you can finish Activity 4 by the end of week 4, you can't finish Activity 1 until the end of week 5. Therefore, the earliest you can start Activity 5 is the beginning of week 6.

If two or more activities or milestones lead to the same activity, the earliest you can start that activity is the latest of the earliest finish dates for those preceding activities or milestones.

Is your head spinning, yet? Take heart; the end's in sight:

- ✓ The earliest you can start Activity 5 is the beginning of week 6.
- ✓ The earliest you can finish Activity 5 is the end of week 7.
- ✓ The earliest you can finish Activity 2 is the end of week 6. Therefore, the earliest you can finish the entire project (and reach the milestone called *End*) is the end of week 7.

So far, you have the following information about your project:

- ✓ The length of the critical path (the shortest time in which you can complete the project) is seven weeks. Only one critical path takes seven weeks; it includes the milestone *Start,* Activity 1, Activity 5, and the milestone *End.*
- ✓ Activity 2, Activity 3, and Activity 4 aren't on critical paths.

The backward pass — determining latest start and finish dates and slack times

You're halfway home. In case resource conflicts or unexpected delays prevent you from beginning all the project activities at their earliest possible start times, you want to know how much you can delay the activities along each path and still finish the project at the earliest possible date. This finish-to-start analysis is called the *backward pass.*

To return to the example started in the preceding section: You found out from the forward pass that the earliest date you can reach the milestone *End* is the end of week 7. However, Rule 2 in the earlier section "Reading a network diagram" says you can't reach the milestone *End* until you've completed Activities 2 and 5. Therefore, to finish your project by the end of week 7, the latest you can finish Activities 2 and 5 is the end of week 7. Again, consider the lower path on the diagram in Figure 5-2 with Activities 3, 4, and 5:

- ✔ You must start Activity 5 by the beginning of week 6 to finish it by the end of week 7 (because Activity 5's estimated duration is two weeks).

- ✔ According to Rule 2, you can't start Activity 5 until you finish Activities 1 and 4. So, you must finish Activities 1 and 4 by the end of week 5.

- ✔ You must start Activity 4 by the beginning of week 3.

- ✔ You must finish Activity 3 before you can work on Activity 4. Therefore, you must finish Activity 3 by the end of week 2.

- ✔ You must start Activity 3 by the beginning of week 2.

Finally, consider the upper path on the network diagram in Figure 5-2:

- ✔ You must start Activity 2 by the beginning of week 7.

- ✔ You can't work on Activity 2 until you finish Activity 1. Therefore, you must finish Activity 1 by the end of week 6.

Here again, you must be careful in your calculations. You must finish Activity 1 by the end of week 5 to start Activity 5 at the beginning of week 6. But, to start work on Activity 2 at the beginning of week 7, you must finish Activity 1 by the end of week 6. So, finishing Activity 1 by the end of week 5 satisfies both requirements.

If two or more arrows leave the same activity or milestone, the latest date you can finish the activity or reach the milestone is the earliest of the latest dates that you must start the next activities or reach the next milestones.

In Figure 5-2, the latest start dates for Activities 2 and 5 are the beginnings of week 7 and week 6, respectively. Therefore, the latest date to finish Activity 1 is the end of week 5. The rest is straightforward: You must start Activity 1 by the beginning of week 1 at the latest.

To organize the dates you calculate in the forward and backward passes, consider writing the earliest and latest start dates and the earliest and latest finish dates at the top of each milestone or activity box in the project's network diagram. Figure 5-3 illustrates how this looks for the example in Figure 5-2.

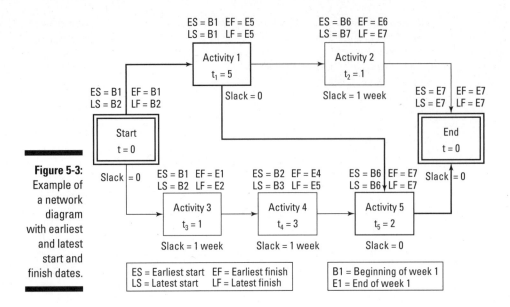

Figure 5-3: Example of a network diagram with earliest and latest start and finish dates.

Now that you have all the earliest and latest start and finish dates for your milestones and activities, you need to determine the slack time for each activity or milestone. (An activity's *slack time* is the amount of time it can be delayed without causing a delay in your overall project completion time.) You can determine slack time in one of two ways:

✔ Subtract the earliest possible start date from the latest allowable start date.

✔ Subtract the earliest possible finish date from the latest allowable finish date.

Thus, you can determine that Activities 2, 3, and 4 have slack times of one week, while Activities 1 and 5 have no slack time. Figure 5-3 displays this information.

Note: If an activity's slack time is zero, the activity is on a critical path.

Although *slack time* is defined as the amount of time an activity or milestone can be delayed without delaying your project's completion time, slack time is actually associated with a sequence of activities rather than with an individual activity. The information in Figure 5-3 indicates that both Activity 3 and Activity 4 (which are on the same path) have slack times of one week. However, if Activity 2 is delayed by a week, Activity 3 will have zero slack time.

A Guide to the Project Management Body of Knowledge, 4th Edition (*PMBOK 4*) identifies the following two types of slack:

✔ **Total slack:** The total amount of time a schedule activity may be delayed without delaying the project end date or a schedule constraint. This is the same as what I refer to as *slack*.

✔ **Free slack:** The amount of time a schedule activity may be delayed without delaying the early start of any immediately following schedule activities.

As an example of these terms, look at the network diagram in Figure 5-3. Consider that Activity 3 is scheduled to start at the beginning of week 1 and Activity 4 is scheduled to start at the beginning of week 3. You can delay the start of Activity 3 by up to one week and Activity 4 will still be able to start at the beginning of week 3. So, Activity 3 has a *free* slack of one week. Coincidently, Activity 3 also has a *total* slack of one week because if you delay its start by more than one week, the completion of the project would be delayed beyond the current scheduled completion date of the end of week 7.

Note: The concept of total slack is more often used in schedule analyses, and that's the concept I use in this book. For simplicity, I refer to this information item simply as *slack* rather than *total slack*.

Working with Your Project's Network Diagram

The preceding sections explain the general rules and procedures for drawing and analyzing any network diagram. This section tells you how to create and analyze the network diagram for your own project.

Determining precedence

To draw your project's network diagram, you first have to decide the order of your project's activities. This section tells you different reasons why you may need to perform activities in a particular order.

Looking at factors that affect predecessors

A *predecessor* to an activity (Activity A, for example) is an activity or milestone that determines when work on Activity A can begin. *PMBOK 4* identifies the following four relationships that can exist between a predecessor and the activity or milestone coming immediately after it (termed its *successor*):

✔ **Finish-to-start:** The predecessor must finish before the successor can start.

✔ **Finish-to-finish:** The predecessor must finish before the successor can finish.

✔ **Start-to-start:** The predecessor must start before the successor can start.

✔ **Start-to-finish:** The predecessor must start before the successor can finish.

The finish-to-start precedence relationship is the one most commonly used, so it's the one I address in this book. In other words, in this book, a *predecessor* is an activity that must be completed before its successor activity can start or its successor milestone can be reached.

Sometimes an activity can't start precisely when its predecessor is finished. A *lag* is the amount of time after its predecessor is completed that you must wait before an activity can start. A *lead* is the amount of time before its predecessor is finished that an activity can begin. In this book, I only consider situations where lead and lag times are zero.

An activity is an *immediate predecessor* to Activity A if you don't have any other activities between it and Activity A. When you determine the immediate predecessors for every activity, you have all the information you need to draw your project's network diagram. The following considerations affect the order in which you must perform your project's activities:

✔ **Mandatory dependencies:** These relationships must be observed if project work is to be a success. They include

- **Legal requirements:** Federal, state, and local laws or regulations require that certain activities be done before others. As an example, consider a pharmaceutical company that has developed a new drug in the laboratory and demonstrated its safety and effectiveness in clinical trials. The manufacturer wants to start producing and selling the drug immediately but can't. Federal law requires that the company obtain Food and Drug Administration (FDA) approval of the drug before selling it.

- **Procedural requirements:** Company policies and procedures require that certain activities be done before others. Suppose you're developing a new piece of software for your organization. You've finished your design and want to start programming the software. However, your organization follows a systems development methodology that requires the management-oversight committee to formally approve your design before you can develop it.

- **Hard logic:** Certain processes must logically occur before others. For example, when building a house, you must pour the concrete for the foundation before you erect the frame.

✔ **Discretionary dependencies:** You may choose to establish these relationships between activities; they aren't required. They include

- **Logical dependencies:** Performing certain activities before others sometimes seems to make the most sense. Suppose you're writing a report. Because much of Chapter 3 depends on what you write in Chapter 2, you decide to write Chapter 2 first. You could write Chapter 3 first or work on both at the same time, but that plan increases the chance that you'll have to rewrite some of Chapter 3 after you finish Chapter 2.

- **Managerial choices:** Sometimes you make arbitrary decisions to work on certain activities before others. Consider that you have to perform both Activity C and Activity D. You can't work on them at the same time, and there's no legal or logical reason why you should work on one or the other first. You decide to work on Activity C first.

✔ **External dependencies:** Starting a project activity may require that an activity outside the project be completed. For example, imagine that your project includes an activity to test a device you're developing. You want to start testing right away, but you can't start this activity until your organization's test laboratory receives and installs a new piece of test equipment they plan to order.

Choosing immediate predecessors

You can decide on the immediate predecessors for your project's activities in one of two ways:

✔ **Front-to-back:** Start with the activities you can perform as soon as your project begins and work your way through to the end. To use this method, follow these steps:

1. **Select the first activity or activities to perform as soon as your project starts.**

2. **Decide which activity or activities you can perform when you finish the first ones (from Step 1).**

3. **Continue in this way until you've considered all activities in the project.**

✔ **Back-to-front:** Choose the activity or activities that will be done last on the project and continue backward toward the beginning. To use this method, follow these steps:

1. **Identify the last project activity or activities you will conduct.**

2. **Decide which activity or activities you must complete right before you can start to work on the last activities (from Step 1).**

3. **Continue in this manner until you've considered all activities in your project.**

Regardless of which method you use to find your project's immediate predecessors, record the immediate predecessors in a simple table like Table 5-1. (This table lists the immediate predecessors in the example shown in Figure 5-2.)

Table 5-1	Immediate Predecessors for Figure 5-2	
Work Breakdown Activity Code	**Activity Description**	**Immediate Predecessors**
1	Activity 1	None
2	Activity 2	1
3	Activity 3	None
4	Activity 4	3
5	Activity 5	1, 4

Determine precedence based on the nature and requirements of the activities, not on the resources you think will be available. Suppose Activities A and B of your project can be performed at the same time but you plan to assign them to the same person. In this case, don't make Activity A the immediate predecessor for B, thinking that the person can work on only one activity at a time. Instead, let your diagram show that A and B can be done at the same time. Later, if you find out you have another person who can help out with this work, you can evaluate the impact of performing Activities A and B at the same time. (See Chapter 6 for a discussion on how to determine when people are overcommitted and how to resolve these situations.)

When you create your network diagram for simple projects, consider writing the names of your activities and milestones on sticky-back notes and attaching them to chart paper or a wall. For more complex projects, consider using an integrated project-management software package. (See Chapter 16 for a discussion of how to use software to support your project planning, and check out *Microsoft Office Project 2007 For Dummies* by Nancy Muir [Wiley] for the lowdown on the most popular project-management software package.)

Using a network diagram to analyze a simple example

Consider the following example of preparing for a picnic to illustrate how to use a network diagram to determine possible schedules while meeting project expectations and satisfying project constraints. (I'm not suggesting that you plan all your picnics this way, but the situation does illustrate the technique rather nicely!)

Deciding on the activities

It's Friday evening, and you and your friend are considering what to do during the weekend to unwind and relax. The forecast for Saturday is for sunny and mild weather, so you decide to go on a picnic at a local lake.

Because you want to get the most enjoyment possible from your picnic, you decide to plan the outing carefully by drawing and analyzing a network diagram. Table 5-2 illustrates the seven activities you decide you must perform to prepare for your picnic and get to the lake.

Table 5-2	Activities for Your Picnic at the Lake		
Activity Identifier Code	*Activity Description*	*Who Will Be Present*	*Duration (In Minutes)*
1	Load car	You and your friend	5
2	Get money from bank	You	5
3	Make egg sandwiches	Your friend	10
4	Drive to the lake	You and your friend	30
5	Decide which lake to go to	You and your friend	2
6	Buy gasoline	You	10
7	Boil eggs (for egg sandwiches)	Your friend	10

In addition, you agree to observe the following constraints:

✔ You and your friend will start all activities at your house at 8 a.m. Saturday — you can't do anything before that time.

✔ You must perform all seven activities to complete your project.

✔ You can't change who must be present during each activity.

✔ The two lakes you're considering are in opposite directions from your house, so you must decide where you're going to have your picnic before you begin your drive.

Setting the order of the activities

Now that you have all your activities listed, you need to decide the order in which you will do them. In other words, you need to determine the immediate predecessors for each activity. The following dependencies are required: Your friend must boil the eggs before he can make the egg sandwiches (duh!), and both of you must load the car and decide which lake to visit before you start your drive.

The order of the rest of the activities is up to you. You may consider the following approach:

✔ Decide which lake before you do anything else.

✔ After you both agree on the lake, you drive to the bank to get money.

✔ After you get money from the bank, you get gasoline.

✔ At the same time, after you agree on the lake, your friend starts to boil the eggs.

✔ After the eggs are boiled, your friend makes the egg sandwiches.

✔ After you get back with the gas and your friend finishes the egg sandwiches, you both load the car.

✔ After you both load the car, you drive to the lake.

Table 5-3 depicts these predecessor relationships.

Table 5-3	Predecessor Relationships for Your Picnic	
Activity Identifier Code	Activity Description	Immediate Predecessors
1	Load car	3, 6
2	Get money from bank	5
3	Make egg sandwiches	7
4	Drive to lake	1
5	Decide which lake	None
6	Buy gasoline	2
7	Boil eggs (for egg sandwiches)	5

Creating the network diagram

Now that you have your immediate predecessors in mind, you can draw the network diagram for your project from the information in Table 5-5. To do so, follow these steps:

1. **Begin your project with a single milestone and label it *Start*.**

2. **Find all activities in the table that have no immediate predecessors — they can all start as soon as you begin your project.**

   In this case, only Activity 5 has no immediate predecessors.

3. **Begin your diagram by drawing the relationship between the Start of your project and the beginning of Activity 5 (see Figure 5-4).**

   Depict Activity 5 with a box and draw an arrow to it from the Start box.

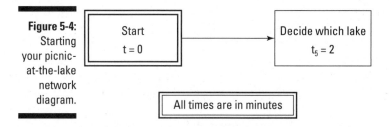

Figure 5-4:
Starting
your picnic-
at-the-lake
network
diagram.

4. **Find all activities that have your first activity as an immediate predecessor.**

   In this case, Table 5-3 shows that Activities 2 and 7 have Activity 5 as an immediate predecessor. Draw boxes to represent these two activities, and draw arrows from Activity 5 to Activities 2 and 7 (see Figure 5-5).

5. **Continue in the same way with the remaining activities.**

   Recognize from Table 5-5 that only Activity 6 has Activity 2 as an immediate predecessor. Therefore, draw a box to represent Activity 6 and draw an arrow from Activity 2 to that box.

   Table 5-3 also shows that only Activity 3 has Activity 7 as an immediate predecessor. So draw a box to represent Activity 3, and draw an arrow from Activity 7 to Activity 3. Figure 5-5 depicts your diagram in progress.

   Now realize that Activity 1 has both Activities 3 and 6 as immediate predecessors. Therefore, draw a box representing Activity 1 and draw arrows from Activities 3 and 6 to this box.

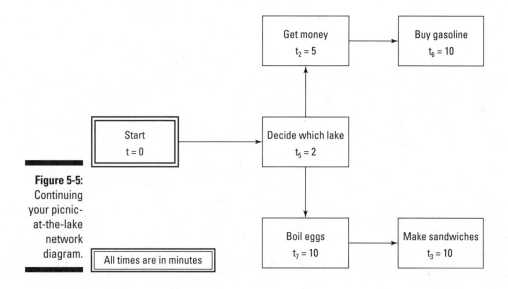

Figure 5-5:
Continuing
your picnic-
at-the-lake
network
diagram.

The rest is pretty straightforward. Because only Activity 4 has Activity 1 as its immediate predecessor, draw a box representing Activity 4 and draw an arrow from Activity 1 to Activity 4.

6. **After adding all the activities to the diagram, draw a box to represent *End*, and draw an arrow from Activity 4 (the last activity you have to complete) to that box (see Figure 5-6 for the complete network diagram).**

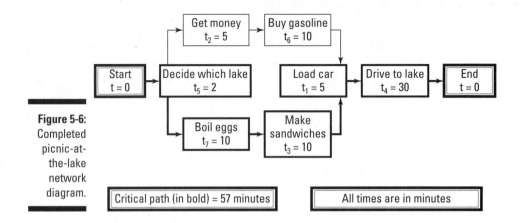

Figure 5-6:
Completed
picnic-at-
the-lake
network
diagram.

Now for the important timing-related questions. First, how long will you and your friend take to get to the lake for your picnic? The upper path (*Start*, Activities 5, 2, 6, 1, 4, and *End*) takes 52 minutes to complete, and the lower path (*Start,* Activities 5, 7, 3, 1, 4, and *End*) takes 57 minutes to complete. Thus, it will take 57 minutes from the time you start until you arrive at the lake for your picnic, and the lower path is the critical path.

The second timing-related question you have to answer is: Can you delay any activities and still get to the lake in 57 minutes? If so, which ones can you delay and by how much? To answer these questions, consider the following:

✔ The network diagram reveals that Activities 5, 7, 3, 1, and 4 are all on the critical path. Therefore, you can't delay any of them if you want to get to the lake in 57 minutes.

✔ Activities 2 and 6 aren't on the critical path, and they can be performed at the same time as Activities 7 and 3. Activities 7 and 3 take 20 minutes to perform, while Activities 2 and 6 take 15 minutes. Therefore, Activities 2 and 6 have a total slack time of 5 minutes.

Developing Your Project's Schedule

Developing your project's schedule requires the combination of activities, resources, and activity-performance sequences that gives you the greatest chance of meeting your client's expectations with the least amount of risk. This section helps you start making a project schedule. It also focuses on some potential pitfalls and solutions for meeting time crunches.

Taking the first steps

After you specify your project's activities (see the discussion on creating Work Breakdown Structures in Chapter 4), take the following steps to develop an initial project schedule:

1. **Identify immediate predecessors for all activities.**

   Immediate predecessors define the structure of your network diagram.

2. **Determine the personnel and nonpersonnel resources required for all activities.**

   The type, amount, and availability of resources affect how long you need to perform each activity.

3. **Estimate durations for all activities.**

   See the section "Estimating Activity Duration" for details on how to do so.

4. **Identify all intermediate and final dates that must be met.**

   These dates define the criteria that your schedule must meet.

5. **Identify all activities or milestones outside your project that affect your project's activities.**

   After you identify these external activities and milestones, you can set up the appropriate dependencies between them and your project's activities and milestones.

6. **Draw your network diagram.**

   Use the network diagram to determine what schedules your project can achieve.

7. **Analyze your project's network diagram to identity all critical paths and their lengths and to identify the slack times of noncritical paths.**

   This information helps you choose which project activities to monitor and how often to monitor them. It also suggests strategies for getting back on track if you encounter unexpected schedule delays. (See the section "Interpreting a network diagram" earlier in this chapter for additional information on critical and noncritical paths.)

If the completion date is acceptable to your client, you're done with your scheduling. However, if your client wants you to finish faster than your initial schedule allows, your analyses are just beginning.

Avoiding the pitfall of backing in to your schedule

Beware of developing a schedule by *backing in,* that is, starting at the end of a project and working your way back toward the beginning to identify activities and estimate durations that allow you to meet your client's desired end date. Using this approach substantially decreases the chances that you'll meet the schedule for the following reasons:

- ✔ You may miss activities because your focus is on meeting a time constraint, not ensuring that you've identified all required work.

- ✔ You base your duration estimates on what you can *allow* activities to take rather than what they'll *require.*

- ✔ The order for your proposed activities may not be the most effective one.

I was reviewing a colleague's project plan a while back and noticed that she had allowed one week for her final report's review and approval. When I asked her whether she thought this estimate was realistic, she replied that it certainly wasn't realistic but that she had to use that estimate for the project plan to work out. In other words, she was using time estimates that totaled to the number she *wanted* to reach rather than ones she thought she *could* meet.

Meeting an established time constraint

Suppose your initial schedule has you finishing your project in three months, but your client wants the results in two months. Consider the following options for reducing the length of your critical paths:

- ✔ **Recheck the original duration estimates.**
  - • Be sure you have clearly described the activity's work.
  - • If you used past performance as a guide for developing the durations, recheck to be sure all characteristics of your current situation are the same as those of the past performance.
  - • Ask other experts to review and validate your estimates.
  - • Ask the people who'll actually be doing the work on these activities to review and validate your estimates.

- ✔ **Consider using more-experienced personnel.** Sometimes more-experienced personnel can get work done in less time. Of course, using more-experienced people may cost you more money. Further, you're not the only one in your organization who needs those more-experienced personnel; they may not always be available to help with your project!

> ✔ **Consider different strategies for performing the activities.** As an example, if you estimate a task you're planning to do internally to take three weeks, see if you can find an external contractor who can perform it in two weeks.
>
> ✔ **Consider *fast tracking* — performing tasks that are normally done sequentially at the same time.** While fast tracking can shorten the overall time to perform the tasks, it also increases the risk of having to redo portions of your work, so be ready to do so.

As you reduce the lengths of critical paths, monitor paths that aren't initially critical to ensure that they haven't become critical. If one or more paths have become critical, use these same approaches to reduce their lengths.

Applying different strategies to arrive at your picnic in less time

Consider the example of preparing for a picnic (which I introduce in the "Using a network diagram to analyze a simple example" section) to see how you can apply these approaches for reducing a project's time to your own project.

Figure 5-6 illustrates your initial 57-minute plan. If arriving at the lake in 57 minutes is okay, your analysis is done. But suppose you and your friend agree that you must reach the lake no later than 45 minutes after you start preparing on Saturday morning. What changes can you make to save you 12 minutes?

You may be tempted to change the estimated time for the drive from 30 minutes to 18 minutes, figuring that you'll just drive faster. Unfortunately, doing so doesn't work if the drive really takes 30 minutes. Remember, your plan represents an approach that you believe has a chance to work (though not necessarily one that's guaranteed). If you have to drive at speeds in excess of 100 miles per hour over dirt roads to drive to the lake in 18 minutes, reducing the duration estimate has no chance of working. (However, doing so does have an excellent chance of getting you a speeding ticket.)

To develop a more realistic plan to reduce your project's schedule, take the following steps:

1. **Start to reduce your project's time by finding the critical path and reducing its time until a second path becomes critical.**

2. **To reduce your project's time further, shorten both critical paths by the same amount until a third path becomes critical.**

3. **To reduce the time still further, shorten all three critical paths by the same amount of time until a fourth path becomes critical, and so on.**

Performing activities at the same time

One way to shorten the time it takes to do a group of activities is by taking one or more activities off the critical path and doing them in parallel with the remaining activities. However, often you have to be creative to simultaneously perform activities successfully.

Consider the 57-minute solution to the picnic example in Figure 5-6. Assume an automatic teller machine (ATM) is next to the gas station that you use. If you use a full-service gas island, you can get money from the ATM while the attendant fills your gas tank. This strategy allows you to perform Activities 2 and 6 at the same time — in a total of 10 minutes rather than the 15 minutes you indicated in the initial network diagram.

At first glance, it appears you can cut the total time down to 52 minutes by making this change. But look again. These two activities aren't on the critical path, so completing them more quickly has no impact on the overall project schedule. (Before you think you can save five minutes by helping your friend make the sandwiches, remember: You agreed that you can't swap jobs.)

Now you have to try again. This time, remember you must reduce the length of the *critical path* if you want to save time. Here's another idea: On your drive to the lake, you and your friend are both in the car, but only one of you is driving. The other person is just sitting there. If you agree to drive, your friend can load the fixings for the sandwiches into the car and make the sandwiches while you drive. This adjustment appears to take ten minutes off the critical path. But does it really?

The diagram in Figure 5-6 reveals that the upper path (Activities 2 and 6) takes 15 minutes and the lower path (Activities 7 and 3) takes 20 minutes. Because the lower path is the critical path, removing five minutes from it can reduce the time to complete the overall project by five minutes. However, reducing the lower path by five minutes makes it the same length (15 minutes) as the upper path. As a result, both paths take 15 minutes, and both are now critical.

Taking an additional five minutes off the lower path (because the sandwiches take ten minutes to make) doesn't save more time for the overall project because the upper path still takes 15 minutes. However, removing the extra five minutes from the lower path does add five minutes of slack to the lower path.

Figure 5-7 reflects this change in your network diagram. Now you can consider using your first idea to get money at the ATM while an attendant fills your car with gas. This time, this move can save you five minutes because the upper path is now critical.

Finally, you can decide which lake to visit and load the car at the same time, which saves you an additional two minutes. Figure 5-8 illustrates the final 45-minute solution.

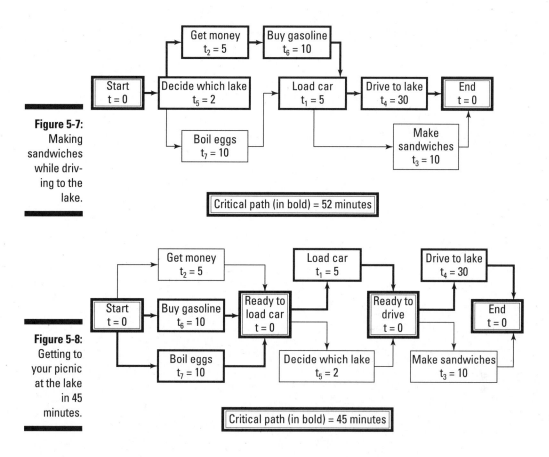

Figure 5-7: Making sandwiches while driving to the lake.

Critical path (in bold) = 52 minutes

Figure 5-8: Getting to your picnic at the lake in 45 minutes.

Critical path (in bold) = 45 minutes

Consider a situation in which you have to complete two or more activities before you can work on two or more new ones. Show this relationship in your diagram by defining a milestone that represents completion of the activities, drawing arrows from the activities to this milestone and then drawing arrows from that milestone to the new activities (refer to Figure 5-8).

In the example, you first complete the activities *Get money, Buy gasoline,* and *Boil eggs,* and then you can perform the activities *Load car* and *Decide which lake.* You represent this relationship by drawing arrows from each of the first three activities to a newly defined milestone, *Ready to load car,* and by drawing arrows from that milestone to the activities *Load car* and *Decide which lake.*

If you think this analysis is getting complicated, you're right. You pay a price to perform a group of activities faster. This price includes

✔ **Increased planning time:** You have to detail precisely all the activities and their interrelationships because you can't afford to make mistakes.

✔ **Increased risks:** The list of assumptions grows, increasing the chances that one or more will turn out to be wrong.

In the picnic-at-the-lake example, you make the following assumptions to arrive at a possible 45-minute solution:

- ✔ You can get right into the full-service island at a little after 8 a.m.
- ✔ Attendants are available to fill up your tank as soon as you pull into the full-service island.
- ✔ The ATM is free and working when you pull into the full-service island.
- ✔ You and your friend can load the car and make a decision together without getting into an argument that takes an hour to resolve.
- ✔ Your friend can make sandwiches in the moving car without totally destroying the car's interior in the process.

At the same time that making assumptions can increase the risks involved in your possible project schedule, identifying the assumptions you make can increase the chances that those assumptions will come true — or at least convince you to develop contingency plans in case they don't.

Consider your assumption that you can get right into a full-service island at about 8 a.m. on Saturday. You can call the gas station owner and ask whether your assumption is reasonable. If the gas station owner tells you he has no idea how long you'll have to wait for someone to pump your gas, you may ask him whether it would make a difference if you paid him $200 in cash. When he immediately promises to cordon off the full-service island from 7:55 a.m. until 8:20 a.m. and assign two attendants to wait there, one with a nozzle and the other with a charge receipt ready to be filled out (so you'll be out in ten minutes), you realize you can reduce most uncertainties for a price! Your job is to determine how much you can reduce the uncertainty and what price you have to pay to do so.

Devising an entirely new strategy

So you have a plan for getting to the lake in 45 minutes. You can't guarantee the plan will work, but at least you have a chance. However, suppose your friend now tells you he really needs to get to the lake in 10 minutes, not 45! Your immediate reaction is probably "Impossible!" You figure creative planning is one thing, but how can you get to the lake in 10 minutes when the drive alone takes 30 minutes?

By deciding that you absolutely can't arrive at the lake in 10 minutes when the drive alone takes 30 minutes, you've forgotten that the true indicator of success in this project is arriving at the lake for your picnic, not performing a predetermined set of activities. Your original seven activities were fine, as long as they allowed you to get to the lake within your set constraints. But if the activities won't allow you to achieve success as you now define it (arriving at the lake in ten minutes), consider changing the activities.

Suppose you decide to find a way other than driving to get from your home to the lake. After some checking, you discover that you can rent a helicopter for $500 per day that'll fly you and your friend to the lake in ten minutes. However, you figure that you both were thinking about spending a total of $10 on your picnic (for admission to the park at the lake). You conclude that it makes no sense to spend $500 to get to a $10 picnic, so you don't even tell your friend about the possibility of renting the helicopter. Instead, you just reaffirm that getting to the lake in ten minutes is impossible. Unfortunately, when you decided not to tell your friend about the helicopter option, you didn't know your friend found out that he could make a $10,000 profit on a business deal if he could get to the lake in ten minutes. Is it worth spending $500 to make $10,000? Sure. But you didn't know about the $10,000 when you gave up on getting to the lake in ten minutes.

When developing schedule options, it's not your job to preempt someone else from making a decision. Instead, you want to present all options and their associated costs and benefits to the decision maker so he can make the best decision. In this instance, you should've told your friend about the helicopter option so he could've considered it when he made the final decision.

Subdividing activities

You can often reduce the time to complete a sequence of activities by subdividing one or more of the activities and performing parts of them at the same time. To relate back to the picnic-at-the-lake example, your friend can save seven minutes when boiling the eggs and preparing the egg sandwiches by using the approach I illustrate in Figure 5-9. Here's what your friend needs to do:

✔ **Divide the activity of boiling the eggs into two parts:**

- **Prepare to boil the eggs:** Remove the pot from the cupboard, take the eggs out of the refrigerator, put the water and eggs in the pot, put the pot on the stove, and turn on the heat — estimated duration of three minutes.

- **Boil the eggs in water:** Allow the eggs to boil in a pot until they're hard — estimated duration of seven minutes.

✔ **Divide the activity of making the egg sandwiches into two parts:**

- **Perform the initial steps to make the sandwiches:** Take the bread, mayonnaise, lettuce, and tomatoes out of the refrigerator; take the wax paper out of the drawer; put the bread on the wax paper; put the mayonnaise, lettuce, and tomatoes on the bread — estimated duration of seven minutes.

- **Finish making the sandwiches:** Take the eggs out of the pot; shell, slice, and put them on the bread; slice and finish wrapping the sandwiches — estimated duration of three minutes.

✔ **First prepare to boil the eggs; next boil the eggs in water and perform the initial steps to make sandwiches at the same time; finally, finish making the sandwiches.**

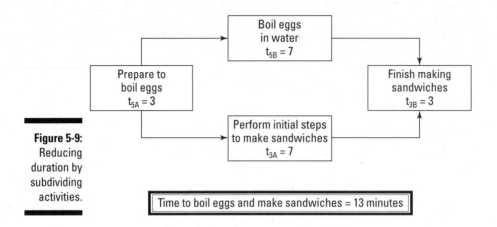

Figure 5-9:
Reducing
duration by
subdividing
activities.

As Figure 5-9 illustrates, the total time to boil the eggs and prepare the sandwiches is: 3 minutes + 7 minutes + 3 minutes = 13 minutes. ***Note:*** The total time for the original activity to boil the eggs is still ten minutes (three minutes to prepare and seven minutes in the water), and the total time for the original activity to make the sandwiches is also still ten minutes (seven minutes for the initial steps and three minutes to finish up). But by subdividing the activities and scheduling them in greater detail, you can complete them in 13 minutes rather than 20.

Estimating Activity Duration

A *duration estimate* is your best sense of how long you need to actually perform an activity. The estimate is not how long you want the activity to take or how long someone tells you it must take; the estimate is how long you think it really will take.

Overly optimistic or unrealistically short duration estimates can cause an activity to take longer than necessary for the following two reasons:

 ✔ Because unrealistic estimates appear to meet your schedule targets, you don't seek realistic alternative strategies that increase the chances of accomplishing activities in their declared durations.

 ✔ If people believe duration estimates are totally unrealistic, they'll stop trying to achieve them. When delays occur during an activity, people will accept them as inevitable instead of seeking ways to overcome them.

This section looks more closely at what you need to estimate activity duration accurately, including an understanding of the activity's components and processes and the resources required to support these processes.

Determining the underlying factors

The underlying makeup of an activity determines how long it will take to complete. Therefore, accurately estimating that activity's duration requires you to describe its different aspects and determine the effect of each one on the activity's length.

When estimating an activity's duration, consider past experience, expert opinion, and other available sources of information to clarify the following components of the activity:

- ✔ **Work performed by people:** Physical and mental activities that people perform, such as writing a report, assembling a piece of equipment, and thinking of ideas for an ad campaign

- ✔ **Work performed by nonhuman resources:** Activities that computers and other machines perform, such as testing software on a computer and printing a report on a high-speed copy machine

- ✔ **Physical processes:** Physical or chemical reactions, such as concrete curing, paint drying, and chemical reactions in a laboratory

- ✔ **Time delays:** Time during which nothing is happening, such as needing to reserve a conference room two weeks before holding a meeting (Time delays are typically due to the unavailability of resources.)

Considering resource characteristics

Knowing the types of resources an activity requires can help you improve your estimate of the activity's duration. For example, not all copy machines generate copies at the same rate. Specifying the characteristics of the particular machine you'll use to make copies can improve the activity's duration estimate.

To support project work, you may need the following types of resources: personnel, equipment, facilities, raw materials, information, and funds. For each resource you need, you have to determine its

- ✔ **Capacity:** Productivity per unit time period
- ✔ **Availability:** When a resource will be available

For example, a copy machine that produces 1,000 copies per minute can complete a job in half the time a machine that produces 500 copies per minute requires. Likewise, a large printing job can take half as long if you have access to a copy machine for four hours a day rather than two hours a day. (See Chapter 7 for more information on estimating project requirements for nonhuman resources.)

Finding sources of supporting information

The first step toward improving your estimate's accuracy is to take into account the right kinds of information, such as determining how long similar activities have actually taken in the past rather than how long people thought they would or should take. However, your estimate's accuracy also depends on the accuracy of the information you use to derive it.

The information you need often has no single authoritative source. Therefore, compare information from the following sources as you prepare your duration estimates:

✔ Historical records of how long similar activities have taken in the past

✔ People who've performed similar activities in the past

✔ People who'll be working on the activities

✔ Experts familiar with the type of activity, even if they haven't performed the exact activity before

Improving activity duration estimates

In addition to ensuring accurate and complete data, do the following to improve the quality of your duration estimates (see Chapter 4 for more details about how to define and describe your project's activities):

✔ **Define your activities clearly.** Minimize the use of technical jargon, and describe work processes fully.

✔ **Subdivide your activities until your lowest-level activity estimates are two weeks or less.**

✔ **Define activity start and end points clearly.**

✔ **Involve the people who'll perform an activity when estimating its duration.**

✔ **Minimize the use of fudge factors.** A *fudge factor* is an amount of time you add to your best estimate of duration "just to be safe." Automatically estimating your final duration estimates to be 50 percent greater than your initial ones is an example. Fudge factors compromise your project planning for the following reasons:

   • Work tends to expand to fill the allotted time. If you're able to finish an activity in two weeks but use a 50-percent fudge factor to indicate a duration of three weeks, the likelihood that you'll finish in less than three weeks is almost zero.

   • People use fudge factors to avoid studying activities in sufficient depth; as a result, they can't develop viable performance strategies.

- Team members and other project audiences lose faith in your plan's accuracy and feasibility because they know you're playing with numbers rather than thinking activities through in detail.

No matter how hard you try, estimating duration accurately can be next to impossible for some activities. For example, you may have an exceptionally difficult time coming up with accurate duration estimates for activities you haven't done before, activities you'll perform in the future, and activities with a history of unpredictability. In these cases,

✔ Make the best estimate you can by following the approaches and guidelines in this section.

✔ Monitor activities closely as your project unfolds to identify details that may affect your initial estimate.

✔ Reflect any changes in your project schedule as soon as you become aware of them.

In situations where you've performed an activity many times before and have historical data on how long it took each time, you may be able to estimate with confidence how long the activity will take the next time you perform it. In less certain situations, however, you may choose to consider the activity's duration as a random variable that can have a range of values with different probabilities.

The *Program Evaluation and Review Technique* (PERT) is a network analysis methodology that treats an activity's duration as a random variable with the probability of the variable having different values being described by a Beta distribution. According to the characteristics of a Beta distribution, you determine the *average value* (also called the *expected value*) of the activity's duration from the following three time estimates:

✔ **Optimistic estimate (t_o):** If you perform the activity 100 times, its duration would be greater than or equal to this number 99 times.

✔ **Most likely estimate (t_m):** If you perform the activity 100 times, the duration would be this number more times than any other.

✔ **Pessimistic estimate (t_p):** If you perform this activity 100 times, its duration would be less than or equal to this number 99 times.

The expected value of the duration (t_e) is then defined by the following formula:

$$\text{Expected value} = t_e = (t_o + 4t_m + t_p) \div 6$$

If only a small number of activities in your network are uncertain, you may assign their durations to be equal to their expected values and determine the critical path, earliest and latest start and finish times, and slack times as before. However, if all activities in your network are uncertain, you may choose to develop three time estimates for each activity. In this case, you can use the properties of the Beta distribution to determine the probability that the length of the critical path falls within specified ranges on either side of the expected value.

Displaying Your Project's Schedule

Unless all your activities are on a critical path, your network diagram doesn't specify your exact schedule. Rather, it provides information for you to consider when you develop your schedule. After you select your actual dates, choose one of the following formats in which to present your schedule:

- ✔ **Milestone list:** A table that lists milestones and the dates you plan to reach them
- ✔ **Activity list:** A table that lists activities and the dates you plan to start and end them
- ✔ **Combined milestone/activity list:** A table that includes milestone and activity dates
- ✔ **Gantt chart:** A timeline that illustrates when each activity starts, how long it continues, and when it ends
- ✔ **Combined milestone and Gantt chart:** A timeline that illustrates when activities start, how long they continue, when they end, and when selected milestones are achieved

Figure 5-10 presents the 45-minute schedule for your picnic at the lake (from Figure 5-8) in a milestone/activity list.

You may combine two or more formats into a single display. Figure 5-11 illustrates a combined WBS, Responsibility Assignment Matrix (see Chapter 10), and Gantt chart (in which triangles represent milestones) for the picnic-at-the-lake example. In addition to requiring less paperwork to prepare and being easier to update and maintain than separate information documents, a combined display can provide greater insight into the plan by presenting two or more aspects together for ready comparison.

Each format can be effective in particular situations. Consider the following guidelines when choosing the format in which to display your schedule:

- ✔ Milestone lists and activity lists are more effective for indicating specific dates.
- ✔ The Gantt chart provides a clearer picture of the relative lengths of activities and times when they overlap.
- ✔ The Gantt chart provides a better high-level overview of a project.

Milestone/Activity	Person Responsible	Start Date (minutes after project start)	End Date (minutes after project start)	Comments
1. Get money	You	0	5	
2. Buy gasoline	You	0	10	Critical path
3. Boil eggs	Your friend	0	10	Critical path
A. Ready to load car	**You and your friend**	-	**10**	**Critical path**
4. Load car	You and your friend	10	15	Critical path
5. Decide which lake	You and your friend	10	12	
B. Ready to drive	**You and your friend**	-	**15**	**Critical path**
6. Make egg sandwiches	Your friend	15	25	
7. Drive to lake	You and your friend	15	45	Critical path
C. End – arrived at lake	**You and your friend**	-	**45**	**Critical path**

Figure 5-10: Representing your picnic-at-the-lake schedule in a milestone/activity list.

Note: Events are in bold.

Figure 5-11: Representing your picnic-at-the-lake schedule in a combined WBS, Responsibility Assignment Matrix, and Gantt chart.

Work Breakdown Structure			Responsibility Assignment Matrix		Gantt Chart	
Activity/Milestone			Personnel		Time (in minutes after start)	
ID	WBS code	Title	You	Friend	0 5 10 15 20 25 30 35 40 45 50 55	
10	1.0.	Start	P	S		
8	2.0.	Preparations	S	P		
2	2.1.	Money	P	-		
6	2.2.	Gas	P	-		
7	2.3.	Eggs	-	P		
3	2.4.	Egg sandwiches	-	P	Summary activities	
5	3.0.	Decide which lake	S	P		
9	4.0.	Travel	P	S		
1	4.1.	Loading car	P	S		
4	4.2.	Driving to lake	P	S	Critical path is outlined in bold	
11	5.0.	End	P	S		

P = Primary responsibility
S = Secondary responsibility

Relating This Chapter to the PMP Exam and PMBOK 4

Table 5-4 notes topics in this chapter that may be addressed on the Project Management Professional (PMP) certification exam and that are also included in *A Guide to the Project Management Body of Knowledge*, 4th Edition (*PMBOK 4*).

Table 5-4	Chapter 5 Topics in Relation to the PMP Exam and *PMBOK 4*	
Topic	*Location in PMBOK 4*	*Comments*
Definition of network diagram (see the section "Picture This: Illustrating a Work Plan with a Network Diagram")	6.2.2. Sequence Activities: Tools and Techniques	The terms and approaches in this book are the same as those used in *PMBOK 4*.
Reading and interpreting a network diagram (see the section "Analyzing a Network Diagram")	6.5.2.2. Critical Path Method	The terms and approaches in this book are the same as those used in *PMBOK 4*.
Understanding precedence (see the section "Determining precedence")	6.2.2. Sequence Activities: Tools and Techniques	The terms and approaches in this book are the same as those used in *PMBOK 4*.
Developing the schedule (see the section "Developing Your Project's Schedule")	6.5.2. Develop Schedule: Tools and Techniques	The terms and approaches in this book are the same as those used in *PMBOK 4*.
Estimating duration (see the section "Estimating Activity Duration")	6.4. Estimate Activity Durations	The terms and approaches in this book are the same as those used in *PMBOK 4*.
Displaying the schedule (see the section "Displaying Your Project's Schedule")	6.5.3.1. Project Schedule	The terms and approaches in this book are the same as those used in *PMBOK 4*.

Chapter 6

Establishing Whom You Need, How Much, and When

1 remember reading the following declaration by a stressed-out project manager: "We've done so much with so little for so long [that] they now expect us to do everything with nothing!"

The truth is, of course, you can't accomplish anything with nothing; everything has a price. You live in a world of limited resources and not enough time, which means you always have more work to do than time and resources allow. After you decide which tasks to pursue, you need to do everything possible to perform them successfully.

Carefully planning for the personnel you need to perform your project increases your chances of succeeding by enabling you to

✔ Ensure the most qualified people available are assigned to each task.

✔ Explain more effectively to team members what you're asking them to contribute to the project.

✔ Develop more accurate and realistic schedules.

✔ Ensure that people are on hand when they're needed.

✔ Monitor resource expenditures to identify and address possible overruns or underruns.

Some organizations have procedures that detail and track every resource on every project. Other organizations don't formally plan or track project resources at all. However, even if your organization doesn't require you to plan your resource needs and track your resource use, doing so is invaluable to your project's success.

This chapter helps you figure out whom you need on your project, when, and for how long. It also discusses how you can identify and manage conflicting demands for people's time.

Getting the Information You Need to Match People to Tasks

Your project's success rests on your ability to enlist the help of appropriately qualified people to perform your project's work. You begin your project planning by determining your project's required results and major deliverables (see Chapter 2 for details on how to do this). You continue your planning by detailing the intermediate and final deliverables that your project must generate in a Work Breakdown Structure (WBS; see Chapter 4 for more information). Your next step is to decide which activities you'll need performed to create the deliverables identified in your project's work packages (the lowest-level components in the WBS) and to determine the skills and knowledge people must have to perform them.

As you find out in the following sections, getting appropriately qualified people to perform your project's activities entails the following two steps:

✔ Determining the skills and knowledge that each activity requires

✔ Confirming that the people assigned to those activities possess the required skills and knowledge and that they're genuinely interested in working on their assignments

A *skill* is something you must be able to do to perform an activity successfully. *Knowledge* is information you must have in your head to be able to perform an activity successfully. *Interest* is your personal desire to know about and be involved with the subject matter of an activity and to have a part in successfully producing the result of the activity. Possessing the necessary skills and knowledge means you're capable of doing a task. Being interested in the task increases the chances you'll apply your skills and knowledge to actually accomplish the task successfully.

Deciding the skills and knowledge that team members must have

To begin deciding the skills and knowledge that people must have for your project, obtain a complete list of all your project's activities. Specify your project's activities by decomposing all the work packages (the lowest-level WBS components) in your project's WBS into the individual actions required to complete them.

You may find information to help you complete this task in your project's WBS dictionary; you identify and describe your project's activities and their important characteristics — such as a unique name and identifier code, duration, predecessors, and successors — in this document. (See Chapter 4 for details on WBS dictionaries and decomposition.)

Next, determine each activity's skill and knowledge requirements by reviewing activity descriptions and consulting with subject-matter experts, your human resources department, and people who have worked on similar projects and activities in the past.

Because you'll ask functional managers and others in the organization to assign staff to your project who have the specified skills and knowledge that your project work requires, you should check with these people before you prepare your list of required skills and knowledge to see whether they have developed any skills rosters and, if they haven't, the schemes (if any) that they or the organization currently uses to describe staff's skills and knowledge. Then, if possible, you can use the same or a similar scheme to describe your project's skill and knowledge requirements to make it easier for the managers to identify those people who are appropriately qualified to address your project's requirements.

For most situations, you need to know two pieces of information about a task to determine the qualifications that a person must have to perform it:

✔ The required levels of proficiency in the needed skills and knowledge

✔ Whether the assignment will entail working under someone else's guidance when applying the skills or knowledge, working alone to apply the skills or knowledge, or managing others who are applying the skills or knowledge.

An example of a scheme that describes these two aspects of a skill or knowledge requirement is *(X, Y)*. *X* is the required level of proficiency in the skill or knowledge and has the following values:

✔ 1 = requires a basic level of proficiency

✔ 2 = requires an intermediate level of proficiency

✔ 3 = requires an advanced level of proficiency

Y is the required working relationship when applying the skill or knowledge and has the following values:

✔ *a* = doesn't entail managing others using the skill or knowledge

✔ *b* = entails managing others using the skill or knowledge

In addition to providing a basis for assigning appropriately qualified people to project teams, information about employees' skills and knowledge can also support

- ✔ **Training:** The organization can develop or make available training in areas in which the organization has shortages.

- ✔ **Career development:** The organization can encourage individuals to develop skills and knowledge that are in short supply to increase their opportunities for assuming greater responsibilities in the organization.

- ✔ **Recruiting:** Recruiters can look to hire people who have the capabilities that will qualify them for specific job needs in the organization.

- ✔ **Proposal writing and new business development:** Information about people's skills and knowledge can be included in proposals to demonstrate the organization's capability to perform particular types of work.

Representing skills, knowledge, and interests in a Skills Matrix

Whether you're able to influence the people assigned to your project team, people are assigned to your team without your input, or you assume the role of project manager of an existing team, you need to confirm the skills, knowledge, and interest of your team members.

If you have a team that was assembled without considering your opinion on the capabilities needed to perform your project's work, it's essential that you find out team members' skills, knowledge, and interests so you can make the most appropriate task assignments. If some or all of your team has been chosen in response to the specific skills and knowledge needs that you discussed with the organization's management, you should document people's skills and knowledge and verify their interests, in case you need to assign people to unanticipated tasks that crop up or if you have to replace a team member unexpectedly.

A *Skills Matrix* is a table that displays people's proficiency in specified skills and knowledge, as well as their interest in working on assignments using these skills and knowledge. Figure 6-1 presents an example of a portion of a Skills Matrix. The left-hand column identifies skill and knowledge areas, and the top row lists people's names. At the intersection of the rows and columns, you identify the level of each person's particular skills, knowledge, and interests.

Figure 6-1 shows that Sue has an advanced level of proficiency in technical writing and can work independently with little or no supervision. In addition, she's interested in working on technical writing assignments. Ed has an advanced level of proficiency in the area of legal research and is capable of managing others engaged in legal research. However, he'd prefer not to work on legal research tasks. Instead, he would like to work on questionnaire design activities, but he currently has no skills or knowledge in this area.

	Bill		Mary		Sue		Ed	
	Proficiency	Interest	Proficiency	Interest	Proficiency	Interest	Proficiency	Interest
Technical writing	(0,0)	0	(0,0)	0	(3,2)	1	(0,0)	1
Legal research	(0,0)	1	(0,0)	1	(0,0)	0	(3,3)	0
Graphic design	(3,3)	1	(0,0)	0	(0,0)	1	(3,3)	1
Questionnaire design	(1,0)	0	(0,0)	0	(0,0)	0	(0,0)	1

Proficiency rating is expressed as (X, Y), where   X = Person's level of skill or knowledge
Y = Level of responsibility applying the skill
or knowledge

Figure 6-1:
Displaying
people's
skills,
knowl-
edge, and
interests
in a Skills
Matrix.

Skill or Knowledge Level (X)	Application of Skills/Knowledge (Y)	Interest
0 = No capability		0 = Has no interest in applying this skill or knowledge
1 = Basic level of capability	1 = Must work under supervision	1 = Is interested in applying this skill or knowledge
2 = Intermediate level of capability	2 = Can work independently with little or no direct supervision	
3 = Advanced level of capability	3 = Can manage others applying the skill or knowledge	

By the way, you may assume that you'll never assign Ed to work on a questionnaire design activity because he has no relevant skills or knowledge. However, if you're trying to find more people who can develop questionnaires, Ed is a prime candidate. Because he wants to work on these types of assignments, he is most likely willing to put in extra effort to acquire the skills needed to do so.

Take the following steps to prepare a Skills Matrix for your team:

1. **Discuss with each team member his or her skills, knowledge, and interests related to the activities that your project entails.**

   Explain that you seek this information so you can assign people to the tasks that they're most interested in and qualified to perform.

2. **Determine each person's level of interest in working on the tasks for which he or she has been proposed.**

   At a minimum, ask people whether they're interested in the tasks for which they've been proposed. If a person isn't interested in a task, try to find out why and whether there is anything you can do to modify the assignment to make it more interesting to him or her.

If a person isn't interested in a task, you can either not ask and not know the reason, or ask and (if you get an honest response) know the reason. Knowing that a person isn't interested is better than not knowing, because you can consider the possibility of rearranging assignments or modifying the assignment to address those aspects of it that the person doesn't find appealing.

3. **Consult with team members' functional managers and/or the people who assigned them to your project to determine their opinions of the levels of each team member's skills, knowledge, and interests.**

   You want to understand the reasons why these managers assigned the people they did to your project.

4. **Check to see whether any areas of your organization have already prepared Skills Matrices.**

   Find out whether they reflect any information about the extent to which team members have skills and knowledge that you feel are required for your project's activities.

5. **Incorporate all the information you gather in a Skills Matrix, and review with each team member the portion of the matrix that contains his or her information.**

   This review gives you the opportunity to verify that you correctly recorded the information you found and the team member a chance to comment on or add to any of the information.

Estimating Needed Commitment

Just having the right skills and knowledge to do a task doesn't necessarily guarantee that a person will successfully complete it. The person must also have sufficient time to perform the necessary work. This section tells you how to prepare a Human Resources Matrix to display the amount of effort people will have to put in to complete their tasks. In addition, this section explains how you can take into account productivity, efficiency, and availability to make your work-effort estimates more accurate.

Using a Human Resources Matrix

Planning your personnel needs begins with identifying whom you need and how much effort they have to invest. You can use a Human Resources Matrix to display this information (see Figure 6-2 for an example of this matrix). The *Human Resources Matrix* depicts the people assigned to each project activity and the work effort each person will contribute to each assignment.

Activity		Personnel (Person-hours)		
Work Breakdown Structure Code	**Description**	**J. Jones**	**F. Smith**	**Analyst**
2.1.1	Questionnaire design	32	0	24
2.1.2	Questionnaire pilot test	0	40	60
2.2.1	Questionnaire instructions	40	24	10

Figure 6-2: Displaying personnel needs in a Human Resources Matrix.

Work effort or *person effort* is the actual time a person spends doing an activity. You can express work effort in units of person-hours, person-days, person-weeks, and so forth. (You may still hear people express work effort as *man*-hours or *man*-days. Same concept — just outdated and politically incorrect!)

Work effort is related to, but different from, duration. *Work effort* is a measure of resource use; *duration* is a measure of time passage (see Chapter 5 for more discussion of duration). Consider the work effort to complete the *questionnaire design* work package in the Human Resources Matrix in Figure 6-2. According to the matrix, J. Jones works on this activity for 32 person-hours, and an unnamed analyst works on it for 24 person-hours.

Knowing the work effort required to complete a work package alone, however, doesn't tell you the duration of the work package. For example, if both people assigned to the *questionnaire design* work package in Figure 6-2 can do their work on it at the same time, if they're both assigned 100 percent to the project, and if no other aspects of the task take additional time, the activity may be finished in four days. However, if either person is available for less than 100 percent of the time, if one or both people must work overtime, or if one person has to finish her work before the other can start, the duration won't be four days.

Identifying needed personnel in a Human Resources Matrix

Begin to create your Human Resources Matrix by specifying in the top row the different types of personnel you need for your project. You can use three types of information to identify the people you need to have on your project team:

✔ **Skills and knowledge:** The specific skills and knowledge that the person who'll do the work must have

✔ **Position name or title:** The job title or the name of the position of the person who'll do the work

✔ **Name:** The name of the person who'll do the work

Eventually, you want to specify all three pieces of information for each project team member. Early in your planning, try to specify needed skills and knowledge, such as *must be able to develop work process flow charts* or *must be able to use Microsoft PowerPoint*. If you can identify the exact skills and knowledge that a person must have for a particular task, you increase the chances that the proper person will be assigned.

Often, you want to identify people you want on your project by name. The reason is simple: If you've worked with someone before and he's done a good job, you want to work with him again. Although it's great for that person's ego, this method, unfortunately, often reduces the chances that you'll get an appropriately qualified person to work on your project. People who develop reputations for excellence often get more requests to participate on projects than they can handle. When you don't specify the skills and knowledge needed to perform the particular work on your project, the manager — who has to find a substitute for that overextended person — doesn't know what skills and knowledge that the alternate needs to have.

On occasion, you may use a position description or title (such as *operations specialist*) to identify a needed resource. In doing so, you assume anyone with that title has the necessary skills and knowledge. Unfortunately, titles are often vague, and position descriptions are frequently out of date. Therefore, using titles or position descriptions are risky ways to get the right person for the job.

Estimating required work effort

For all work packages, estimate the work effort that each person has to invest, and enter the numbers in the appropriate boxes in the Human Resources Matrix (refer to Figure 6-2). As you develop your work-effort estimates, do the following:

- ✔ **Describe in detail all work related to performing the activity.** Include work directly and indirectly related:

  - Examples of work directly related to an activity include writing a report, meeting with clients, performing a laboratory test, and designing a new logo.

  - Examples of indirectly related work include training to perform activity-related work and preparing periodic activity-progress reports.

- ✔ **Consider history.** Past history doesn't guarantee future performance, but it does provide a guideline for what's possible. Determine whether a work package has been done before. If it has, review written records to determine the work effort spent on it. If written records weren't kept, ask people who've done the activity before to estimate the work effort they invested.

When using prior history to support your estimates, make sure

- The people who performed the work had qualifications and experience similar to those of the people who'll work on your project.

- The facilities, equipment, and technology used were similar to those that'll be used for your project.

- The time frame was similar to the one you anticipate for your project.

✔ **Have the person who'll actually do the work participate in estimating the amount of work effort that will be required.** Having people contribute to their work-effort estimates provides the following benefits:

- Their understanding of the activity improves.

- The estimates are based on their particular skills, knowledge, and prior experience, which makes them more accurate.

- Their commitment to do the work for that level of work effort increases.

If you know who'll be working on the activity, have those people participate during the initial planning. If people don't join the project team until the start of or during the project, have them review and comment on the plans you've developed. Then update your plans as needed.

✔ **Consult with experts familiar with the type of work you need done on your project, even if they haven't performed work exactly like it before.** Incorporating experience and knowledge from different sources improves the accuracy of your estimate.

Factoring productivity, efficiency, and availability into work-effort estimates

Being assigned to a project full time doesn't mean a person can perform project work at peak productivity 40 hours per week, 52 weeks per year. Additional personal and organizational activities reduce the amount of work people produce. Therefore, consider each of the following factors when you estimate the number of hours that people need to complete their project assignments:

✔ **Productivity:** The results a person produces per unit of time that he spends on an activity. The following factors affect a person's productivity:

- **Knowledge and skills:** The raw talent and capability a person has to perform a particular task

- **Prior experience:** A person's familiarity with the work and the typical problems of a particular task

- **Sense of urgency:** A person's drive to generate the desired results within established time frames (urgency influences a person's focus and concentration on an activity)

- **Ability to switch among several tasks:** A person's level of comfort moving to a second task when he hits a roadblock in his first one so that he doesn't sit around stewing about his frustrations and wasting time

- **The quality and setup of the physical environment:** Proximity and arrangement of a person's furniture and the support equipment he uses; also the availability and condition of the equipment and resources

✔ **Efficiency:** The proportion of time a person spends on project work as opposed to organizational tasks that aren't related to specific projects. The following factors affect a person's efficiency:

- **Non-project-specific professional activities:** The time a person spends attending general organization meetings, handling incidental requests, and reading technical journals and periodicals about his field of specialty

- **Personal activities:** The time a person spends getting a drink of water, going to the restroom, organizing his work area, conducting personal business on the job, and talking about non-work-related topics with coworkers

The more time a person spends each day on non-project-specific and personal activities, the less time he has to work on his project assignments. (Check out the nearby sidebar "The truth is out: How workers really spend their time" for more info. I also discuss efficiency in the upcoming two sections.)

✔ **Availability:** The portion of time a person is at the job as opposed to on leave. Organizational policy regarding employee vacation days, sick days, holidays, personal days, mental health days, administrative leave, and so on define a person's availability.

When deciding how many work-hours to budget for a person to do a particular task, adjust the number required at peak performance to allow for actual levels of productivity, efficiency, and availability.

Reflecting efficiency when you use historical data

How you reflect efficiency in your estimates depends on whether and how you track work effort. If you base your work-effort estimates on historical data from time sheets and if either of the following situations is true, you don't have to factor in a separate measure for efficiency:

✔ **Your time sheets have one or more categories to show time spent on non-project-specific work, *and* people accurately report the actual time they spend on their different activities.**

In this case, the historical data represent the actual number of hours people worked on the activity in the past. Thus, you can comfortably use the numbers from your time sheets to estimate the actual level of effort this activity will require in the future, as long as people continue to record in separate categories the hours they spend on non-project-specific activities.

✔ **Your time sheets have no category for recording time spent on non-project-specific work. However, you report accurately (by activity) the time you spend on work-related activities, and you apportion in a consistent manner your non-project-specific work among the available project activities.**

In this case, the historical data reflect the number of hours that people *recorded* they spent on the activity in the past, which includes time they actually spent on the activity and a portion of the total time they spent on non-project-specific work.

Again, if people's time-recording practices haven't changed, you can use these numbers to estimate the hours that people will record doing this same activity in the future.

The truth is out: How workers really spend their time

A number of years ago, I read a study that determined that the typical employee spends an average of four hours of an eight-hour work day on preplanned project activities and work assignments. The interviewers in this study spoke with people with a wide range of job responsibilities from more than 100 organizations. In other words, the typical employee in this study averaged a work efficiency of 50 percent!

Since then I have found several organizations that conducted similar studies of their own operations. These organizations all found workers' efficiency to be about 75 percent. You may think the workers in these companies were more efficient than the ones in the previous study, but, in fact, these studies were biased. The people surveyed wanted their organizations to think they were spending most of their time working on project assignments, and the organizations wanted to believe their employees were doing so. Still, the organization studies found that people spent about 25 percent of each day doing something other than preplanned, project-related activities!

When collected properly, time sheets provide the most reliable source of past experience. However, the following time-sheet practices can cause the data on them to be inaccurate:

✔ People aren't allowed to record overtime, so some hours actually spent on an activity may never be known.

✔ People fill out their time sheets for a period several days before the period is over, so they must guess what their hourly allocations for the next several days will be.

✔ People copy the work-effort estimates from the project plan onto their time sheets each period instead of recording the actual number of hours they spend.

If any of these situations exist in your organization, don't use historical data from time sheets to support your work-effort estimates for your current project. Instead, use one or more of the approaches discussed in the earlier section "Estimating required work effort."

Accounting for efficiency in personal work-effort estimates

If you base work-effort estimates on the opinions of people who'll do the activities or who have done similar activities in the past instead of on historical records, you have to factor in a measure of efficiency.

First, ask the person from whom you're getting your information to estimate the required work effort assuming he could work at 100 percent efficiency. (In other words, ask him not to worry about normal interruptions during the day, having to work on multiple tasks at a time, and so on.) Then modify the estimate to reflect efficiency by doing the following:

✔ If the person will use a time sheet that has one or more categories for non-project-specific work, use his original work-effort estimate.

✔ If the person will use a time sheet that doesn't have categories to record non-project-specific work, add an additional amount to his original estimate to account for his efficiency.

As an example, suppose a person estimates that he needs 30 person-hours to perform a task (if he can be 100 percent efficient) and his time sheets have no categories for recording non-project-specific work. If you estimate that he'll work at about 75 percent efficiency, allow him to charge 40 person-hours to your project to complete the task. (75 percent of 40 person-hours is 30 person-hours — the amount you really need.)

Failure to consider efficiency when estimating and reviewing project work effort can lead to incorrect conclusions about people's performance. Suppose your boss assigns you a project on Monday morning. He tells you the project will take about 40 person-hours, but he really needs it by Friday close of business. Suppose further that you work intensely all week and finish the task by Friday close of business. In the process, you record 55 hours for the project on your time sheet.

If your boss doesn't realize that his initial estimate of 40 person-hours was based on your working at 100 percent efficiency, he'll think you took 15 hours longer than you should have. On the other hand, if your boss recognizes that 55 person-hours *on the job* translates into about 40 person-hours of work *on specific project tasks,* your boss will appreciate that you invested extra effort to meet his aggressive deadline.

Although your performance is the same, overlooking the impact of efficiency makes you appear less capable, while correctly considering it makes you appear intensely dedicated.

The longer you're involved in an assignment, the more important efficiency and availability become. Suppose you decide you have to spend one hour on an assignment. You can reasonably figure your availability is 100 percent and your efficiency is 100 percent, so you charge your project one hour for the assignment. If you need to spend six hours on an assignment, you can figure your availability is 100 percent, but you must consider 75 percent efficiency (or a similar planning figure). Therefore, charge one workday (eight work hours) to ensure that you can spend the six hours on your assignment.

However, if you plan to devote one month or more to your assignment, you'll most likely take some leave days during that time. Even though your project budget doesn't have to pay for your annual or sick leave, one person-month means you have about 97 hours for productive work on your assignment, assuming 75 percent efficiency and 75 percent availability (2,080 hours total in a year ÷ 12 months in a year × 0.75 × 0.75).

The numbers in Table 6-1 depict productive person-hours available at different levels of efficiency and availability. If your organization uses different levels of efficiency or availability, develop your own planning figures.

Table 6-1	Person-Hours Available for Project Work		
	Productive Person-Hours Available		
	100 Percent Efficiency, 100 Percent Availability	*75 Percent Efficiency, 100 Percent Availability*	*75 Percent Efficiency, 75 Percent Availability*
1 person-day	8	6	4.5
1 person-week	40	30	22.5
1 person-month	173	130	98
1 person-year	2,080	1,560	1,170

In addition to reflecting the influence of efficiency and availability, improve the accuracy of your work-effort estimates by doing the following:

- **Define your work packages clearly.** Minimize the use of technical jargon, and describe associated work processes (see Chapter 4 for more details).

- **Subdivide your work.** Do so until you estimate that your lowest-level activities will take two person-weeks or less.

- **Update work-effort estimates when project personnel or task assignments change.**

Ensuring Your Project Team Members Can Meet Their Resource Commitments

If you work on only one activity at a time, determining whether you're over-committed can be straightforward. But suppose you plan to work on several activities that partially overlap during a particular time period. Then you must decide when to work on each activity to see whether your multitasking has left you overcommitted.

This section shows you how to schedule your work effort for a task, how to identify resource overloads, and how to resolve those overloads.

Planning your initial allocations

The first step in making sure you can handle all your project commitments is to decide when you'll work on each activity. If your initial plan has you working on more than one activity at the same time, your next task is to determine the total level of effort you'll have to devote each time period to meet your multiple commitments.

Begin planning out your workload by developing

- ✔ A Human Resources Matrix (see the earlier section "Using a Human Resources Matrix" for more info)
- ✔ A Person-Loading Graph or Chart for each individual in the Human Resources Matrix

A *Person-Loading Graph* (also called a *Resource Histogram*) is a bar graph that depicts the level of work effort you'll spend each day, week, or month on an activity. A *Person-Loading Chart* presents the same information in a table. The graphical format highlights peaks, valleys, and overloads more effectively, while the tabular format presents exact work-effort amounts more clearly. Prepare a Person-Loading Chart or Graph for each project team member.

Suppose you plan to work on Activities 1, 2, and 3 of a project. Table 6-2 shows you plan that Activity 1 will take three weeks, Activity 2 will take two weeks, and Activity 3 will take three weeks. Table 6-2 also shows you estimate that you'll spend 60 person-hours on Activity 1 (50 percent of your available time over the task's three-week period), 40 person-hours on Activity 2 (50 percent of your available time over the task's two-week period), and 30 person-hours on Activity 3 (25 percent of your available time over the task's three-week period). (Consider that you've already accounted for efficiency in these estimates — see the earlier section "Estimating Needed Commitment" for more on efficiency.) If you don't have to work on more than one activity at a time, you should have no problem completing each of your three assignments.

Table 6-2   Planned Duration and Work Effort for Three Activities

Activity	Duration (In Weeks)	Work Effort (In Person-Hours)
Activity 1	3	60
Activity 2	2	40
Activity 3	3	30

The Gantt chart in Figure 6-3 illustrates your initial schedule for completing these three activities (check out Chapter 5 for more on Gantt charts). However, instead of having you work on these activities one at a time, this initial schedule has you working on both Activities 1 and 2 in week 2 and on all three activities in week 3. You have to decide how much effort you'll put in each week on each of the three tasks to see whether you can work on all three activities as they're currently scheduled.

As a starting point, assume you'll spend your time evenly over the life of each activity. That means you'll work 20 hours a week on Activity 1 during weeks 1, 2, and 3, 20 hours a week on Activity 2 during weeks 2 and 3, and 10 hours a week on Activity 3 during weeks 3, 4, and 5, as depicted in the Gantt chart in Figure 6-3.

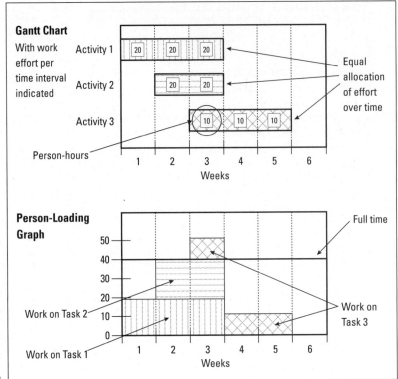

Figure 6-3:
Planning
to work
on several
activities
during the
same time
period.

Determine the total effort you'll have to devote to the overall project each week by adding up the person-hours you'll spend on each task each week as follows:

- In week 1, you'll work 20 person-hours on Activity 1 for a total commitment to the project of 20 person-hours.

- In week 2, you'll work 20 person-hours on Activity 1 and 20 person-hours on Activity 2 for a total commitment to the project of 40 person-hours.

- In week 3, you'll work 20 person-hours on Activity 1, 20 person-hours on Activity 2, and 10 person-hours on Activity 3 for a total commitment to the project of 50 person-hours.

- In weeks 4 and 5, you'll work 10 person-hours on Activity 3 for a total commitment to the project each week of 10 person-hours.

The *Person-Loading Graph* in Figure 6-3 shows these commitments. A quick review reveals that this plan has you working 10 hours of overtime in week 3. If you're comfortable putting in this overtime, this plan works. If you aren't, you have to come up with an alternative strategy to reduce your week 3 commitments (see the next section for how to do so).

Resolving potential resource overloads

If you don't change your time allocations for Activity 1 or 2 and you're willing to work only a total of 40 person-hours in week 3, you'll accomplish less than you planned on one or both of the activities that you work on that week. Therefore, consider one or more of the following strategies to eliminate your overcommitment:

✔ **Allocate your time unevenly over the duration of one or more activities.** Instead of spending the same number of hours on an activity each week, plan to spend more hours some weeks than others.

Suppose you choose to spend your hours unevenly over the duration of Activity 1 by increasing your commitment by 10 hours in the first week and reducing it by 10 hours in the third week, as depicted in the Gantt chart in Figure 6-4. The Person-Loading Graph in Figure 6-4 illustrates how this uneven distribution removes your overcommitment in week 3.

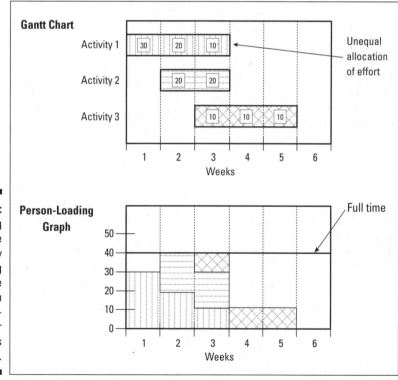

Figure 6-4: Eliminating a resource overload by changing the allocation of person-hours over the activity's life.

✔ **Take advantage of any slack time that may exist in your assigned activities.** Consider starting one or more activities earlier or later.

Figure 6-5 illustrates that if Activity 3 has at least one week of slack time remaining after its currently planned end date, you can reduce your total work on the project in week 3 to 40 person-hours by delaying both the start and the end of Task 3 by one week. (See Chapter 5 for a detailed definition and discussion of slack time.)

✔ **Assign some of the work you were planning to do in week 3 to someone else currently on your project, to a newly assigned team member, or to an external vendor or contractor.** Reassigning 10 person-hours of your work in week 3 removes your overcommitment.

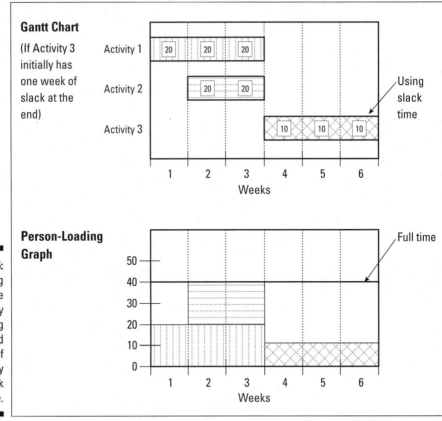

Figure 6-5: Eliminating a resource overload by changing the start and end dates of an activity with slack time.

Show the total hours that each person will spend on your project in a *Summary Person-Loading Chart,* a chart that allows you to do the following (see Figure 6-6):

✔ Identify who may be available to share the load of overcommitted people.

✔ Determine the personnel budget for your project by multiplying the number of hours people work on the project by their weighted labor rates. (See Chapter 7 for more information on setting labor rates.)

Figure 6-6: Showing total person-hours for a project in a Summary Person-Loading Chart.

| | Person-hours | | | | | |
	Week 1	Week 2	Week 3	Week 4	Week 5	Total
You	20	40	50	10	10	130
Bill	10	20	10	30	10	80
Mary	15	10	20	10	30	85
Total	45	70	80	50	50	295

Coordinating assignments across multiple projects

Working on overlapping tasks can place conflicting demands on a person, whether the tasks are on one project or several. Although successfully addressing these conflicts can be more difficult when more than one project manager is involved, the techniques for analyzing them are the same whether you're the only project manager involved or you're just one of many. This section illustrates how you can use the techniques and displays from the previous sections to resolve resource conflicts that arise from working on two or more projects at the same time.

In general, people on any of your project teams may also be assigned to other projects you're managing or to other project managers' projects. If Summary Person-Loading Charts are available for each project your people are assigned to, you can manage each person's overall resource commitments by combining the information from the projects' Summary Person-Loading Charts into an Overall Summary Person-Loading Chart.

Figure 6-7 illustrates an Overall Summary Person-Loading Chart that shows the commitments for each person on one or more of your project teams. This Overall Summary Person-Loading Chart (titled "All Projects") is derived from the Summary Person-Loading Charts for each of your team members' projects.

Figure 6-7 indicates that you're currently scheduled to work on Projects A, B, and C in February for 40, 20, and 40 person-hours, respectively. If someone requests that you be assigned to work on Project D for 60 person-hours in February, you have several options.

If you assume that you have a total of 160 person-hours available in February, you can devote 60 person-hours to Project D with no problem, because only 100 person-hours are currently committed.

However, you don't currently have available in February the other 20 person-hours the person is requesting. Therefore, you can consider doing one of the following:

✔ Find someone to assume 20 person-hours of your commitments to Projects A, B, or C in February.

✔ Shift your work on one or more of these projects from February to January or March.

✔ Work overtime.

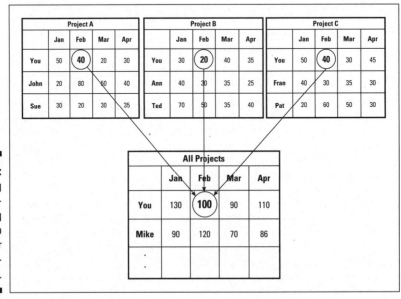

Figure 6-7:
Using Person-Loading Charts to plan your time on several projects.

Relating This Chapter to the PMP Exam and PMBOK 4

Table 6-3 notes topics in this chapter that may be addressed on the Project Management Professional (PMP) certification exam and that are also included in *A Guide to the Project Management Body of Knowledge,* 4th Edition (*PMBOK 4*).

Table 6-3   Chapter 6 Topics in Relation to the PMP Exam and *PMBOK 4*

Topic	Location in PMBOK 4	Comments
Specifying the competencies required to perform the different project activities (see the section "Deciding the skills and knowledge that team members must have")	6.3.1.2. Activity Attributes 6.3.3.1. Activity Resource Requirements 9.1.3.1. Human Resource Plan 9.2.1.1. Project Management Plan 9.2.1.2. Enterprise Environmental Factors	Both books emphasize the need to specify the competencies required to perform the project's activities. This book discusses how to determine the needed competencies.
Maintaining a record of team members' skills, knowledge, and interests (see the section "Representing team members' skills, knowledge, and interests in a Skills Matrix")	9.2.1.2. Enterprise Environmental Factors	Both books note the need to obtain information about the skills and knowledge of people who might be assigned to your project team. This book discusses the details and provides an example of a Skills Matrix.
Specifying and making available the appropriate type and amount of human resources (see the section "Using a Human Resources Matrix")	9.1.3.1. Human Resource Plan 9.2. Acquire Project Team (Introduction) 9.2.2.2. Negotiation	Both books address the importance of having qualified personnel resources assigned to your project team. This book explains how a Human Resources Matrix can be used to record the required characteristics and amounts of needed personnel.

(continued)

Table 6-3 *(continued)*

Topic	*Location in PMBOK 4*	*Comments*
Estimating required work effort (see the section "Estimating required work effort")	6.3.2. Estimate Activity Resources: Tools and Techniques 9.1.3.1. Human Resource Plan	Both books specify several of the same techniques for estimating the amount of needed personnel and displaying when they are required. This book discusses how to reflect productivity, efficiency, and availability in the estimates.
Handling multiple resource commitments (see the section "Ensuring Your Project Team Members Can Meet Their Resource Commitments")	9.1. Develop Human Resource Plan (Introduction) 9.1.3.1. Human Resource Plan	Both books emphasize the importance of handling conflicting demands for the same resources. This book discusses and presents examples of specific tools and strategies for addressing and resolving these conflicting demands.

Chapter 7

Planning for Other Resources and Developing the Budget

In This Chapter

▶ Accounting for your project's nonpersonnel resources

▶ Preparing a detailed budget for your project

A key part of effective project management is ensuring that nonpersonnel resources are available throughout the project when and where they're needed and according to specifications. When people are available for a scheduled task but the necessary computers and laboratory equipment aren't, your project can have costly delays and unanticipated expenditures. Also, your team members may experience frustration that leads to reduced commitment.

In addition to clearly defined objectives, a workable schedule, and adequate resources, a successful project needs sufficient funds to support the required resources. All major project decisions (including whether to undertake it, whether to continue it, and — after it's done — whether it was successful) must consider the project's costs.

This chapter looks at how you can determine, specify, and display your nonpersonnel resource needs and then how to develop your project budget.

Determining Nonpersonnel Resource Needs

In addition to personnel, your project may require a variety of other important resources (such as furniture, fixtures, equipment, raw materials, and information). Plan for these nonpersonnel resources the same way you plan to meet your personnel requirements. (Check out Chapter 6 for more on meeting your personnel needs.) As part of your plan, develop the following:

✔ A nonpersonnel resources matrix

✔ Nonpersonnel usage charts

✔ A nonpersonnel summary usage chart

A *nonpersonnel resources matrix* displays the following information for every lowest-level component (or *work package*) in your project Work Breakdown Structure, or WBS (see Chapter 4 for a discussion of a WBS):

✔ The nonpersonnel resources needed to perform the activities that comprise the work package (For example, Figure 7-1 shows that you need computers, copiers, and use of a test laboratory to complete the three listed work packages.)

✔ The required amount of each resource (For example, Figure 7-1 suggests that you need 40 hours of computer time and 32 hours of the test laboratory to create a device. The shaded computer usage numbers in Figure 7-1 are detailed by week in Figure 7-2, later in this chapter.)

Activity			Amount of Resource Required (Hours)		
Work Breakdown Structure Code	**Description**		**Computer**	**Copier**	**Test Lab**
1.2.1.	Presentation		32	0	0
2.1.4.	Report		0	40	0
3.3.1.	Device		40	0	32

Figure 7-1: An illustration of a nonpersonnel resources matrix.

To estimate the amount of each resource you need, examine the nature of the task and the capacity of the resource. For example, determine the amount of copier time you need to reproduce a report by doing the following:

1. **Estimate the number of report copies.**

2. **Estimate the number of pages per copy.**

3. **Specify the copier capacity in pages per unit of time.**

4. **Multiply the first two numbers and divide the result by the third number to determine the amount of copier time needed to reproduce your reports.**

Ensuring that nonpersonnel resources are available when needed requires that you specify the times that you plan to use them. You can display this information in separate usage charts for each resource. Figure 7-2 illustrates a computer usage chart that depicts the amount of computer time each task requires during each week of your project. For example, the chart indicates that Task 1.2.1 requires six hours of computer time in week 1, four hours in week 2, six hours in week 3, and eight hours in each of weeks 4 and 5. You would prepare similar charts for required copier time and use of the test lab.

Work Package		Amount of Computer Time Required (Hours)					
WBS Code	Description	Week 1	Week 2	Week 3	Week 4	Week 5	Total
1.2.1.	Presentation	6	4	6	8	8	32
2.1.4.	Report	0	0	0	4	0	4
3.3.1.	Device	10	8	16	6	0	40
Totals		15	12	22	18	8	76

Figure 7-2:
An example of a computer usage chart.

Finally, you display the total amount of each nonpersonnel resource you require during each week of your project in a nonpersonnel summary usage chart, as illustrated in Figure 7-3. The information in this chart is taken from the weekly totals in the individual usage charts for each nonpersonnel resource.

	Amount of Resource Required (Hours)					
	Week 1	Week 2	Week 3	Week 4	Week 5	Total
Computer	16	12	22	18	8	76
Copier	0	0	0	30	10	40
Test Lab	0	0	24	8	0	32

Figure 7-3:
An example of a nonpersonnel summary usage chart.

Making Sense of the Dollars: Project Costs and Budgets

In a world of limited funds, you're constantly deciding how to get the most return for your investment. Therefore, estimating a project's costs is important for several reasons:

✔ It enables you to weigh anticipated benefits against anticipated costs to see whether the project makes sense.

✔ It allows you to see whether the necessary funds are available to support the project.

✔ It serves as a guideline to help ensure that you have sufficient funds to complete the project.

Although you may not develop and monitor detailed budgets for all your projects, knowing how to work with project costs can make you a better project manager and increase your chances of project success. This section looks at different types of project costs that you may encounter. It then offers helpful tips for developing your own project budget.

Looking at different types of project costs

A *project budget* is a detailed, time-phased estimate of all resource costs for your project. You typically develop a budget in stages — from an initial rough estimate to a detailed estimate to a completed, approved project budget. On occasion, you may even revise your approved budget while your project is in progress (check out "Refining your budget as you move through your project's stages" later in this chapter for more info).

Your project's budget includes both direct and indirect costs. *Direct costs* are costs for resources solely used for your project. Direct costs include the following:

✔ Salaries for team members on your project

✔ Specific materials, supplies, and equipment for your project

✔ Travel to perform work on your project

✔ Subcontracts that provide support exclusively to your project

Indirect costs are costs for resources that support more than one project but aren't readily identifiable with or chargeable to any of the projects individually. Indirect costs fall into the following two categories:

- ✓ **Overhead costs:** Costs for products and services for your project that are difficult to subdivide and allocate directly. Examples include employee benefits, office space rent, general supplies, and the costs of furniture, fixtures, and equipment.

  You need an office to work on your project activities, and office space costs money. However, your organization has an annual lease for office space, the space has many individual offices and work areas, and people work on numerous projects throughout the year. Because you have no clear records that specify the dollar amount of the total rent that's just for the time you spend in your office working on just this project's activities, your office space is treated as an indirect project cost.

- ✓ **General and administrative costs:** Expenditures that keep your organization operational (if your organization doesn't exist, you can't perform your project). Examples include salaries of your contracts department, finance department, and top management as well as fees for general accounting and legal services.

Suppose you're planning to design, develop, and produce a company brochure. Direct costs for this project may include the following:

- ✓ **Labor:** Salaries for you and other team members for the hours you work on the brochure
- ✓ **Materials:** The special paper stock for the brochure
- ✓ **Travel:** The costs for driving to investigate firms that may design your brochure cover
- ✓ **Subcontract:** The services of an outside company to design the cover art

Indirect costs for this project may include the following:

- ✓ **Employee benefits:** Benefits (such as annual, sick, and holiday leave; health and life insurance; and retirement plan contributions) in addition to salary while you and the other team members are working on the brochure
- ✓ **Rent:** The cost of the office space you use when you're developing the copy for the brochure
- ✓ **Equipment:** The computer you use to compose the copy for the brochure
- ✓ **Management and administrative salaries:** A portion of the salaries of upper managers and staff who perform the administrative duties necessary to keep your organization functioning

Recognizing the three stages of a project budget

Organization decision makers would love to have a detailed and accurate budget on hand whenever someone proposes a project so they can assess its relative benefits to the organization and decide whether they have sufficient funds to support it. Unfortunately, you can't prepare such an estimate until you develop a clear understanding of the work and resources the project will require.

In reality, decisions of whether to go forward with a project and how to undertake it must be made before people can prepare highly accurate budgets. You can develop and refine your project budget in the following stages to provide the best information possible to support important project decisions:

- ✓ **Rough order-of-magnitude estimate:** This stage is an initial estimate of costs based on a general sense of the project work. You make this estimate without detailed data. Depending on the nature of the project, the final budget may wind up 100 percent (or more!) higher than this initial estimate.

  Prepare a rough order-of-magnitude estimate by considering the costs of similar projects (or similar activities that will be part of your project) that have already been done, applicable cost and productivity ratios (such as the number of assemblies that can be produced per hour), and other methods of approximation.

  This estimate sometimes expresses what someone *wants* to spend rather than what the project will really *cost*. You typically don't detail this estimate by lowest-level project activity because you prepare it in a short amount of time before you've identified the project activities.

  Whether or not people acknowledge it, initial budget estimates in annual plans and long-range plans are typically rough order-of-magnitude estimates. As such, these estimates may change significantly as the planners define the project in greater detail.

- ✓ **Detailed budget estimate:** This stage entails an itemization of the estimated costs for each project activity. You prepare this estimate by developing a detailed WBS (see Chapter 4) and estimating the costs of all lowest-level work packages. (Turn to Chapter 6 for information on estimating work effort, and see the section "Determining Nonpersonnel Resource Needs" earlier in this chapter for ways to estimate your needs for nonpersonnel resources.)

- ✓ **Completed, approved project budget:** This final stage is a detailed project budget that essential people approve and agree to support.

Refining your budget as you move through your project's stages

A project moves through four stages as it evolves from an idea to a reality: starting the project, organizing and preparing, carrying out the work, and closing the project. (See Chapter 1 for more discussion of these phases.) Prepare and refine your budget as your project moves through these different stages by following these steps:

1. **Prepare a rough order-of-magnitude estimate in the starting the project stage.**

   Use this estimate (which I introduce in the preceding section) to decide whether the organization should consider your project further by entering the organizing and preparing stage.

   Rather than an actual estimate of costs, this number often represents an amount that your project can't exceed in order to have an acceptable return for the investment. Your confidence in this estimate is low because you don't base it on detailed analyses of the project activities.

2. **Develop your detailed budget estimate and get it approved in the organizing and preparing stage after you specify your project activities.**

   See the next section for more information on estimating project costs for this stage.

   Check with your organization to find out who must approve project budgets. At a minimum, the budget is typically approved by the project manager, the head of finance, and possibly the project manager's supervisor.

3. **Review your approved budget in the carrying out the work stage — when you identify the people who will be working on your project and when you start to develop formal agreements for the use of equipment, facilities, vendors, and other resources.**

   Pay particular attention to the following items that often necessitate changes in the budget approved for the project:

   - People actually assigned to the project team are more or less experienced than originally anticipated.

   - Actual prices for goods and services you'll purchase have increased.

   - Some required project nonpersonnel resources are no longer available when you need them.

   - Your clients want additional or different project results than those they originally discussed with you.

4. **Get approval for any required changes to the budget or other parts of the approved plan before you begin the actual project work.**

   Submit requests for any changes to the original plan or budget to the same people who approved them.

5. **Monitor project activities and related occurrences throughout the carrying out the work and closing the project stages to determine when budget revisions are necessary.**

   Check out Chapter 12 for how to monitor project expenditures during your project's performance and how to determine whether budget changes are needed. Submit requests for necessary budget revisions as soon as possible to the same people you submitted the original budget to in Step 2.

 You may not personally participate in all aspects of developing your project budget. If you join your project after the initial planning, be sure to review the work that has been done on the budget and resolve any questions you may have and issues you may identify.

Determining project costs for a detailed budget estimate

After you prepare your rough order-of-magnitude estimate and move into the organizing and preparing stage of your project, you're ready to create your detailed budget estimate. Use a combination of the following approaches to develop this budget estimate (see the following sections for more on these approaches):

- ✔ **Bottom-up:** Develop detailed cost estimates for each lowest-level work package in the WBS (refer to Chapter 4 for more information on the WBS), and total these estimates to obtain the total project budget estimate.

- ✔ **Top-down:** Set a target budget for the entire project and apportion this budget among all Level 2 components in the WBS. Then apportion the budgets for each of the Level 2 components among its Level 3 components. Continue in this manner until a budget has been assigned to each lowest-level WBS work package.

The bottom-up approach

Develop your bottom-up budget estimate by doing the following:

1. **For each lowest-level work package, determine direct labor costs by multiplying the number of hours each person will work on it by the person's hourly salary.**

You can estimate direct labor costs by using either of the following two definitions for salary:

- The actual salary of each person on the project

- The average salary for people with a particular job title, in a certain department, and so on

Suppose you need a graphic artist to design overheads for your presentation. The head of the graphics department estimates the person will spend 100 person-hours on your project. If you know Harry (with a salary rate of $30 per hour) will work on the activity, you can estimate your direct labor costs to be $3,000. However, if the director doesn't know who'll work on your project, use the average salary of a graphic artist in your organization to estimate the direct labor costs.

2. **For each lowest-level work package, estimate the direct costs for materials, equipment, travel, contractual services, and other nonpersonnel resources.**

See the section "Determining Nonpersonnel Resource Needs" earlier in this chapter for information on how to determine the nonpersonnel resources you need for your project. Consult with your procurement department, administrative staff, and finance department to determine the costs of these resources.

3. **Determine the indirect costs associated with each work package.**

You typically estimate indirect costs as a fraction of the planned direct labor costs for the work package. In general, your organization's finance department determines this fraction annually by doing the following:

- Estimating organization direct labor costs for the coming year

- Estimating organization indirect costs for the coming year

- Dividing the estimated indirect costs by the estimated direct labor costs

You can estimate the total amount of indirect costs either by considering that they are all in a single category labeled "indirect costs" or that they can be in one of the two separate categories labeled "overhead costs" and "general and administrative costs" (see the earlier section "Looking at different types of project costs" and the nearby sidebar "Two approaches for estimating indirect costs" for more information). Choose your method of estimating indirect costs by weighing the potential accuracy of the estimate against the effort to develop it.

Suppose you're planning a project to design and produce a company brochure. You already have the following information (Table 7-1 illustrates this information in a typical detailed budget estimate):

- ✔ You estimate that you'll spend 200 person-hours on the project at $30 per hour and that Mary will spend 100 person-hours at $25 per hour.

✔ You estimate that the cost of the stationery for the brochures will be $1,000.

✔ You estimate $300 in travel costs to visit vendors and suppliers.

✔ You expect to pay a vendor $5,000 for the brochure's artwork.

✔ Your organization has a combined indirect cost rate of 60 percent of direct labor costs.

Table 7-1	Project Budget Estimate for a Company Brochure	
Cost Category	*Cost in Personnel and Nonpersonnel Resources*	*Total Monetary Cost*
Direct labor	You: 200 hours ($30 per hour)	$6,000
	Mary: 100 hours ($25 per hour)	$2,500
	Total direct labor	**$8,500**
Indirect costs (60 percent of direct labor costs)		**$5,100**
Other direct costs	Materials	$1,000
	Travel	$300
	Subcontract	$5,000
	Total other direct costs	**$6,300**
Total project costs		**$19,900**

The top-down approach

You develop a top-down budget estimate by deciding how much you want the total project to cost and then dividing that total cost in the appropriate ratios among the lower-level WBS components until you've allocated amounts to all the work packages.

Suppose you plan to develop a new piece of equipment. You develop a bottom-up cost estimate that suggests the budget for each Level 2 component in your WBS should be as follows, with the total budget being determined by adding together the amounts to be $100,000:

✔ Design: $60,000 (60 percent of the resulting total budget)

✔ Development: $15,000 (15 percent of the resulting total budget)

✔ Testing: $5,000 (5 percent of the resulting total budget)

✔ Production: $20,000 (20 percent of the resulting total budget)

However, experience with similar projects suggests that approximately 40 percent of the total budget is typically devoted to design, not 60 percent, as you've developed using your bottom-up approach. In other words, the relative allocations of your total budget among the four major project phases aren't in agreement with the amounts recommended from prior experience. Your numbers indicate that you've planned a design phase for a $150,000 project rather than a $100,000 project.

To fix this discrepancy, you have two options:

> ✔ Try to scale down your design approach so that it can be implemented for $40,000.

> ✔ Request an additional $50,000 for your project.

But whichever approach you choose, you can't just arbitrarily change the numbers without specifying how you will perform the necessary work!

Two approaches for estimating indirect costs

Accurately determining the true cost of a project requires that you appropriately allocate all activity and resource costs. However, the cost of tracking and recording all expenditures can be considerable. Therefore, organizations have developed methods for approximating the amounts of certain expenses assigned to different projects.

Following are two approaches for estimating the indirect costs associated with an activity: The first approach defines two different indirect rates; it's more accurate but requires more detailed record keeping, so it's also more costly. The second defines a single rate for all indirect costs.

Option 1: Use one rate for overhead costs and another rate for general and administrative costs.

✔ Your finance department determines the overhead rate by calculating the ratio of all projected overhead costs to all projected direct salaries.

✔ Your finance department determines the general-and-administrative-cost rate by calculating the ratio of all projected general and administrative costs to the sum of all projected direct salaries, overhead costs, and other direct costs.

✔ You determine overhead costs of an activity by multiplying its direct salaries by the overhead rate.

✔ You determine general and administrative costs of an activity by multiplying the sum of its direct salaries, overhead costs, and other direct costs by the general-and-administrative-cost rate.

Option 2: Use one indirect-cost rate for all overhead and general and administrative costs.

✔ Your finance department determines the combined indirect-cost rate by calculating the ratio of all projected overhead costs to all projected direct salaries.

✔ You determine an activity's indirect costs by multiplying its direct salaries by the indirect-cost rate.

Some organizations develop *weighted labor rates*, which combine hourly salary and associated indirect costs. As an example, suppose your salary is $30 per hour and your organization's indirect-cost rate is 50 percent. Your weighted labor rate is $45 per hour ($30 + 0.5 × $30).

Relating This Chapter to the PMP Exam and PMBOK 4

Table 7-2 notes topics in this chapter that may be addressed on the Project Management Professional (PMP) certification exam and that are included in *A Guide to the Project Management Body of Knowledge,* 4th Edition (*PMBOK 4*).

Table 7-2	Chapter 7 Topics in Relation to the PMP Exam and *PMBOK 4*	
Topic	*Location in PMBOK 4*	*Comments*
Techniques for determining and displaying nonpersonnel resources (see the section "Determining Nonpersonnel Resource Needs")	7.1.3.1. Activity Cost Estimates	Both books specify the same types of resources that should be planned and budgeted for. This book discusses formats for arraying and presenting information about needed nonpersonnel resources.
Techniques and approaches for estimating project costs and developing the project budget (see the sections "Recognizing the three stages of a project budget," "Refining your budget as you move through your project's stages," and "Determining project costs for a detailed budget estimate")	7.1. Estimate Costs 7.2. Determine Budget	Both books mention similar categories of costs to be considered and the same evolving approach to developing a budget estimate that starts with rough estimates and refines them as more information is acquired.

Chapter 8

Venturing into the Unknown: Dealing with Risk and Uncertainty

*Y*our first step in managing a successful project is to develop a plan to produce the desired results on time and within budget. If your project lasts a relatively short time and you're thorough and realistic in your planning, your project will most likely be a success.

However, the larger, more complex, and longer your project is, the more likely you are to encounter some aspects that don't work out as you envisioned. Thus, you have the greatest chance for success if you confront the possibility of such changes head-on *and* if you plan to minimize their undesirable consequences from your project's outset.

This chapter discusses how to consider potential risks when you're deciding whether you'll undertake your project, when you're developing your project plan, and while you're performing your project's work. It shows you how to identify and assess the impact of project risks, and it explores strategies for minimizing their consequences. Finally, this chapter gives pointers for preparing your own risk-management plan.

Defining Risk and Risk Management

Risk is the possibility that you may not achieve your product, schedule, or resource targets because something unexpected occurs or something planned doesn't occur. All projects have some degree of risk because predicting the future with certainty is impossible. However, project risk is greater

- The longer your project lasts
- The longer the time is between preparing your project plan and starting the work
- The less experience you, your organization, or your team members have with similar projects
- The newer your project's technology is

A Guide to the Project Management Body of Knowledge, 4th Edition (*PMBOK 4*), asserts that risk can be either negative or positive:

- *Negative risks,* also referred to as *threats,* potentially have a detrimental effect on one or more of the project objectives, such as causing you to miss a deadline.
- *Positive risks,* also referred to as *opportunities,* potentially have a beneficial effect on project objectives, such as allowing you to complete a task with fewer personnel than you originally planned.

In other words, anything that can cause you either to fall short of or to exceed your established project targets, if it occurs, is considered a risk. While some approaches for analyzing and responding to both types of risks are similar, this chapter presents approaches for identifying, evaluating, and managing negative risks. In this chapter, the term *risk* always refers to a negative risk or threat, unless otherwise noted.

Risk management is the process of identifying possible risks, assessing their potential consequences, and then developing and implementing plans for minimizing any negative effects. Risk management can't eliminate risks, but it offers the best chance for successfully accomplishing your project despite the uncertainties of a changing environment.

So how can you address your project's risks? Take the following steps to determine, evaluate, and manage the risks that may affect your project:

1. **Identify risks.**

   Determine which aspects of your plan or project environment may change.

2. **Assess the potential effects of those risks on your project.**

   Consider what can happen if those aspects don't work out the way you envision.

3. **Develop plans for mitigating the effects of the risks.**

   Decide how you can protect your project from the consequences of risks.

4. **Monitor the status of your project's risks throughout performance.**

   Determine whether existing risks are still present, whether the likelihood of these risks is increasing or decreasing, and whether new risks are arising.

5. **Inform key audiences of all risks involved with your project.**

   Explain the status and potential effect of all project risks — from the initial concept to the project's completion.

The rest of this chapter describes these steps in more detail.

Focusing on Risk Factors and Risks

The first step toward controlling risks is identifying them. However, not all risks pose the same degree of concern to all projects, and using a scatter-gun approach to identify risks that may affect your project leaves a significant chance that you'll overlook some important ones.

This section shows you how to identify potential risks on your project by recognizing the special situations that are most likely to create them.

Don't put all your eggs in one basket

I once met a man who was starting a large project that was a top priority for his organization. His project's success depended heavily on one person who would work on the project full time for six months and perform all the technical-development tasks. I asked whether he had considered the consequences of this person's leaving the project before it was finished. He said he didn't have to worry about that risk because he simply wouldn't allow the man to leave.

It occurred to me that his approach for dealing with risk was similar to the one of a woman who canceled her health insurance for a year — because she wasn't planning to get sick! He may have gotten top management to agree that the person would have no other assignments for the duration of his project. However, he still couldn't guarantee that the person wouldn't get sick or decide to leave the organization.

Recognizing risk factors

A *risk factor* is a situation that may give rise to one or more project risks. A risk factor itself doesn't cause you to miss a product, schedule, or resource target. However, it increases the chances that something may happen that will cause you to miss one.

For example: The fact that you and your organization haven't undertaken projects similar to the present one is a risk factor. Because you have no prior experience, you may overlook activities you need to perform, or you may underestimate the time and resources you need to perform them. Having no prior experience doesn't guarantee you'll have these problems, but it does increase the chance that you may.

Start to manage risks at the outset of your project, and continue to do so throughout its performance. At each point during your project, identify risks by recognizing your project's risk factors. Use your project phases as well as your overall project plan to help you identify risk factors.

All projects progress through the following four life cycle stages, and each stage can present new risk factors for your project (see Chapter 1 for a detailed discussion of these stages):

- ✔ Starting the project
- ✔ Organizing and preparing
- ✔ Carrying out the work
- ✔ Closing the project

Table 8-1 illustrates possible risk factors that may arise in each of these stages.

Table 8-1	Possible Risk Factors That May Arise during Your Project's Evolution
Life Cycle Stage	**Possible Risk Factors**
All	You or your team spends insufficient time on one or more stages.
	Key information isn't in writing.
	You or your team moves to a subsequent stage without completing one or more of the earlier stages.

Life Cycle Stage	Possible Risk Factors
Starting the project	Some background information and/or plans aren't in writing.
	No formal benefit-cost analysis has been done.
	No formal feasibility study has been done.
	You don't know who the originator of the project idea is.
Organizing and preparing	People unfamiliar with similar projects prepare your project plan.
	Your plan isn't in writing.
	Parts of the plan are missing.
	Some or all aspects of the plan aren't approved by all key audiences.
Carrying out the work	People on the project team didn't prepare the plan.
	Team members who didn't participate in the development of the project plan don't review it.
	You haven't made an effort to establish team identity and focus.
	You haven't developed any team procedures to resolve conflicts, reach decisions, or maintain communication.
	Needs of your primary clients change.
	You have incomplete or incorrect information regarding schedule performance and resource expenditures.
	Project-progress reporting is inconsistent.
	One or more key project supporters are reassigned.
	Team members are replaced.
	Marketplace characteristics or demands change.
	Changes are handled informally, with no consistent analysis of their effect on the overall project.
Closing the project	Project results aren't formally approved by one or more project drivers.
	Project team members are assigned to new projects before the current project is completed.

Table 8-2 depicts risk factors that different parts of your project plan may suggest.

Table 8-2	Possible Risk Factors Related to Different Parts of Your Project Plan
Part of Project Plan	*Possible Risk Factors*
Project audiences	Your project has a new client.
	You've had prior problems with a client.
	Upper management or other key drivers show only mild interest in your project.
	Your project doesn't have a project champion.
	Not all project audiences have been identified.
Project background	Your project derived from a spontaneous decision rather than a well-thought-out assessment.
	You don't have conclusive proof that your project will eliminate the problem it addresses.
	Your project can't start until one or more other planned activities are completed.
Project scope	Your project is unusually large.
	Your project requires a variety of skills and knowledge.
	Your project involves different organizational units.
Project strategy	You have no declared strategy.
	Your project involves a new, untested technology or approach.
Project objectives and deliverables	One or more objectives or deliverables are missing.
	Some performance measures are unclear or missing.
	Some performance measures are difficult to quantify.
	One or more performance targets or specifications are missing.
	One or more objectives or deliverables haven't been approved by all drivers.
Constraints	Your constraints aren't written down.
	Your constraints are vague.
	Note: In general, all constraints are potential risk factors.
Assumptions	Assumptions aren't written down.
	Your assumptions are vague.

Part of Project Plan	Possible Risk Factors
	Note: In general, all risk factors in all assumptions are potential risk factors.
Work packages and activities	Work packages or activities are insufficiently detailed.
	Not all team members participated in preparing descriptions of their assigned work packages and activities.
Roles and responsibilities	Not all supporters were involved in developing their roles and responsibilities.
	You have an overdependence on one or more people.
	No primary responsibility is assigned for one or more activities.
	Two or more people have primary responsibility for the same activity.
	No one person has overall responsibility for the project.
Schedule (activity-duration estimates)	Time estimates are backed into from an established end date.
	You have no historical database of activity durations.
	Your project involves new procedures or technologies for some activities.
	Activities are performed by team members you haven't worked with before.
Schedule (activity interdependencies)	Interdependencies aren't specifically considered during schedule development.
	Partially related activities are scheduled simultaneously to save time.
	Your project plan uses no formal analytical approach to assess the effect of interdependencies on the schedule.
Personnel	Your project plan has no estimates for actual work effort required to perform activities.
	Your project plan doesn't formally consider availability or efficiency.
	Your project plan has no detailed work schedules for people working simultaneously on two or more tasks.
	Your team includes one or more new or inexperienced team members.
Other resources	You have no plans to identify the type, amount, or timing of required nonpersonnel resources.
Funds	You have no project budget.

Identifying risks

After you recognize your project's risk factors, the next step in your risk assessment is to identify the specific risks that may result from each of your risk factors. With this information in hand, you can determine the particular effects each risk may have on your project and decide how you want to manage that risk.

Describe how each risk factor may cause you to miss your product, schedule, or resource targets. Suppose, for example, that you plan to use a new technology in your project. Using a new technology is a risk factor (as you see in Table 8-2). Possible product, schedule, and resource risks that may arise from this risk factor include the following:

- ✔ **Product risk:** The technology may not produce the desired results.

- ✔ **Schedule risk:** Tasks using the new technology may take longer than you anticipate.

- ✔ **Resource risk:** Existing facilities and equipment may not be adequate to support the use of the new technology.

To identify specific potential risks for each risk factor, do the following:

- ✔ **Review past records of problems encountered in similar situations.** If a risk factor actually resulted in an unexpected occurrence in the past, you definitely want to be prepared for it this time.

- ✔ **Brainstorm with experts and other people who have related experiences.** The more sources of expert opinion you consult, the less chance you have of overlooking something important.

- ✔ **Be specific.** The more specifically you describe a risk, the better you can assess its potential effect. Here's an example of a nonspecific risk compared to a specific one:

  - • **Nonspecific:** Activities may be delayed.

  - • **Specific:** Delivery may take three weeks rather than two.

Try to eliminate potential risk factors as soon as possible. For example, suppose a key audience hasn't approved your project's objectives. Instead of just noting the risk that you may not correctly address this audience's needs, try to get the audience's approval!

Assessing Risks: Probability and Consequences

The expected consequences of a risk depend on the effect of the risk if it becomes a reality and the probability that the risk will become a reality. Consider the expected consequences of different risks to choose which risks you want to actively manage and which risks you'll leave alone. This section discusses how to determine the probability that a particular risk will occur on your project and how to estimate the extent of that risk's consequences.

Gauging the likelihood of a risk

A meteorologist's forecast that it may snow isn't sufficient reason to go out and buy a $1,000 snow thrower. First, you want to know the chances that it'll snow, and second, you want to know how much snow is likely to fall. If the meteorologist is sure that, if it snows, the total accumulation will be at least 20 inches but the chances of it snowing at all are only one in 1,000, you may decide it's not worth it to spend $1,000 to be prepared for a situation that is so unlikely to occur.

The first step in deciding whether to deal proactively with a risk is assessing the likelihood that it will occur. Use one of the following schemes to describe the chances that a risk will occur:

- ✔ **Probability of occurrence:** You can express the likelihood that a risk will occur as *probability*. Probability is a number between 0 and 1, with 0.0 signifying that a situation will never happen, and 1.0 signifying that it will always occur. (You may also express probability as a percentage, with 100 percent meaning the situation will always occur.)

- ✔ **Category ranking:** Classify risks into categories that represent their likelihood. You may use *high, medium,* and *low,* or *always, often, sometimes, rarely,* and *never.*

- ✔ **Ordinal ranking:** Order the risks so the first is the most likely to occur, the second is the next most likely, and so on.

- ✔ **Relative likelihood of occurrence:** If you have two possible risks, you can express how much more likely one is to occur than the other. For example, you can declare that the first risk is *twice as likely* to occur as the second.

If you have objective data on the number of times a risk has occurred in similar situations in the past, use the first scheme in the preceding list to determine the likelihood that the risk will occur again in the future. If you don't have objective data available, use one of the other three schemes that are based on personal opinion to describe the likelihood particular risks will occur.

The following sections explain how to describe the likelihood a risk occurring using each of the preceding approaches.

Relying on objective info

You can estimate the probability of a risk occurring by considering the number of times the risk actually occurred on similar projects. Suppose, for example, that you designed 20 computer-generated reports over the past year for new clients. Eight times, when you submitted your design for final approval, new clients wanted at least one change. If you're planning to design a computer-generated report for another new client, you may conclude the chances are 40 percent that you'll have to make a change in the design you submit (8 divided by 20, then multiplied by 100).

When using objective information, such as past project reports, to determine the likelihood of different risks,

✔ Consider previous experience with similar projects.

✔ Consider as many similar situations as possible.

✔ Keep in mind that the more similar situations you consider, the more confidence you can have in your conclusions.

Counting on personal opinions

In the absence of objective data, solicit the opinions of experts and people who have worked on similar projects in the past. You can estimate the likelihood of a particular risk by soliciting the opinions of ten people who have worked on projects similar to yours. For example, ask them to rate the likelihood of a specific risk as *high, medium,* or *low.* Suppose six people choose *high,* two choose *medium,* and two choose *low.* You may then develop your estimate of the likelihood by assigning values of 3, 2, and 1, to *high, medium,* and *low,* respectively, and determining the weighted average of the responses as follows:

$$(6 \times 3) + (2 \times 2) + (2 \times 1) = (18 + 4 + 2) \div 10 = 2.4$$

This formula suggests the risk has medium to high likelihood of occurring (because 2.4 is between 2 and 3).

To increase the accuracy of the likelihood estimates you make based on personal opinions, try the following:

- ✔ **Define the category name as clearly as possible.** You may suggest that *low* means the likelihood of the risk is between 0 and 33 percent, *medium* means 33 to 66 percent, and *high* means 66 to 100 percent.

- ✔ **Consider the opinions of as many people as possible.** The more data points you have, the more confident you can be in the estimate.

- ✔ **Be sure the projects your respondents have worked on are truly similar to yours.** Otherwise, you have no reason to assume you can use their experience to predict what'll happen on your project.

- ✔ **Don't allow people to discuss their estimates with each other before they share them with you.** You're looking for individual opinions, not a group consensus.

- ✔ **After they've submitted their initial estimates to you, consider having the people discuss their reasons for their estimates with one another and then asking them whether they want to revise their estimates.** Some people may choose to modify their original estimates if they realize they failed to take into account certain important considerations.

Precision is different from accuracy. *Precision* refers to the detail of a number. *Accuracy* refers to how correct the number is. You may estimate the likelihood of a particular risk to be 67.23 percent. However, even though you express the risk precisely to two decimal places, your guess has little chance of being accurate if you have no prior experience with similar projects. Unfortunately, people often assume that more precise numbers are also more accurate. You can help avoid misinterpretations when you share your assessments of likelihood by using round numbers, categories, or relative rankings.

The more risk factors that suggest a particular risk may occur, the higher the likelihood that the risk will occur. For example, ordering from a vendor you haven't worked with before increases the chances that it'll take longer to receive your order than promised. However, the likelihood of a longer-than-promised wait for delivery is even greater if the item is also a special order, if you want delivery during a busy period for the vendor, and if the vendor has to order several parts from different manufacturers to make the item.

Estimating the extent of the consequences

Not long ago, I was waiting to see my doctor when the nurse came out and told me the doctor had to attend to an emergency and would be slightly delayed. Imagine my shock when, after waiting for three hours for the doctor,

I learned that, several hours earlier, he had gone to a hospital that was an hour away and was currently in the middle of an emergency operation! If I'd known the doctor was going to be gone for several hours, I would've rescheduled my appointment. Instead, because I didn't know how long the delay would be, I wasted three hours. And, unless I wanted to wait the rest of the afternoon, I'd have to make a new appointment anyway.

In this simple example, going for my annual checkup is my project, and beginning my checkup at the scheduled time is one of my project's targets. The doctor being called away on an emergency shortly before my scheduled appointment is a risk factor — it increases the chances that my checkup won't start at the scheduled time. My estimate of the magnitude of the consequences (how long I expect the start of my appointment to be delayed) affects what I choose to do (wait for the doctor to return or reschedule my appointment for another time).

After you identify the likelihood that a particular risk will affect your project, be sure to determine the magnitude of the consequences or effects that may result. That magnitude directly influences how you choose to deal with the risk. Determine the specific effect that each risk may have on your project's product, schedule, and resource performance. When evaluating these effects, do the following:

✔ **Consider the effect of a risk on the total project rather than on just part of it.** Taking one week longer than you planned to complete an activity may cause you to miss intermediate milestones (and cause the personnel waiting for the results of that activity to sit idle). However, the effect on the project is even greater if the delayed activity is on your project's critical path (see Chapter 5), which means the weeklong delay on that one activity also causes a weeklong delay for your entire project.

✔ **Consider the combined effect of related risks.** The likelihood that your schedule will slip is greater if three activities on the same critical path have a significant risk of delay rather than just one.

Be sure to describe risks and their associated consequences as specifically as possible. For example, suppose a key piece of equipment you ordered for your project may arrive later than expected. You can describe that risk as *the delivery may be late,* or as *the delivery may be delayed by two weeks.* Just stating that the delivery may be late doesn't give you enough information to assess the likely effect of that delay on the overall project. It also makes estimating the probability of that risk's occurrence more difficult. Are you talking about a delay of one day? One month? Stating that the delivery may be delayed by two weeks allows you to determine more precisely the likely effect the delay will have on the overall schedule and resources. It also allows you to decide how much you're willing to spend to avoid that delay.

You can use a variety of formal techniques to support your risk estimation and assessment, including the following:

✔ **Decision trees:** These diagrams illustrate different situations that may occur as your project unfolds, the likelihood of each situation's occurrence, and the consequences of that occurrence to your project.

Figure 8-1 illustrates a simple decision tree to help determine from which of two vendors to buy a piece of equipment. Both vendors have proposed a price of $50,000 if the equipment is delivered on the agreed-on date. Both vendors have also proposed they receive an incentive for delivering early and absorb a penalty for delivering late, but the amounts of the incentives and penalties differ. The decision tree depicts the probabilities that each vendor will deliver the equipment early, on time, and late, respectively, and the resulting price you pay in each case.

Multiplying the base price plus the performance incentive for early delivery by the probability of early delivery yields the expected value of the price you pay if delivery is early. You can calculate the total expected prices for Vendors A and B by totaling the expected prices if each is early, on time, and late, respectively.

This analysis suggests that you can expect to pay Vendor A $45,000 and have a 70 percent chance he'll deliver on time or early. You can expect to pay Vendor B $56,000 and have a 70 percent chance he'll deliver on time or early. So you can see that Vendor A is the better choice!

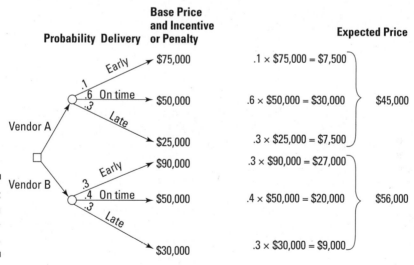

Figure 8-1: Illustrating a simple decision tree.

✔ **Risk-assessment questionnaires:** These formal data-collection instruments elicit expert opinion about the likelihood of different situations occurring and their associated effects.

✔ **Automated impact assessments:** These computerized spreadsheets consider — in combination — the likelihood that different situations will occur and the consequences if they do.

Getting Everything under Control: Managing Risk

Recognizing risks that pose a threat to your project is the first step toward controlling them. But you can't stop there. You also have to develop specific plans for reducing their potential negative effects on your project. This section helps you select the risks you'll proactively manage, develop a plan for addressing them, and share your plan with your project's audiences.

Choosing the risks you want to manage

All identified risks affect your project in some way *if they occur* (after all, that's the definition of a risk). However, you may determine that anticipating and minimizing the negative consequences of some risks if they occur takes more time and effort than just dealing with the situations when they arise.

So your first step in developing a risk-management strategy is choosing the risks that you want to address proactively and which ones you'll just accept. When making this decision, do the following:

✔ **Consider the likelihood of a risk *and* its potential effect on your project.** If the potential effect of a risk is great and if the chances it will occur are high, you probably want to develop plans to manage that risk. If both the effect and the likelihood are low, you may decide not to worry about it.

When the potential effect is high but the likelihood is low or vice versa, you must consider the situation more carefully. In these more complex situations, you can use a more formal approach for considering the combined effect of likelihood of occurrence and potential consequence by defining the *expected value of risk,* as follows:

Expected value of risk = (quantitative measure of the effect if it occurs) × (probability it will occur)

Suppose you need to buy certain materials for a device you're planning to build. When you place your order, you think you have an 80 percent chance of receiving the materials by the date promised. However, this means you have a 20 percent chance that something will go wrong and that you'll have to pay a premium to get the materials from another vendor by the date you need them. You estimate that the materials normally cost $1,000 and that you'll have to pay an additional $500 to get them from another vendor at the last minute. Determine the expected value of this risk as follows:

> Expected value of risk = Additional cost incurred if you use another vendor at the last minute × probability that you'll have to use this vendor
>
> Expected value of risk = $500 × 0.2 = $100

You may conclude that, all things being equal, spending more than $100 to reduce the chances of this risk isn't a wise financial decision.

✔ **Decide whether a potential consequence is so unacceptable that you're not willing to take the chance even if it's very unlikely to occur.**

Suppose your company wants to build a new plant in an area that has been hit hard by hurricanes. The estimated cost of the new plant is $50 million, and the likelihood that a hurricane will totally destroy the building is 0.1 percent. The expected value of this risk is $50,000 ($50,000,000 × 0.001), which the company can easily absorb. However, if a hurricane actually destroys the building, the associated $50 million loss would put the company out of business. So, even though the expected value of the loss is relatively small, the company may feel that even a 0.1 percent chance of its new building being destroyed by a hurricane is unacceptable.

If you choose to build the plant, be sure you develop a strategy to manage the risk of the plant being totally destroyed (see the next section). You may want to reconsider whether you want to undertake the project at all.

Developing a risk-management strategy

Choose one or more of the following approaches for dealing with the risks you decide to manage:

> ✔ **Avoidance:** Act to eliminate the risk factor that gave rise to the risk. An example is deciding not to use a new, untested procedure that you're concerned may not produce the desired project results.

✔ **Transfer:** Pay someone else to assume some or all of the effect of the risk. Suppose you choose to proceed with your plans to build a new $50 million facility (see the example in the preceding section). You can buy disaster insurance on the facility so the company doesn't have to assume the full burden of a total loss if a hurricane destroys the facility.

✔ **Mitigation:** Either reduce the likelihood that a risk occurs, or minimize the negative consequences if it does occur. The following are examples of risk mitigation:

- **Minimize the chances that the risk will occur.** Take actions to reduce the chances that an undesirable situation will come to pass. For example, consider that you have a person on your project who's new to your organization. Consequently, you feel the person may take longer to do her assigned task than you planned. To reduce the chances that the person will require more time, explain the task and the desired results very clearly to the person before she begins to work on it, develop frequent milestones and monitor the person's performance often so that you can deal with any problems as soon as they occur, and have her attend training to refresh the skills and knowledge she needs to perform the assignment.

- **Develop contingencies to minimize the negative consequences if an undesirable situation does come to pass.** Suppose you plan to have your organization's publication department reproduce 100 copies of the manual for your training program. If you're concerned that the department may have higher-priority projects at the same time, locate an external vendor that can reproduce the manuals if the need arises. Finding the vendor beforehand can reduce any time delay resulting from the need to switch to another resource.

Keep in mind that if these approaches are to work, you must choose your strategies and plan their implementation as early as possible in your project.

Although the following approaches may sometimes seem appealing as you consider all the risks involved in a particular project, they don't work, so don't use them:

✔ **The ostrich approach:** Ignoring all risks, or pretending they don't exist

✔ **The prayer approach:** Looking to a higher being to solve all your problems or to making them disappear

✔ **The denial approach:** Recognizing that certain situations may cause problems for your project but refusing to accept that these situations may occur

Though it may require a bit of work upfront, proactively managing your project's risks always pays dividends down the line.

Communicating about risks

People often share information about project risks ineffectually or not at all. As a result, their projects suffer unnecessary problems and setbacks that proper communication may have avoided.

You may be reluctant to deal with risk because the concept is hard to grasp. If your project's a one-time deal, what difference does it make that, in the past, a particular risk has occurred 40 times out of 100? You may also feel that focusing on risks suggests you're looking for excuses for failure rather than ways to succeed.

Communicate about project risks early and often. In particular, share information with drivers and supporters at the following points in your project (see Chapter 1 for more about these project life cycle stages):

✔ **Starting the project:** To support the process of deciding whether or not to undertake the project

✔ **Organizing and preparing:** To guide the development of all aspects of your project plan

✔ **Carrying out the work:**

- To allow team members to discuss potential risks and to encourage them to recognize and address problems as soon as those problems occur

- To update the likelihood that identified risks will occur, to reinforce how people can minimize the negative effects of project risks, and to guide the assessment of requests to change parts of the current approved project plan

You can improve your risk-related communications with your project's drivers and supporters by

✔ Explaining in detail the nature of a risk, how it may affect your project, and how you estimated the likelihood of its occurrence

✔ Telling people the current chances that certain risks will occur, how you're minimizing the chances of problems, and how they can reduce the chances of negative consequences

✔ Encouraging people to think and talk about risks, always with an eye toward minimizing the negative effects of those risks

✔ Documenting in writing all the information about the risks

You can discuss this information at regularly scheduled team meetings, in regularly scheduled progress reports and upper-management reviews, and in special meetings to address issues that arise. (See Chapter 13 for more on sharing project information.)

Preparing a Risk-Management Plan

A *risk-management plan* lays out strategies to minimize the negative effects that uncertain occurrences can have on your project. Develop your risk-management plan in the organizing and preparing stage of your project, refine it at the beginning of the carrying out the work stage, and continually update it during the remainder of the carrying out the work stage (see Chapter 1 for more on these stages). Include the following in your risk-management plan:

- Risk factors
- Associated risks
- Your assessment of the likelihood of occurrence and the consequences for each risk
- Your plan for managing selected risks
- Your plan for keeping people informed about those risks throughout your project

Table 8-3 illustrates a portion of a risk-management plan.

Table 8-3	A Portion of a Risk-Management Plan
Plan Element	**Description**
Risk factor	You haven't worked with this client before.
Risks	**Product:** Chance for miscommunication leads to incorrect or incomplete understanding of the client's needs.
	Schedule: Incomplete understanding of the client's business operation leads to an underestimate of your time to survey the client's current operations.
	Resources: Inaccurate understanding of the client's technical knowledge leads to assigning tasks to the client that he can't perform; you need additional staff to perform these tasks.
Analysis	Chances of misunderstanding the client's needs = high.
	Chances of underestimating the time to survey operations = low.
	Chances of misunderstanding the client's technical knowledge = low.

Plan Element	Description
Strategy	Deal only with the risk of misunderstanding the client's needs. Reduce the chances of this risk by doing the following:
	1. Review past correspondence or written problem reports to identify the client's needs.
	2. Have at least two team members present in every meeting with the client.
	3. Speak with different staff in the client's organization.
	4. Put all communications in writing.
	5. Share progress assessments with the client every two weeks throughout the project.

Relating This Chapter to the PMP Exam and PMBOK 4

Table 8-4 notes topics in this chapter that may be addressed on the Project Management Professional (PMP) certification exam and that are also included in *A Guide to the Project Management Body of Knowledge,* 4th Edition (*PMBOK 4*).

Table 8-4	Chapter 8 Topics in Relation to the PMP Exam and *PMBOK 4*	
Topic	Location in PMBOK 4	Comments
Definitions of project risk and risk management (see the section "Defining Risk and Risk Management")	11. Project Risk Management (Introduction)	The definitions of these terms in both books are essentially the same. This book focuses on addressing risks with negative consequences, while *PMBOK 4* notes that risks can have either negative or positive consequences.

(continued)

Table 8-4 *(continued)*

Identifying project risks (see the sections "Focusing on Risk Factors and Risks" and "Identifying risks")	11.2. Identify Risks	The risk identification processes and the areas that may give rise to project risks addressed in both books are almost the same.
Choosing risks to address in depth (see the section "Assessing Risks: Probability and Consequences"	11.3. Perform Qualitative Risk Analysis	Both books recommend determining risks to consider in depth by taking into account consequences and probability of occurrence.
Techniques for assessing risks and expected consequences (see the sections "Estimating the extent of the consequences" and "Choosing the risks you want to manage")	11.4. Perform Quantitative Risk Analysis	This book explores in depth several techniques that are mentioned in *PMBOK 4*.
Approaches for dealing with risks (see the section "Developing a risk-management strategy")	11.5.2.1. Strategies for Negative Risks or Threats	This book examines in depth the different approaches mentioned in *PMBOK 4*.

Part III

Group Work: Putting Your Team Together

The 5th Wave   By Rich Tennant

"Before we start this project, I'd like to clarify what metaphors we'll be speaking in. Last time we used sports metaphors. How about using cooking metaphors? 'Half baked,' 'burnt,' 'simmering,' that sort of thing?"

In this part . . .

The key to successful projects is people — using their capabilities to the fullest, encouraging their mutually supportive work efforts, and sustaining their ongoing commitment to your project's success.

In this part, I identify the people who affect the work environment in a project-oriented organization. I also suggest ways to define team member roles, and I offer approaches that encourage team members to maintain a supportive environment. Finally, I describe how to start your project off on the right foot.

Chapter 9

Aligning the Key Players for Your Project

In This Chapter
▶ Comparing three organizational structures in terms of their pros and cons
▶ Defining the actors and their roles in the matrix structure
▶ Being successful in a matrix organization

*I*n the traditional work environment, you have one direct supervisor who assigns your work, completes your performance appraisals, approves your salary increases, and authorizes your promotions. However, increasing numbers of organizations are moving toward a structure in which a variety of people direct your work assignments. What's the greatest advantage of this new structure? When all is said and done, it supports faster and more-effective responses to the diverse projects in an organization.

Success in this new project-oriented organization requires you to do the following:

✔ Recognize the people who define and influence your work environment.

✔ Understand their unique roles.

✔ Know how to work effectively with them to create a successful project.

This chapter helps you define your organization's environment and understand individual roles. It also provides tips to help you successfully accomplish your project in a matrix-structured organization.

Defining Three Organizational Environments

Over the years, projects have evolved from organizational afterthoughts to major vehicles for conducting business and developing future capabilities. Naturally, the approaches for organizing and managing projects have evolved, as well.

This section explains how projects are handled in the traditional functional structure, the project-focused projectized structure, and the extensively used matrix structure, which combines aspects of both the functional and projectized structures.

The functional structure

The *functional organization structure* (see Figure 9-1 for an example) brings together people who perform similar tasks or who use the same kinds of skills and knowledge in *functional groups*. In this structure, people are managed through clear lines of authority that extend through each group to the head of the group and, ultimately, to a single person at the top. For example, in Figure 9-1, you see that all people who perform human resources functions for the organization (such as recruiting, training, and benefits management) are located in the human resources group, which reports to the chief executive.

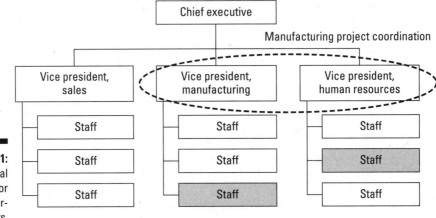

Figure 9-1:
A functional structure for administering projects.

□ Shaded boxes indicate staff working on a manufacturing project

Depending on the nature of the project and the skills and knowledge required for it, a project in the functional structure may be handled completely by staff within a particular functional group. However, as illustrated in Figure 9-1, if the manufacturing group is performing a project that requires the expertise of a person from the human resources group, the vice president of manufacturing must make a formal agreement with the vice president of human resources to make the necessary human resources staffer available to work on the project. The vice president of human resources must then manage this person as he performs his tasks for the project.

The project manager has less authority over project team members in the functional structure than in any other form of project organization. In fact, he serves more as a project coordinator than a project manager because the functional managers maintain all authority over the project team members and the project budget.

Advantages of the functional structure

The functional structure has the following advantages:

- **Functional groups are reservoirs of skills and knowledge in their areas of expertise.** Group members are hired for their technical credentials and continue to develop their capabilities through their work assignments.

- **Functional groups' well-established communication processes and decision-making procedures provide timely and consistent support for the group's projects.** From the beginning of their assignments, group members effectively work with and support one another because they know with whom, how, and when to share important task information. Decisions are made promptly because areas of authority are clearly defined.

- **Functional groups provide people with a focused and supportive job environment.** Group members work alongside colleagues who share similar professional interests. Each member has a well-defined career path and one boss who gives his assignments and reviews his performance. The established interpersonal relationships among the group's members facilitate effective collaborative work efforts.

Disadvantages of the functional structure

The functional structure has the following drawbacks:

- **The functional structure hampers effective collaboration between different functional groups.** Group members' working relationships are mainly with others in their group, and management assesses their performance on how well they perform in the group's area of specialization. This makes effective collaboration with other groups on a project difficult.

- **The functional group members' main interest is to perform the tasks in their group's specialty area effectively, rather than to achieve goals and results that may involve and affect other groups in the organization.** Group members' professional interests and working relationships are mostly with others in their group, and their boss, who gives them their work assignments and evaluates their performance, is the head of the functional group. This environment encourages members to be most concerned with and to give the highest priority to their functional group's task assignments.

✔ **A functional group may have difficulty getting buy in and support for its project from other functional groups that must support or will be affected by the project.** Each functional group can initiate a project without consulting other functional groups. As a result, people in these other areas may be reluctant to support such a project when it doesn't address their needs in the most effective way. They may also be reluctant to support it because the project may be competing with projects from their own functional group for scarce resources.

The projectized structure

The *projectized organization structure* groups together all personnel working on a particular project. Project team members are often located together and under the direct authority of the project manager for the duration of the project. As an example, you see in Figure 9-2 that a design engineer, an IT specialist, and a test engineer all work on Project A, while a different design engineer and a different test engineer work on Project B.

The project manager has almost total authority over the members of her team in the projectized structure. She makes assignments and directs team members' task efforts; she controls the project budget; she conducts team members' performance assessments and approves team members' raises and bonuses; and she approves annual leave.

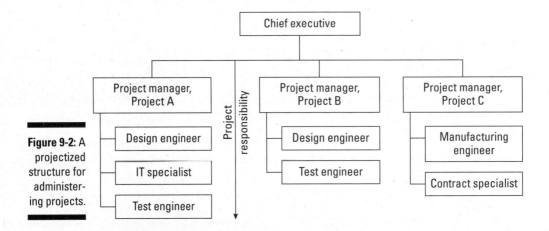

Figure 9-2: A projectized structure for administering projects.

Advantages of the projectized structure

The projectized structure has the following advantages:

▌ ✔ **All members of a project team report directly to the project manager.** This clarified and simplified reporting structure reduces the potential for conflicting demands on team members' time and results in fewer and shorter lines of communication. In addition, it facilitates faster project decision making.

✔ **Project team members can more easily develop a shared sense of identity, resulting in a stronger commitment to one another and to the success of the project.** Consistent focus on a single project with the same group of team members gives people a greater appreciation of one another's strengths and limitations, as well as a deeper understanding of and a stronger belief in the value of the intended project results.

✔ **Everyone on the team shares the processes for performing project work, communication, conflict resolution, and decision making.** The projectized structure enhances project productivity and efficiency because more time can be devoted to doing work rather than creating systems to support doing the work.

Disadvantages of the projectized structure

The projectized structure has the following disadvantages:

✔ **Higher personnel costs:** Even when several projects have similar personnel needs, different people with the same skill set have to be assigned to each one. As a result, chances are greater that projects won't be able to fully support people with specialized skills and knowledge, which can lead to either keeping people on projects longer than they're actually needed or having to cover people's salaries when their project doesn't have enough work to support them full time.

✔ **Reduced technical interchange between projects:** Providing all the skills and knowledge required to perform a project by assigning people full time to the project team reduces the need and the opportunity for sharing work experiences with people on other teams.

✔ **Reduced career continuity, opportunities, and sense of job security:** Because people are hired to work on one specific project team, they have no guarantee that the organization will need their services when their current project comes to an end.

The matrix structure

With increasing frequency, projects today involve and affect many functional areas within an organization. As a result, personnel from these different areas must work together to successfully accomplish the project work. The matrix organization structure combines elements of both the functional and projectized structures to facilitate the responsive and effective participation of people from different parts of the organization on projects that need their specialized expertise.

As Figure 9-3 illustrates, in a *matrix organization structure,* people from different areas of the organization are assigned to lead or work on projects. Project managers guide the performance of project activities while people's direct supervisors (from groups such as finance, manufacturing, and sales, as in Figure 9-3) perform administrative tasks like formally appraising people's performance and approving promotions, salary increases, or requests for leave. Because an individual can be on a project for less than 100 percent of his time, he may work on more than one project at a time. (I discuss the key players in a matrix structure in more detail later in the "Recognizing the Key Players in a Matrix Environment" section.)

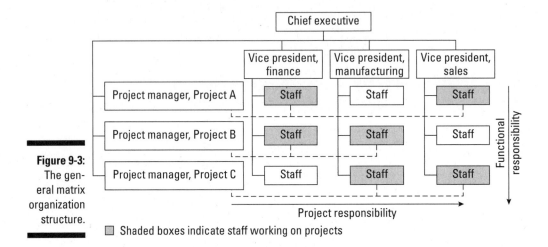

Figure 9-3: The general matrix organization structure.

Shaded boxes indicate staff working on projects

A matrix environment is classified as *weak, strong,* or *balanced,* depending on the amount of authority the project managers have over their teams. Here's a little more info about each of these classifications:

✔ **Weak matrix:** Project team members receive most of their direction from their functional managers. Project managers have little, if any, direct authority over team members and actually function more like project coordinators than managers.

✔ **Strong matrix:** Companies with strong matrix structures choose project managers for new projects from a pool of people whose only job is to manage projects. The companies never ask these people to serve as team members. Often these project managers form a single organizational unit that reports to a manager of project managers. In addition to directing and guiding project work, these project managers have certain administrative authority over the team members, such as the right to participate in their performance appraisals.

✔ **Balanced matrix:** This type of matrix environment is a blend of the weak and strong environments. People are assigned to lead projects or serve as team members based on the projects' needs rather than on their job descriptions. Although the project manager may have some administrative authority over team members (such as approving leave requests), for the most part, the project manager guides, coordinates, and facilitates the project.

Check out the later section "Working Successfully in a Matrix Environment" for more information on the matrix structure.

Advantages of the matrix structure

A matrix environment offers many benefits, including the following:

✔ **Teams can assemble rapidly.** Because you have a larger resource pool from which to choose your project team, you don't have to wait for a few people to finish current assignments before they can start on your project. Additionally, this approach reduces the time-consuming process of hiring someone new from the outside.

✔ **Specialized expertise can be available for several different projects.** Projects often require a small amount of effort from a person with highly specialized knowledge or skills. If your project alone can't provide sufficient funds to hire this person full time, perhaps several projects together, each using a portion of the expert's time, can.

✔ **Getting buy in from team members' functional units is easier with the matrix structure than with the functional or projectized structures.** Unit members who work on a project or who are affected by its outcome are more likely to support the project if they're confident that the team hears their concerns and issues.

Disadvantages of the matrix structure

A matrix environment introduces the following challenges, which the project manager must successfully address:

✔ **Team members working on multiple projects respond to two or more managers.** Each team member has at least two people giving her direction — a project manager (who coordinates project work and team support) and a functional manager (who coordinates the team member's project assignments, completes her performance appraisal, and approves requests for leave). When these two managers are at similar levels in the organization, resolving conflicting demands for the team member's time can be difficult.

✔ **Team members may not be familiar with one another's styles and knowledge.** Because team members may not have worked extensively together, they may require some time to become comfortable with one another's work styles and behaviors.

✔ **Team members may focus more on their individual assignments and less on the project and its goals.** For example, a procurement specialist may be responsible for buying equipment and supplies for all her projects. In such a case, the specialist may be less concerned about a project's target date for the purchases and more concerned about correctly following her department's procurement procedures.

Recognizing the Key Players in a Matrix Environment

The matrix structure that I introduce earlier in this chapter makes it easier for people from diverse parts of the organization to contribute their expertise to different projects. However, working in a matrix environment requires that the project manager deal with the styles, interests, and demands of more people who have some degree of control over his project's resources, goals, and objectives than in a functional or projectized structure.

In a matrix environment, the following people play critical roles in every project's success:

✔ **Project manager:** The person ultimately responsible for the successful completion of the project

✔ **Project team members:** People responsible for successfully performing individual project activities

✔ **Functional managers:** The team members' direct-line supervisors

✔ **Upper management:** People in charge of the organization's major business units

The following sections discuss how each of these people can help your project succeed.

The project manager

If you're the project manager, you're responsible for all aspects of the project. Being responsible doesn't mean you have to do the whole project yourself, but you do have to see that every activity is completed satisfactorily.

(See Chapter 10 for definitions of authority, responsibility, and accountability.) In this role, you're specifically responsible for the following:

- Determining objectives (see Chapter 2), schedules (see Chapter 5), and resource budgets (see Chapters 6 and 7)

- Ensuring you have a clear, feasible project plan to reach your performance targets (see Chapter 4)

- Identifying and managing project risks (see Chapter 8)

- Creating and sustaining a well-organized, focused, and committed team (see Part III)

- Selecting or creating your team's operating practices and procedures (see Chapter 11)

- Monitoring performance against plans and dealing with any problems that arise (see Chapter 12)

- Resolving priority, work approach, or interpersonal conflicts (see Chapter 14)

- Identifying and facilitating the resolution of project issues and problems (see Chapter 12)

- Controlling project changes (see Chapter 12)

- Reporting on project activities (see Chapter 13)

- Keeping your clients informed and committed (see Chapter 13)

- Accomplishing objectives within time and budget targets (see Part IV)

- Contributing to your team members' performance appraisals (see Chapter 15)

On occasion, you may hear people use the terms project *director* and project *leader,* both of which sound similar to project *manager.* Check with your organization, but usually *manager* and *director* describe the same position. Project *leader,* however, is a different story. People often think of *management* as focusing on issues and *leadership* as focusing on people; *management* also deals with established procedures, while *leadership* deals with change. Therefore, calling someone a project *leader* emphasizes her responsibility to focus and energize the people supporting the project, as opposed to the more technical tasks of planning and controlling. But again, check with your organization to be sure the term *leader* is meant to convey this message. (Often *project leader* is just another term for *project manager* — go figure!)

Project team members

Project team members must satisfy the requests of both their functional managers and their project managers. As a team member, your responsibilities related to project assignments include the following:

- ✔ Performing tasks in accordance with the highest standards of technical excellence in your field
- ✔ Performing assignments on time and within budget
- ✔ Maintaining the special skills and knowledge required to do the work well

In addition, you're responsible for working with and supporting your team members' project efforts. Such help may entail the following:

- ✔ Considering the effect your actions may have on your team members' tasks
- ✔ Identifying situations and problems that may affect team members' tasks
- ✔ Keeping your team members informed of your progress, accomplishments, and any problems you encounter

Functional managers

Functional managers are responsible for orchestrating their staff's assignments among different projects. In addition, they provide the necessary resources for their staff to perform their work in accordance with the highest standards of technical excellence. Specifically, functional managers are responsible for the following:

- ✔ Developing or approving plans that specify the type, timing, and amount of resources required to perform tasks in their area of specialty
- ✔ Ensuring team members are available to perform their assigned tasks for the promised amount of time
- ✔ Providing technical expertise and guidance to help team members solve problems related to their project assignments
- ✔ Providing the equipment and facilities needed for a person to do his work
- ✔ Helping people maintain their technical skills and knowledge
- ✔ Ensuring members of the functional group use consistent methodological approaches on all their projects
- ✔ Completing team members' performance appraisals

✔ Recognizing performance with salary increases, promotions, and job assignments

✔ Approving team members' requests for annual leave, administrative leave, training, and other activities that take time away from the job

Upper management

Upper management creates the organizational environment; oversees the development and use of operating policies, procedures, and practices; and encourages and funds the development of required information systems. More specifically, upper management is responsible for the following:

✔ Creating the organizational mission and goals that provide the framework for selecting projects

✔ Setting policies and procedures for addressing priorities and conflicts

✔ Creating and maintaining labor and financial information systems

✔ Providing facilities and equipment to support project work

✔ Defining the limits of managers' decision-making authority

✔ Helping to resolve project issues and decisions that can't be handled successfully at lower levels in the organization

Working Successfully in a Matrix Environment

Achieving success in a matrix environment requires that you effectively align and coordinate the people who support your project, deflecting any forces that pull those people in different directions. This section can help you, as a project manager, get the highest-quality work from your team members in a matrix environment, along with timely and effective support from the functional and senior managers.

Creating and continually reinforcing a team identity

Committing to work with others to achieve a common goal encourages people to overcome problems they may encounter along the way. The following tips can help clarify your team's purpose and encourage team members to support

one another as you work together to achieve it (see Chapter 11 for additional guidelines):

- ✔ **Clarify team vision and working relationships.** As soon as you have a team, work with the team members to develop a project mission that members can understand and support. Give people an opportunity to become familiar with each other's work styles.

- ✔ **Define team procedures.** Encourage your team to develop its own work procedures instead of allowing people to use the approaches of their respective functional groups.

- ✔ **Clarify each person's authority.** Team members may have to represent their functional areas when making project decisions. Clarify each team member's level of independent authority to make such decisions, and determine who outside the team can make any decisions that are beyond the purview of the team member.

- ✔ **Be aware of and attend to your team's functioning.** Help people establish comfortable and productive interpersonal relationships. Continue to support these relationships throughout your project.

- ✔ **Be sure one person is assigned the role of project manager — with overall coordinative responsibilities.** The project manager continually reminds team members of the overarching project goals and focuses their attention on how they influence and affect each other's work.

Getting team member commitment

Team members typically have little or no authority over each other in a matrix environment. Therefore, they perform their project assignments because they choose to, not because they have to. Work with people initially and throughout your project to encourage them to commit to your project's goals (see Chapter 14 for more on how to encourage team member buy in).

Eliciting support from other people in the environment

The project manager's authority over team members is frequently limited; for the most part, he must rely on suggestion, encouragement, and persuasion to help team members address issues and accomplish their assignments. Therefore, it's important that you identify and establish relationships with others who can help you deal with situations that you're unable to resolve yourself. Here's how:

- ✓ **Get a champion.** Because you most likely don't have authority over all the people who affect the chances for your project's success, get an ally who does have that authority — and do so as soon as possible. This *project champion* can help resolve team members' schedule and interpersonal conflicts and raise your project's visibility in the organization. (See Chapter 3 for more information.)

- ✓ **Ask for and acknowledge your team members' functional managers' support.** By thanking functional managers for supporting their staff and allowing the staff to honor their project commitments, you're encouraging those managers to provide similar support for you and others in the future.

Heading off common problems before they arise

Take the following steps upfront and throughout your project to head off potential conflicts and concerns before they arise:

- ✓ **Plan in sufficient detail.** Work with team members to clearly and concisely define the project work and each person's specific roles and responsibilities for all activities. This planning helps people more accurately estimate the amount of effort they need to give and the timing of that effort for each assignment.

- ✓ **Identify and address conflicts promptly.** Conflicts frequently arise in a matrix environment, given people's diverse responsibilities, different styles, and lack of experience working together. Encourage people to identify and discuss conflicts as soon as they arise. Develop systems and procedures to deal with conflicts promptly — before they get out of hand.

- ✓ **Encourage open communication among team members, especially regarding problems and frustrations.** The earlier you hear about problems, the more time you have to deal with them. Discussing and resolving team issues encourages working relationships that are more enjoyable and productive.

- ✓ **Encourage upper management to establish an oversight committee to monitor project performance and to address resource and other conflicts.** Project and functional managers must focus on the goals for their respective areas of responsibility. Often, both groups rely on the same pool of people to reach these goals. But these diverse needs can place conflicting demands on people's time and effort. An upper-management oversight committee can ensure that the needs of the entire organization are considered when addressing these conflicts.

Relating This Chapter to the PMP Exam and PMBOK 4

Table 9-1 notes topics in this chapter that may be addressed on the Project Management Professional (PMP) certification exam and that are included in *A Guide to the Project Management Body of Knowledge,* 4th Edition (*PMBOK 4*).

Table 9-1	Chapter 9 Topics in Relation to the PMP Exam and *PMBOK 4*	
Topic	*Location in PMBOK 4*	*Comments*
Functional, projectized, and matrix organizational structures (see the section "Defining Three Organizational Environments"	2.4.2. Organizational Structure	Both books identify the same three organizational structures for handling projects as being the most common.
Roles of project manager, project team members, functional managers, and upper management (see the section "Recognizing the Key Players in a Matrix Environment")	1.6. Role of a Project Manager 2.3. Stakeholders	This book discusses in more detail than *PMBOK 4* how each entity can support a project team's successful performance.

Chapter 10

Defining Team Members' Roles and Responsibilities

---

*Y*our project team typically includes people with different skill sets and operating styles who work in different parts of the organization. Thus, you may not have worked extensively with your team members before. In addition, your project usually has a tight time schedule, and team members most likely are working on several other assignments at the same time.

Success in this kind of environment requires that you and your team members agree on how to work with each other to maximize contributions and minimize wasted time and mistakes. The team needs an approach that gives everyone confidence that members will live up to their commitments. The project manager and every team member must understand and be comfortable with their planned roles.

This chapter explains how to distinguish between the different degrees of team member task involvement, make key assignments, encourage people to keep their promises, present an overall picture of team members' roles and responsibilities, and, finally, handle a micromanager.

Understanding the Key Roles

A typical project entails performing specific pieces of work, making decisions, and coordinating the activities of others. To accomplish the project with a minimum of time and resources, each piece of work must be done in the correct order, and each person must work at peak efficiency, being sure not to repeat or duplicate unnecessarily work that others have already done. The more complex the project and the greater the number of people working on it, the more difficult it is to ensure people don't step on each other's toes along the way.

To help you start coordinating people's efforts, this section defines three different roles that team members can play when working on a project activity and takes a look at their similarities and differences.

Distinguishing authority, responsibility, and accountability

The following concepts can help you define and clarify how team members should relate to each other and to their assigned tasks:

- **Authority:** The ability to make binding decisions about your project's products, schedule, resources, and activities. Examples include your ability to sign purchase orders that don't exceed $3,000 and your ability to change a scheduled date by no more than two weeks.

- **Responsibility:** The commitment to achieve specific results. An example is your promise to have a draft report ready by March 1.

- **Accountability:** Bringing consequences to bear in response to people's performance, such as your boss noting in your annual performance appraisal that you solved a tough manufacturing problem.

  Unfortunately, many people think accountability means only paying the price when you foul up. This fear of having to be accountable for their mistakes often leads people to avoid situations in which they would be accountable for their performance. Paying a price when you foul up is certainly half of the concept, but the other half is being rewarded for doing a good job. This positive reinforcement is far more effective than negative reinforcement for encouraging high-quality results.

Although these three terms are related, each term is a distinct and necessary element of defining and reinforcing team roles.

Comparing authority and responsibility

Both authority and responsibility are upfront agreements. Before you start your project, you agree who can make which decisions and who will ensure particular results. However, authority focuses on processes, while responsibility focuses on outcomes:

- Authority defines the decisions you can make but doesn't mention the results you have to achieve.

✔ Responsibility addresses the results you must accomplish but doesn't mention the decisions you can make to reach those results.

Remember, too, that you can transfer the authority to make decisions to another person, but you can't transfer the responsibility for the results of those decisions. (For more about delegating authority and sharing responsibility, check out the next section.)

Suppose you have the authority to issue purchase orders up to $5,000 for your project. Assume no policy or instructions specifically prevent you from giving some or all of this authority to someone else, so you give Matt, one of your team members, authority to sign purchase orders for your project not to exceed $4,000. However, if Matt mistakenly issues a $3,000 purchase order for ten reams of specialty paper instead of a $1,500 purchase order for the five reams that he really needs, you're still responsible for his error.

You can always take back authority that you gave to someone else, but you can't blame the person for exercising that authority while he has it.

Making Project Assignments

Effectively eliciting the help and support of others in the work you do is essential to get the most out of all team members. This section focuses specifically on what you need to know about defining project roles, including deciding what can and can't be delegated, assigning roles with confidence, sharing responsibility, and holding everyone accountable.

Delving into delegation

Delegating is giving away something you have. (I know other definitions of delegating exist, but to keep it simple: *to delegate* is to give away.) In the following sections, I help you decide what to delegate and understand different degrees of delegation; I also explain how to support your delegations and achieve the best results possible.

You can delegate authority, but you can only share responsibility. You can completely transfer your decision-making power to someone else so she can make the decisions with no involvement or approval from you. However, when another person agrees to assume a responsibility of yours, you're still obligated to ensure that she achieves the desired results. See the later section "Sharing responsibility" for more details.

Deciding what to delegate

You delegate authority for four reasons:

- ✔ To free yourself up to do other tasks
- ✔ To have the most qualified person make decisions
- ✔ To get another qualified person's perspective on an issue
- ✔ To develop another person's ability to handle additional assignments prudently and successfully

Although the potential benefits of delegating can be significant, not every task can or should be delegated. Consider the following guidelines when deciding which tasks are appropriate candidates for delegation:

- ✔ **Assign yourself to the tasks that you do best.** Suppose you're the best lawyer in town and there's more demand for your services at a fee of $500 per hour than you can meet. Suppose also that you can type twice as fast as the next fastest typist in town, who charges $200 per hour. Should you type all your own legal briefs?

  The answer is no. If you spend an hour typing, you'd save the $400 you'd have to pay the typist (who'd require two hours at a cost of $200 per hour to do the same work). However, if you spend the same one hour providing legal services, you'd earn $500, which would allow you to pay the typist $400 for the work and still have $100 left over. (This concept is referred to as the *law of comparative advantage.*)

- ✔ **If possible, assign yourself to tasks that aren't on a project's critical path.** (See Chapter 5 for a discussion of critical paths.) A delay on any activity on a project's critical path pushes back the estimated date for project completion. Therefore, when you have to stop working on a task that's on your project's critical path to deal with problems on another task, you immediately delay the entire project.

  Suppose you're managing a project to develop and present a training program. Part of the project entails preparing the content for the training manual and reserving the facilities where you'll present the training. Each activity is on one of the project's critical paths, and both are scheduled to be performed at the same time. Because you're so concerned that the training manual has the correct content and is completed on time, you assign yourself to finish developing it, and you assign Marty, a member of your project team, to reserve the facilities.

  When Marty encounters an unexpected problem while trying to use the organization's credit card to pay for the deposit to hold the facilities, you feel you need to help him resolve it. However, if you stop working on your critical path activity of completing the training manual to help him, your project's completion will be delayed.

- ✔ **Don't assign other people to work on a task that you can't clearly describe.** The time you save by not working on the task is more than offset by the time you spend answering questions and continually redirecting the person to whom you've assigned the unclear task.

Understanding degrees of delegation

Delegation doesn't have to be an all-or-nothing proposition, where you either make all decisions yourself or you withdraw from the situation entirely. Consider the following six degrees of delegation, each of which builds on and extends the ones that come before it:

- ✔ **Get in the know.** Get the facts and bring them to me for further action.

- ✔ **Show me the way to go.** Develop alternative actions to take based on the facts you've found.

- ✔ **Go when I say so.** Be prepared to take one or more of the actions you've proposed, but don't do anything until I say so.

- ✔ **Go unless I say** *no*. Tell me what you propose to do and when, and take your recommended actions unless I tell you otherwise.

- ✔ **How'd it go?** Analyze the situation, develop a course of action, take action, and let me know the results.

- ✔ **Just go!** Here's a situation; deal with it.

Each level of delegation entails some degree of independent authority. For example, as your manager, when I ask you to find the facts about a situation, you choose what information sources to consult, which information to share with me, and which to discard. The primary difference between the levels of delegation is the degree of checking with the manager before taking action.

Supporting your delegations of authority

You must reinforce and support your delegations of authority, or you can find yourself doing the task you thought you had assigned to someone else.

Suppose you've been a manager of a project for the past two months, and Mary, who has been your assistant, has been dealing with people's technical issues. When someone comes to Mary with a technical problem, she analyzes the problem, decides how to address it, and passes the problem and her proposed solution by you. If you agree with her solution, you ask her to implement it. If you don't, you help her develop a more acceptable one.

Yesterday, you told Mary that, from now on, she doesn't have to pass her proposed solutions by you before implementing them. After discussing this with her, you told the other team members about the new procedure.

This morning Joe came to Mary to discuss a problem he was having with a contractor, and after listening to the problem, she gave Joe very specific instructions for how to deal with it. When Joe left Mary's office, he called you, recounted the problem he had discussed with Mary and her proposed solution, and asked you whether you agreed with Mary's approach.

You now have a dilemma. On the one hand, you want to support Mary's newly delegated authority. On the other hand, you want to ensure that your project goes smoothly and successfully. What should you do?

The only response you can make to Joe that supports your delegation of authority to Mary is: "Do whatever Mary told you to do."

Responding to Joe with, "Yes, Mary's solution sounds good to me," doesn't work because, by declaring that you like Mary's solution, you undercut Mary's authority to make the decision on her own! Perhaps you intend your words to assure Joe that you have full confidence in Mary's ability to develop an appropriate solution and that the one she proposed is an example of her good judgment. In reality, your response suggests to Joe that you're still in the approval process because you gave your approval to Mary's *decision* rather than to her exercising her *authority to make the decision*.

You want to support your delegation, but you also want to ensure your project's success. So how do you deal with the following situations?

- **You don't agree with Mary's recommendation.** If you fear that following Mary's recommendation will have catastrophic consequences, you must suggest to Joe that he wait until you can discuss the issue with Mary. In this instance, protecting your project and your organization is more important than supporting your delegation of authority.

 In all other instances, though, you need to tell Joe to follow Mary's suggestion because she has the authority to make that decision. Here are several reasons to do so, even if you don't agree with her choice:

  • She may know more about the situation than Joe told you.

  • Maybe she's right and you're wrong.

  • If Mary believes that you'll jump in to save her every time she makes a bad decision, she'll be less concerned about making the correct decision the first time.

 You can always ask Mary later to explain to you privately the rationale for her decision, and you can offer your thoughts and opinions when you feel they're necessary.

- **Joe's call indicates a more general problem with the team's procedures and working relationships.**

  • Perhaps you weren't clear when you explained the new working procedures with Mary to your team. Explain and reinforce the new procedures to Joe and the other team members.

  • Perhaps Joe didn't like Mary's answer and is trying to go behind her back to get his way. Again, you must reinforce that the decision is Mary's to make.

- Perhaps Mary didn't adequately explain to Joe why she recommended what she did. Suggest to Mary that she discuss with Joe the reasons behind her solutions and that she verifies that he understands and is comfortable with the information she shares.

- Perhaps some interpersonal conflict exists between Joe and Mary. Talk with both of them to determine whether such a conflict exists and, if it does, how it came about. Work with Joe and Mary to help them address and resolve the conflict.

Delegating to achieve results

Delegation always involves some risk — you have to live with the consequences of someone else's decisions. However, you can take the following steps to improve the person's chances for successful performance:

1. **Clarify what you want to delegate.**

   Describe in unambiguous terms the activity you want the other person to perform and the results you want her to achieve. If necessary, also explain what you don't want the person to do.

2. **Choose the right person.**

   Determine the skills and knowledge you feel a person must have to perform the task successfully, and don't delegate the task to a person who lacks these skills and knowledge. (See Chapter 6 for more on describing the skills and knowledge people need to do different jobs.)

3. **Make the delegation correctly.**

   Explain the activity to be performed, the effort you expect the person to expend, and the date she should have the activity completed. Put this information in writing for clarity and future reference.

4. **Be available to answer questions.**

   Maintaining contact while the person performs the task allows you to ensure that any ambiguities and unexpected situations encountered are resolved promptly and to your satisfaction. It also conveys to the person that the task is important to you.

5. **Monitor performance.**

   Set up frequent, well-defined checkpoints at which you can monitor the person's performance. Then keep that schedule.

6. **Promptly address problems that arise.**

   If you feel the person's performance isn't satisfactory, discuss your concerns and develop steps to bring it back on track.

Sharing responsibility

The decision to delegate authority is unilateral; it doesn't require the agreement of both parties. You can choose to give someone the authority to make a decision whether or not she wants it. After you give your authority to another person, she's free to pass it on to someone else (if you haven't specifically told her not to).

Responsibility is a two-way agreement. You ask me to respond to a customer inquiry, and I agree that I will. Because you and I agree that I'll handle the inquiry, I can't decide to give the assignment to someone else and then not worry about whether she'll handle it. I committed to you that the inquiry would be addressed; the only way I can free myself from this responsibility is to ask you to agree to change our original understanding.

Suppose Alice, your boss, asks you to prepare a report of your organization's latest sales figures. You know where to get the raw sales data, and you figure that you can prepare the text of the report in Microsoft Word and ask Bill, a member of your staff, to prepare any necessary graphics in Microsoft PowerPoint. So you accept Alice's assignment, and you then ask for and receive Bill's agreement to prepare the graphics for you.

A week later, Alice asks how you're doing on the report. You tell her that you've completed the text, but Bill hasn't finished the graphics, yet. You suggest that she check with Bill to find out how he's doing and when he'll be finished. How do you think Alice will respond to your suggestion?

After a moment's silence, Alice reminds you that you agreed to prepare the report and, therefore, that ensuring all parts of the work are complete is your responsibility, not hers. In other words, because you accepted the responsibility for completing the report, you can't choose unilaterally to give away part of that responsibility to someone else.

Alice was correct in refusing to deal directly with Bill for other reasons:

- ✔ If Alice had agreed to check directly with Bill, she would have tacitly been telling him that whenever you give him assignments in the future, he should be concerned about satisfying her rather than you. In other words, she would have undermined your leadership position.

- ✔ Following up with Bill would've been difficult for Alice to do, even if she had wanted to, because she didn't know exactly what you asked him to do or when you asked him to have it done.

The only way you can relieve yourself of some or all of the responsibility you accepted is to ask Alice to agree to a revised plan.

Holding people accountable when they don't report to you

People who make promises, fail to keep them, and then suffer no consequences create some of the worst frustrations in a project environment. Observe these guidelines to encourage people to honor commitments to you:

✔ **If you're responsible, you should be held accountable.** In other words, if you make a promise, you should always experience consequences based on how well you keep your promise.

✔ **If you're not responsible, you shouldn't be held accountable.** When something goes wrong but you weren't responsible for ensuring that it was handled correctly, you shouldn't face negative consequences. (Of course, you shouldn't receive accolades when it goes well, either.)

Holding people accountable when something they aren't responsible for goes wrong is called *scapegoating*. Assigning blame indiscriminately only encourages people to avoid dealing with you in the future.

When a person who doesn't report to you administratively promises to do something for you, holding her accountable can be a touchy issue. You may not try to hold her accountable because you think it's inappropriate (after all, you're not her boss) or because you don't know how to do so. But remember: Holding people accountable is appropriate and necessary when they've accepted a responsibility. Accountability helps people know that they're on the right track, and it enables you to acknowledge when they've completed the promised assignments. You don't need authority to hold people accountable; the people just have to have accepted the responsibility.

Use the following approaches to hold people accountable when you don't have direct authority over them:

✔ **Find out who has direct authority over the person and bring that supervisor into the process.** Consider soliciting the approval of the person's boss when you ask the person to accept responsibility for a task. When you do so correctly and at the right time, you can improve the chances for success. If a person's boss is unaware that her staff member agreed to perform a task for you, your chances of getting the boss's help when the person fails to perform as promised are small. However, if the boss supported her staff member's offer to help you when it was made, the boss and her staff member shouldn't be surprised if you solicit the boss's help when the staff member doesn't do the task.

✔ **Put it in writing.** Have you ever noticed how strangely people react when you put an informal agreement in writing? All of a sudden, they act as if you don't trust them. Don't let this reaction deter you. Put your agreement in writing to formalize it, to clarify the terms, and to serve as a reminder to both you and the person agreeing to do the task. If the person asks whether you want to have a written agreement because you don't trust that she'll do what she promises, explain to her that if you didn't trust her, you wouldn't work with her at all!

✔ **Be specific.** The clearer you make your request, the easier it is for the person to estimate the effort she needs to respond to the request and to produce the right result the first time. You may feel that being too specific is inappropriate because you have no direct authority over her. But recognize that putting a request in writing doesn't make it an order; it just clarifies its specifics and makes it easier to perform.

✔ **Follow up.** Negotiate a schedule to monitor the person's performance and to address any issues or questions that arise. Be sure to

- Negotiate a follow-up schedule at the outset of the agreement. If you call unannounced at random times, you appear to be checking up because you don't trust the person.

- Base your follow-up schedule on when the person plans to achieve certain intermediate milestones; this timeline gives you more objective criteria for an assessment.

✔ **Make the person accountable to the team.** Your most valuable professional asset is your reputation. When a person promises to do something for you, let others on your team know about the promise. When the person lives up to that promise, acknowledge her accomplishment in front of her colleagues. If the person fails to live up to the promise, let her know you'll share that information with others.

✔ **Get commitment.** When a person indicates that she'll help you out, be sure to get a firm, specific commitment that the desired result will be achieved by a specific time and for a specific cost. Beware of vague declarations like "I'll give it my best effort" or "You can count on me."

✔ **Create a sense of urgency and importance.** You may want to minimize any pressure the person feels by offering to *understand* if she can't perform to your expectations because of one reason or another. Unfortunately, this approach suggests that the work you're asking her to do isn't really that important and actually increases the chance that she won't complete it. Instead, let the person know how her work influences other activities and people on the project. Let her know why she needs to perform to expectations and what the consequences will be — to the project and the organization — if she doesn't.

The nearby sidebar "Holding the line when someone else drops the ball" has an example of holding someone accountable when he isn't your direct report.

Holding the line when someone else drops the ball

Suppose you recently joined a team working on a project to develop and implement an upgraded inventory control system for your organization. When you learn that your friend Eric had been on this team until a month ago, you call him to discuss his experiences on the project.

After listening to his in-depth account of his project involvement, you explain that you and three other team members have been asked to develop the new system's users' manual. You ask him whether, in view of his extensive knowledge of the project's history, he'd be willing to do you a favor and write a draft of Chapter 1 of the manual that recounts the system's background and evolution. Today is Monday, and you explain you need the draft by a week from Friday. Eric agrees, and you both hang up.

Unfortunately, you never receive the draft of Chapter 1 from Eric. He never calls you to explain why he didn't submit the draft, and you never check with him to see what's happening.

You probably make and receive requests like this one several times each day. Unfortunately, too many times people promise to help you out but don't deliver. You have to find ways to hold people accountable when they make agreements to complete assignments for you — even if you have no direct authority over them.

Of course, you can hold people accountable only if they accept responsibility in the first place. Therefore, in the preceding illustration, the first question you have to ask is: After your phone call, did Eric accept the responsibility to write the draft for you and your colleagues?

Very simply, the answer is *yes*. How do you know? Because he said he would. Take note, however, that I'm not suggesting that Eric is responsible for preparing the draft of Chapter 1 and that you and your colleagues are off the hook. Your responsibility to prepare the users' manual hasn't changed, but Eric accepted the responsibility to prepare the Chapter 1 draft for you. That Eric no longer works on the project or that he doesn't report to you or your boss is beside the point. He's responsible because he said he would be.

Eric may argue that he has a personal obligation to complete the draft (because he said he would) but no organizational obligation because the agreement wasn't in writing and he wasn't officially on your project team. That argument doesn't hold up, though; he's responsible because he said he would be. If he didn't want to accept the responsibility, he only had to say *no*.

The second question is: Did you do anything to hold Eric accountable for not keeping his promise? The answer to this question is *no*. If Eric never sent you the draft, your actions (or lack of them) send him the following messages:

- ✔ **The assignment wasn't that important.** What a terrible message to send! You asked Eric to take time away from his busy day to do something for you, and you didn't even care whether he completed the task? He's probably happy that he decided not to spend time on the task because, apparently, it wouldn't have made a difference anyway.

- ✔ **Eric's behavior was okay.** This message is even worse! It confirms that making promises and then not performing and not explaining your reasons for not performing is okay. Circumstances may have arisen that made it impossible for Eric to honor his commitment, but does that justify not calling to tell you about the situation? Unfortunately, this type of behavior, multiplied many times every day, defines

(continued)

(continued)

an organizational environment in which promises mean little and breaking them becomes an accepted part of business as usual.

Most likely, you didn't intend to convey these messages. You probably figured that Eric didn't send the draft because he was busy with other work, and you didn't want to make a big deal about it because he agreed to go out of his way to help you. Unfortunately, he can't know what's in your mind because you didn't tell him.

Maybe he didn't ignore his promise to prepare the draft. Consider some other possibilities:

✔ **He sent you the draft, but it got lost in the delivery system.** Unfortunately, most people figure that no news is good news.

When Eric didn't get a call from you, he probably assumed that you'd received the draft and found it acceptable. Certainly, he reasoned, you would've called if you had any questions!

✔ **He misunderstood you initially; he thought you needed the draft by a month (rather than a week) from Friday.** Maybe he's still working on the draft and plans to give it to you on the date he thought you needed it.

Accountability is a management-control process. Responding to a person's actions lets the person know whether he's on target or whether he needs to make a correction. Not responding to unacceptable performance unfortunately increases the likelihood that it will occur again.

Picture This: Depicting Roles with a Responsibility Assignment Matrix

Defining and sharing team roles and responsibilities upfront can help you improve performance and identify and head off potential difficulties during a project. One way you can display team roles and responsibilities is in a *Responsibility Assignment Matrix* (RAM) — also called a *Linear Responsibility Chart* (LRC). This section helps you understand the elements of a RAM, effectively read a RAM, develop your own chart, and improve your chart to meet your own needs. Your only limit is your creativity!

A *RACI chart* is a particular type of RAM. The RACI chart derives its name from the first letters of the four roles most commonly used in the chart — **R**esponsible, **A**ccountable, **C**onsult, and **I**nform.

Introducing the elements of a RAM

The RAM is a table that depicts each project audience's role in the performance of different project activities (see Chapter 3 for more on project audiences). A RAM's format is as follows (see Figure 10-1, which illustrates a portion of a RAM for designing and conducting a customer-needs survey):

- ✔ Project deliverables are in the left-hand column.
- ✔ Project audiences are in the top row.
- ✔ The role each audience will play in performing the work to produce each deliverable is in the intersections of the rows and columns.

Figure 10-1:
A Respons-
ibility
Assignment
Matrix
(RAM)
displays
project
roles.

Deliverable		Project manager	Task leader	Staffer A	Group director	Purchasing
WBS code	**Title**					
2.3.	Questionnaire design	A	S, A	P		
3.3.	Respondents		P			
4.4.	Pretest		P	S		
6.5.	Final questionnaire printing	A	P		A	A

P = Primary responsibility   S = Secondary responsibility   A = Approval

The RAM in Figure 10-1 indicates which of the following three roles people can have in this project's activities:

- ✔ **Primary responsibility (P):** You'll ensure the results are achieved.
- ✔ **Secondary responsibility (S):** You'll ensure some portion of the results is achieved.
- ✔ **Approval (A):** You're not actually working on the deliverable, but you approve the results produced by others who are.

The RAM is just a format; for each project, you define and assign the roles you feel are appropriate. You may, for example, decide to use the following roles in addition to the three already defined:

- ✔ **Review (R):** You review and comment on the results of an activity, but your formal approval isn't required.
- ✔ **Output (O):** You receive products from the activity.
- ✔ **Input (I):** You provide input for the activity work.

Reading a RAM

To illustrate how you read the RAM, consider the deliverable *questionnaire design* in Figure 10-1. The chart suggests that three people work together on this activity as follows:

- ✔ Staffer A has primary responsibility for the questionnaire's content, format, and layout. On this project, Staffer A reports to the task leader who, in turn, reports to the project manager.

- ✔ The task leader performs selected parts of the questionnaire design under the general coordination of Staffer A. Also, the task leader must approve all aspects of the questionnaire design before work can proceed to the next step.

- ✔ The project manager must approve the entire questionnaire, even though he isn't doing any of the actual design or layout himself.

You can analyze any RAM vertically by audience and horizontally by activity for situations that may give rise to problems. For an example, check out Table 10-1, which notes some observations about the assignments displayed in Figure 10-1 and issues they may suggest. After you identify these situations, you can decide how to address them.

Table 10-1   Situations and Issues Suggested in Figure 10-1

Situation	*Possible Issues*
The project manager has no direct responsibilities for individual project deliverables.	Will the project manager fully understand the substance and status of the project work?
The task leader is heavily committed.	The task leader won't have enough time to handle all these duties.
	The task leader is making all key decisions.
	What if the task leader leaves during the project?
The group director doesn't get involved until he is asked to approve the funds for printing the questionnaires.	The group director will slow down the approval process by asking questions about the purpose of the project, the use of the results, and so on.

Situation	Possible Issues
The task leader is the only person involved in selecting the respondents.	Do you want a key decision (that can determine the validity of the entire pretest) to be made by only one person?
The deliverable *final questionnaire printing* requires three approvals.	Does anyone else have to approve the questionnaire before it can be used?
	Are too many people approving the questionnaire? Would it be acceptable just to notify one or two of these people rather than to require their sign-off?
	The activity may take longer than estimated because the people approving the questionnaire aren't under the project manager's direct control.

After identifying a potential issue with your project's role assignments, you can choose how to deal with it. Possibilities include

✔ **Ignoring the issue:** For example, you may decide that three approvals are necessary to print the questionnaires.

✔ **Taking simple steps to minimize the risk of a problem:** For example, you may ask the task leader to thoroughly document all important information in case he leaves the project unexpectedly.

✔ **Addressing the issue further in a formal risk-management plan:** See Chapter 8 for a discussion of how to analyze and plan to manage risks.

Developing a RAM

Despite the straightforward nature of the information included in the RAM, getting everyone to agree on people's roles can be time-consuming. The following steps can help you get people's input and approval with the least time and effort:

1. **Identify all people who'll participate in or support your project.**

   See the discussion of project audiences in Chapter 3 for details.

2. **Develop a complete list of deliverables for your project.**

   See Chapter 4 for details on a Work Breakdown Structure.

3. **Discuss with all team members how they'll each support the work to produce the different project deliverables.**

   For each of their assignments, discuss the level of their responsibility and authority, as well as the specific work they'll perform. Also discuss with them any involvement that others will have on their activities. If specific people haven't yet been identified for certain activities, consult with people who have done those types of activities before.

4. **Prepare an initial draft of your RAM.**

   Draw the table for your chart, and enter your project's deliverables in the left-hand column and the people who will support the activities in the first row. In the cells formed by the intersection of each row and column, enter the roles that each person will have (based on the discussions you have with your team members in Step 3).

5. **Have the people whom you consulted in Step 3 review and approve your draft chart.**

   If people agree with the chart, ask them to indicate their agreement in writing. If they express concerns about some aspects, ask them to note their concerns in a memo or an e-mail.

6. **If some of your team members don't approve the draft chart, revise the chart to address their concerns and ask all people who gave input to review and approve the revised chart.**

   If you make any changes to the draft RAM, have all your team members review and approve the revised chart, especially if they already approved the prior version.

7. **Go back to Step 5 and continue the process until everyone you consulted in Step 3 approves the chart.**

Ensuring your RAM is accurate

For complex projects, the RAM can be quite large. And keeping the chart current and consulting throughout the project with all the people identified can be time-consuming. However, having a chart with incorrect information can result in duplicated efforts and overlooked activities. The following sections offer you suggestions for how you can keep your RAM accurate and current throughout the project.

Developing a hierarchy of charts

Including 50 or more activities on the same RAM can be cumbersome, so consider developing a series of nested charts for larger projects (also known as a *hierarchy* of charts). Prepare a high-level chart that identifies responsibilities for higher-level components in your Work Breakdown Structure (such as project phases and major deliverables), and then develop separate charts that detail responsibilities for lower-level deliverables and work packages. (See Chapter 4 for the definition of phases, deliverables, and work packages in a Work Breakdown Structure.)

Suppose you're planning a project to design and implement an information system. Figure 10-2 illustrates how you may create two layers of RAMs to depict the project team members' roles. Prepare a high-level RAM that details the roles for major phases, such as *requirements, system design,* and *system test.* Display in a second chart the roles of the team leader and his group in terms of the activities that comprise *requirements.*

Design and Implement a New Information System

Deliverable WBS code	People Title	Project manager	Team leader A	Team leader B	Team leader C
1.2.	Requirements	A	P		
2.2.	System design	A		P	S
3.1.	System test	A	S	S	P

Finalize Requirements

Deliverable WBS code	People Title	Team leader A	Staffer X	Staffer Y	Staffer Z
1.2.1.	Literature review	A	P	S	
1.2.2.	Focus groups	P	S		S
1.2.3.	Report	A	S	S	

P = Primary responsibility   S = Secondary responsibility   A = Approval

Figure 10-2:
A hierarchy of Responsibility Assignment Matrices.

Getting input from everyone involved

Involve the entire team when developing your chart. As the project manager, you don't know exactly how people should perform tasks in their areas of specialty, so you need to ask them. And, even if you do know, people have a greater commitment to a plan when they participate in developing it.

Putting your RAM in writing

You may think you can save time by not putting your RAM in writing. However, putting the chart in writing is essential for two reasons:

> ✔ **You can see possible problems in your project that you may have overlooked if you were considering pieces of information separately.**
>
> Refer to the RAM in Figure 10-1. Before preparing the chart, the task leader knew he was primarily responsible for selecting respondents or the questionnaire's pretest, and other team members knew they weren't involved in that activity. But writing this down in the RAM highlights that the task leader is, in fact, the only one involved in this activity.
>
> ✔ **You ensure that people have a common understanding of their roles and relationships.**

Keeping your RAM up to date

The longer your project is, the more likely it is that activities will be added or deleted, that people will leave the team, and that new people will join the team. Periodically reviewing and updating your RAM enables you to

> ✔ Assess whether the current assignments are working out and, if not, where changes may be needed.
>
> ✔ Clarify the roles and responsibilities for new activities.
>
> ✔ Clarify the roles and responsibilities for new people who join the team.

You can develop a RAM at any time during a project. If you join a project that's underway and find that no RAM exists, develop one to clarify the roles and responsibilities from the current point forward.

Dealing with Micromanagement

Micromanagement is a person's excessive, inappropriate, and unnecessary involvement in the details of a task that she asks another person to perform. It can lead to inefficient use of personal time and energy, as well as to tension and low morale. In this section, I help you look at the causes for micromanagement, give you some tips on ways to gain your micromanager's trust and confidence, and suggest how to work with a micromanager.

Realizing why a person micromanages

Unfortunately, no simple rules define when a person is micromanaging. If you think your boss is getting a little too close for comfort, let her know you feel that her oversight is a bit excessive. Try to give her some objective indicators to explain why you feel the way you do.

If the person doesn't change, you need to understand why she continues to micromanage you. Think about whether one or more of the following explanations may be the reason, and try the suggested approaches:

- ✔ **The person is interested in and enjoys the work.** Set up times to discuss interesting technical issues with the person.

- ✔ **The person is a technical expert and feels that she can do the job best.** Review your technical work frequently with the person; give the person opportunities to share her technical insights with you.

- ✔ **The person may feel that she didn't explain the assignment clearly or that unexpected situations may crop up.** Set up a schedule to discuss and review your progress frequently so that the micromanager can promptly uncover any mistakes and help you correct them.

- ✔ **The person is looking for ways to stay involved with you and the team.** Set up scheduled times to discuss project activities. Provide the micromanager with periodic reports of project progress, and make a point to stop by and say "Hello" periodically.

- ✔ **The person feels threatened because you have more technical knowledge than she does.** When talking about your project in front of others, always credit the micromanager for her guidance and insights. Share key technical information with the person on a regular basis.

- ✔ **The person doesn't have a clear understanding of how she should be spending her time.** Discuss with the person the roles she would like you to assume on project activities. Explain how the person can provide useful support as you perform the work.

- ✔ **The person feels that she has to stay up on the work you're doing in case anyone else asks about it.** Discuss with the person what type of information she needs and how frequently she needs it. Develop a schedule to provide progress reports that include this information.

Helping a micromanager trust you

Your boss may be micromanaging you because she doesn't yet have full confidence in your ability to perform. Instead of being angry or resentful, take the following steps to help your boss develop that confidence:

- ✔ **Don't be defensive or resentful when the person asks you questions.** Doing so makes you appear like you're hiding something, which only makes the person worry more. Instead, willingly provide all the information the person asks for.

✔ **Thank the micromanager for her interest, time, and technical guidance.** Complaining about what you perceive to be excessive oversight strains your relationship and increases the person's fears and insecurities. After you explain that you value and will incorporate her input, you can try to develop a more acceptable working relationship.

✔ **Offer to explain how you approach your tasks.** Seeing that you perform your work using appropriate, high-quality techniques increases your manager's confidence that you'll successfully complete the assignment she gave you.

✔ **Work with the person to develop a scheme for sharing progress and accomplishments.** Develop meaningful and frequent checkpoints. Frequent monitoring early in your work reassures both of you that you're performing the assignments successfully.

Working well with a micromanager

You can reduce or even eliminate most micromanagement by improving your communication and strengthening your interpersonal relationships. Consider the following tips as you work with a micromanager:

✔ **Don't assume.** Don't jump to conclusions. Examine the situation and try to understand the motivations of the person who's micromanaging you.

✔ **Listen.** Listen to the micromanager's questions and comments; see if patterns emerge. Try to understand her real interests and concerns.

✔ **Observe the person's behavior with others.** If the person micromanages others, the micromanagement likely stems from her feelings rather than from your actions. Try to find ways to address the person's real interests and concerns.

✔ **If at first you don't succeed, try, try again.** If your first attempts to address the situation are unsuccessful, develop an alternative strategy. Keep at it until you succeed.

Relating This Chapter to the PMP Exam and PMBOK 4

Table 10-2 notes topics in this chapter that may be addressed on the Project Management Professional (PMP) certification exam and that are also included in *A Guide to the Project Management Body of Knowledge,* 4th Edition (*PMBOK 4*).

Table 10-2	Chapter 10 Topics in Relation to the PMP Exam and *PMBOK 4*	
Topic	**Location in PMBOK 4**	**Comments**
Creating and using a Responsibility Assignment Matrix, or RAM (see the section "Picture This: Depicting Roles with a Responsibility Assignment Matrix")	9.1.2.1. Organization Charts and Position Descriptions	In addition to the Responsibility Assignment Matrix, *PMBOK 4* mentions organization charts and the Organizational Breakdown Structure (OBS) as formats for displaying project roles. Organization charts portray staff and reporting relationships, while the OBS displays project assignments by the organizational units responsible for them.

Chapter 11

Starting Your Project Team Off on the Right Foot

· ·

In This Chapter

▶ Making final touches on team member assignments

▶ Developing your team's operating procedures and more

▶ Setting up systems and schedules for project control

▶ Making your project official with an announcement

▶ Planning the post-project review

· ·

*A*fter intense work on a tight schedule, you submit your project plan (the single document that integrates and consolidates your project's Scope Statement, audience list, Work Breakdown Structure, Responsibility Assignment Matrix, schedule, resource requirements, budget, and all subsidiary plans for providing project support services) for review and approval. A few days later, your boss comes to you and says,

> "I have some good news and some bad news. Which would you like to hear first?"

> "Tell me the good news," you respond.

> "Your plan's been approved."

> "So, what's the bad news?" you ask.

> "Now you have to do the project!"

Starting off your project correctly is a key to ultimate success. Your project plan describes what you'll produce, the work you'll do, how you'll do it, when you'll do it, and which resources you'll need to do it. When you write your project plan, you base it on the information you have at the time, and, if information isn't available, you make assumptions. The more time between your plan's completion and its approval, the more changes you're likely to find in your plan's assumptions as you actually start your project.

As you prepare to start your project, you need to reconfirm or update the information in your plan, determine or reaffirm which people will play roles in your project and exactly what those roles will be, and prepare the systems and procedures that will support your project's performance. This chapter tells you how to accomplish these tasks and get your project off to a strong start.

Finalizing Your Project's Participants

A *project audience* is a person or group that supports, is affected by, or is interested in your project. (See Chapter 3 for a detailed discussion of how to identify project audiences.) In your project plan, you describe the roles you anticipate people to play and the amount of effort you expect team members to invest. You identify the people by name, by title or position, or by the skills and knowledge they need to have.

This section shows you how to reaffirm who will be involved in your project. It also helps you make sure everyone's still on board — and tells you what to do if some people aren't.

Are you in? Confirming your team members' participation

As you start your project, you need to confirm the identities of the people who'll work to support your project by verifying that specific people are still able to uphold their promised commitments and, if necessary, by recruiting and selecting new people to fulfill the remaining needs.

As you contact all the people who will support your project, be sure to do the following:

1. **Inform them that your project has been approved and when work will start.**

   Not all project plans are approved. You rarely know in advance how long the approval process will take or how soon your project can start. Inform team members as soon as possible so they can schedule the necessary time.

2. **Confirm that they're still able to support your project.**

   People's workloads and other commitments may change between the time you prepare your plan and your project's approval. If a person is no longer able to provide the promised support, recruit a replacement as soon as possible (see the later section "Filling in the blanks" for guidelines).

3. **Explain what you'll do to develop the project team and start the project work.**

   Provide a list of all team members and others who will support the project. Also mention the steps you'll take to introduce members and kick off the project.

4. **Reconfirm the work you expect them to perform, the schedules and deadlines you expect them to keep, and the amount of time you expect them to spend on the work.**

   Clarify specific activities and the nature of the work.

Depending on the size and formality of your project, you can use any format from a quick e-mail to a formal Work-Order Agreement to share this information with the people who will be involved in your project.

As Figure 11-1 illustrates, a typical *Work-Order Agreement* includes the following information:

✔ **Identifiers:** The identifiers include the project name, project number, activity name, and Work Breakdown Structure (WBS) code. (For more information about the WBS, see Chapter 4.) The project name and number confirm that your project is now official. You use the activity name and WBS code to record work progress as well as time and resource charges.

✔ **Work to be performed and deliverables or results to be produced:** These details describe the different activities and procedures involved in the project, as well as outputs of the project.

✔ **Activity start date, end date, and number of hours to be spent:** Including this information reaffirms

   • The importance of doing the work within the schedule and budget

   • Acknowledgement from the person who'll do the work that he expects to do the described work within these time and resource constraints

   • The criteria you'll use to assess the person's performance

✔ **Written approvals from the person who'll do the work, his supervisor, and the project manager:** Including these written approvals increases the likelihood that everyone involved has read and understood the project's elements and is committed to support it.

Be sure you specify all this information when reconfirming a person's commitment to your project. The longer you wait to specify any of this information, the greater the chances are that the person won't provide the support you had hoped for.

Work-Order Agreement		
Project name:	Project number:	
Activity name:	Work Breakdown Structure code:	
Description of work to be performed:		
Deliverables or results to be produced:		
Start date	End date	Number of hours to be spent
Approvals		
Project manager: Name (Print) Name (Signature)　　　Date	Team member: Name (Print) Name (Signature)　　　Date	Team member's supervisor: Name (Print) Name (Signature)　　　Date

Figure 11-1:
A typical
Work-Order
Agreement.

If you choose not to use a formal Work-Order Agreement, be sure to write down all key information that clarifies your agreement and get signed approvals from the team member and his supervisor. Asking for signed approvals encourages people to consider carefully before they make any commitments and serves as a reference and reminder of exactly what was promised.

Assuring that others are on board

Other people may also play a role in your project's success, even though they may not officially be members of your project team. Two such groups are *drivers* (people who have a say in defining the results of your project) and *supporters* (people who will perform a service or provide resources for your team).

Another special audience is your *project champion,* a person in a high position in the organization who strongly supports your project; who will advocate for your project in disputes, planning meetings, and review sessions; and who will take necessary actions to help ensure your project's success. (See Chapter 3 for a detailed discussion of these different types of project audiences.)

Contact your project champion and all other drivers and supporters to

- ✔ Inform them that your project has been approved and when work will start.
- ✔ Reaffirm your project's objectives.
- ✔ Confirm with identified drivers that the project's planned results still address their needs.
- ✔ Clarify with supporters exactly how you want them to help your project.
- ✔ Develop specific plans for involving each audience throughout the project and keeping them informed of progress.

Some people will be interested in your project but won't define its planned results or directly support your efforts. As you identify these *observers,* as they're often called, choose those individuals you want to keep informed of your progress throughout the project, and plan how you'll do so. (See Chapter 3 for a discussion of how to identify project observers and Chapter 13 for different ways to keep people informed about your progress.)

Filling in the blanks

If your plan identifies proposed project team members only by job title, position description, or skills and knowledge (and not by specific names), you have to find actual people to fill the specified roles. You can fill the empty roles by assigning responsibility to someone already on your organization's staff, by recruiting a person from outside your organization, or by contracting with an external organization.

Whichever method you choose, prepare a written description of the activities you want each person to perform. This description can range from a simple memo for informal projects to a written job description for more formal ones.

Write down your needs for each category of personnel separately. At a minimum, include the following information in your role descriptions:

- ✔ Project name, number, and start date
- ✔ Necessary skills and knowledge
- ✔ Activities to be performed and start and end dates
- ✔ Anticipated level of effort

If you plan to look inside your organization to recruit team members for roles not yet filled, do the following:

- ✔ Identify potential candidates by working with your human resources (HR) department and area managers.
- ✔ Meet with the candidates to discuss your project, describe the work, and assess their qualifications.
- ✔ Choose the best candidates, and ask them to join your team.
- ✔ Document the agreements you make with the new team members.

If you're looking outside the organization, consult with your organization's HR department to identify potential resources. Provide a detailed description of the qualifications, skills, and knowledge needed, the expected tasks, and the anticipated level of effort. Sit in on the interviews and assessment process.

Also, if you plan to obtain the support of external consultants, work with your organization's contracts office. Provide the contracts office with the same information that you provide your HR office. Review the contract document before your contracting officer signs it.

In addition to filling your empty team member roles, work with people in key organizational units to identify people, other than team members, who will support your project (for example, a contracts specialist or a procurement specialist, as long as he or she isn't officially on your project team). After you identify these people, do the following:

- ✔ Meet with them to clarify your project's goals and anticipated outputs and the ways in which they will support your performance.
- ✔ Develop plans for involving them and keeping them informed of progress throughout your project.

Developing Your Team

Merely assigning people to tasks doesn't create a project team. A *team* is a collection of people who are committed to common goals and who depend on one another to do their jobs. Project teams consist of members who can and must make a valuable and unique contribution to the project.

A team is different from other associations of people who work together. For example,

- ✔ A *group* consists of people who work individually to accomplish their particular assignments on a common task.

  ✔ A *committee* consists of people who come together to review and critique issues, propose recommendations for action, and, on occasion, implement those recommendations.

As soon as you identify your project team members, take steps to define and establish your team's identity as well as its operating practices. Develop the following elements, making sure your team understands and accepts them:

  ✔ **Goals:** What the team as a whole and members individually hope to accomplish

  ✔ **Roles:** Each member's areas of specialty, position on the team, authority, and assignments

  ✔ **Processes:** The techniques that team members will use to perform their project tasks

  ✔ **Relationships:** The attitudes and behaviors of team members toward one another

This section discusses how to begin creating your team's identity by having members review and discuss the project plan, examine overall team and individual team member goals, agree on everyone's roles, and start to establish productive working relationships.

Reviewing the approved project plan

As soon as people join the team, have them review the approved project plan to reinforce the project's goals, clarify the work planned, confirm the feasibility of time and resource estimates, and identify any potential problems. Meet as a group to discuss people's thoughts and reactions, after they've reviewed the plan.

Team members who contributed to the proposal can remind themselves of the project's background and purpose, their planned roles, and the work to be done. They can also identify situations and circumstances that may have changed since the proposal was prepared and then review and reassess project risks and risk-management plans.

New team members can understand the project's background and purpose, find out about their roles and assignments, raise concerns about time frames and budgets, and identify issues that may affect the project's success.

Developing team and individual goals

Team members commit to your project when they believe their participation can help them achieve worthwhile professional and personal goals. Help team members develop and buy into a shared sense of the project goals by doing the following:

✔ Discuss the reasons for the project, its supporters, and the impact of its results. (See Chapter 2 for a discussion of how to identify the needs your project will address.)

✔ Clarify how the results may benefit your organization's clients.

✔ Emphasize how the results may support your organization's growth and viability.

✔ Explore how the results may impact each team member's job.

Encourage people to think about how their participation may help them achieve personal goals, such as acquiring new skills and knowledge, meeting new people, increasing their visibility in the organization, and enhancing their opportunities for job advancement. Obviously, projects aren't only about helping team members achieve personal benefits. However, when team members can realize personal benefits while performing valued services for the organization, the members' motivation and commitment to project success will be greater. (See Chapter 14 for more on how to create and sustain team member motivation.)

Specifying team member roles

Nothing causes disillusionment and frustration faster than bringing motivated people together and then giving them no guidance on working with one another. Two or more people may start doing the same activity independently, and other activities may be overlooked entirely. Eventually, these people find tasks that don't require coordination, or they gradually withdraw from the project to work on more rewarding assignments.

To prevent this frustration from becoming a part of your project, work with team members to define the activities that each member works on and the nature of their roles. Possible team member roles include the following:

✔ **Primary responsibility:** Has the overall obligation to ensure the completion of an activity

✔ **Secondary or supporting responsibility:** Has the obligation to complete part of an activity

✔ **Approval:** Must approve the results of an activity before work can proceed

✔ **Consultation resource:** Can provide expert guidance and support if needed

✔ **Required recipient of project results:** Receives either a physical product from an activity or a report of an activity

If you prepared a Responsibility Assignment Matrix (RAM) as part of your project plan, use it to start your discussions of project roles with your team members (see Chapter 10 for more on how to use the RAM). Make sure you don't just present the RAM; take the time to encourage questions and concerns from team members until they're comfortable that the roles are feasible and appropriate.

Defining your team's operating processes

Develop the procedures that you and your team will use to support your day-to-day work. Having these procedures in place allows people to effectively and efficiently perform their tasks; it also contributes to a positive team atmosphere. At a minimum, develop procedures for the following:

✔ **Communication:** These processes involve sharing project-related information in writing and through personal interactions. Communication procedures may include

- When and how to use e-mail to share project information

- Which types of information should be in writing

- When and how to document informal discussions

- How to set up regularly scheduled reports and meetings to record and review progress

- How to address special issues that arise

✔ **Conflict resolution:** These processes involve resolving differences of opinion between team members regarding project work. You can develop the following conflict-resolution procedures:

- *Standard approaches* (normal steps that you take to encourage people to develop a mutually agreeable solution)

- *Escalation procedures* (steps you take if the people involved can't readily resolve their differences)

✔ **Decision making:** These processes involve deciding among alternative approaches and actions. Develop guidelines for choosing the most appropriate choice for a situation, including consensus, majority rule, unanimous agreement, and decision by technical expert. Also develop escalation procedures — the steps you take when the normal decision-making approaches get bogged down.

Supporting the development of team member relationships

On high-performance project teams, members trust each other and have cordial, coordinated working relationships. But, developing trust and effective work practices takes time and concerted effort.

Help your team members get to know and be comfortable with one another as soon as your project starts by encouraging them to do the following:

✔ Work through conflicts together.

✔ Brainstorm challenging technical and administrative issues.

✔ Spend informal personal time together, such as having lunch or participating in non-work-related activities after hours.

All together now: Helping your team become a smooth-functioning unit

When team members trust each other, have confidence in each other's abilities, can count on each other's promises, and communicate openly, they can devote all their efforts to performing their project work instead of spending their time dealing with interpersonal frustrations. Help your team achieve this high-performance level of functioning by guiding them through the following stages:

✔ **Forming:** This stage involves identifying and meeting team members and politely discussing project objectives, work assignments, and so forth. Share the project plan, introduce people to each other, and discuss each person's background, organizational responsibilities, and areas of expertise.

✔ **Storming:** This stage involves raising and resolving personal conflicts about the project or other team members. As part of the storming stage, do the following:

• Encourage people to discuss any concerns they have about the project plan's feasibility, and be sure you address those concerns.

• Encourage people to discuss any reservations they may have about other team members or team members' abilities.

• Focus these discussions on ways to ensure successful task performance — you don't want the talks to turn into unproductive personal attacks.

You can initially speak privately with people about issues you're uncomfortable bringing up in front of the entire team. Eventually, though, you must discuss their concerns with the entire team to achieve a sense of mutual honesty and trust.

✔ **Norming:** This stage involves developing the standards and operating guidelines that govern team member behavior. Encourage members to establish these team norms instead of relying on the procedures and practices they use in their functional areas. Examples of these norms include the following:

- **How people present and discuss different points of view:** Some people present points of view politely, while others aggressively debate their opponents in an attempt to prove their points.

- **Timeliness of meeting attendance:** Some people always show up for meetings on time, while others are habitually 15 minutes late.

- **Participation in meetings:** Some people sit back and observe, while others actively participate and share their ideas.

At a team meeting, encourage people to discuss how team members should behave in different situations. Address the concerns people express, and encourage the group to adopt team norms.

✔ **Performing:** This stage involves doing project work, monitoring schedules and budgets, making necessary changes, and keeping people informed.

As you guide your team through these developmental stages, keep in mind the following guidelines:

- ✔ **Your team won't automatically pass through these stages; you have to guide them.** Left on their own, teams often fail to move beyond the forming stage. Many people don't like to confront thorny interpersonal issues, so they simply ignore them. Your job is to make sure your team members address what needs to be addressed and become a smooth-functioning team.

- ✔ **Your involvement as project manager in your team's development needs to be heavier in the early stages and lighter in the later ones.** During the forming stage, you need to take the lead as new people join the team. Then, in the storming stage, you take a strong facilitative role as you guide and encourage people to share their feelings and concerns. Although you can help guide the team as it develops its standards and norms during the norming stage, your main emphasis is to ensure that everyone participates in the process. Finally, if you've navigated the first three stages successfully, you can step back in the performing stage and offer your support as the team demonstrates its ability to function as a high-performing unit.

✔ **On occasion, you may have to revisit a stage you thought the team had completed.** For example, a new person may join the team, or a major aspect of the project plan may change.

✔ **If everything goes smoothly on your project, it doesn't matter whether the team has successfully gone through the forming, storming, and norming stages.** But when the project runs into problems, your team may become dysfunctional if it hasn't progressed successfully through each stage. Suppose, for example, that the team misses a major project deadline. If team members haven't developed mutual trust for one another, they're more likely to spend time searching for someone to blame than working together to fix the situation.

✔ **As the project manager, you need to periodically assess how the team feels it's performing; then you have to decide which, if any, issues the team needs to work through.** Managing your team is a project in and of itself!

Laying the Groundwork for Controlling Your Project

Controlling your project throughout its performance requires that you collect appropriate information, evaluate your performance compared with your plan, and share your findings with your project's audiences. This section highlights the steps you take to prepare to collect, analyze, and share this information. (See Chapter 12 for full details on maintaining control of your project.)

Selecting and preparing your tracking systems

Effective project control requires that you have accurate and timely information to help you identify problems promptly and take appropriate corrective action. This section highlights the information you need and explains how to get it.

Throughout your project, you need to track performance in terms of the following:

✔ **Schedule achievement:** The assessment of how well you're meeting established dates

✔ **Personnel resource use:** The levels of effort people are spending on their assignments

✔ **Financial expenditures:** The funds you're spending for project resources

See Chapter 12 for a detailed discussion of the information systems you can use to track your project's progress.

If you use existing, enterprise-wide information systems to track your project's schedule performance and resource use, set up your project on these systems as follows (see Chapter 12 for information on how to decide whether to use existing information systems to support your project's monitoring and control):

- ✔ **Obtain your official project number.** Your *project number* is the official company identifier for your project. All products, activities, and resources related to your project are assigned that number. Check with your organization's finance department or project office to find out your project's number, and check with your finance or information technology department to determine the steps you must take to set up your project on the organization's financial tracking system, labor recording system, and/or activity tracking system.

- ✔ **Finalize your project's Work Breakdown Structure (WBS).** Have team members review your project's WBS and make any necessary changes or additions. Assign identifier codes to all WBS elements. (Check out Chapter 4 for a complete explanation of the WBS.)

- ✔ **Set up charge codes for your project on the organization's labor tracking system.** If team members record their labor hours by projects, set up charge codes for all WBS activities. Doing so allows you to monitor the progress of individual WBS elements, as well as the total project.

   If your organization's system can limit the number of hours for each activity, enter those limits (see the "Setting your project's baseline" section later in this chapter and the information in Chapter 12 for how to establish your project's schedule, resource, and budget targets). Doing so ensures that people don't mistakenly charge more hours to activities than your plan allows.

- ✔ **Set up charge codes for your project on your organization's financial system.** If your organization tracks expenditures by project, set up the codes for all WBS activities that have expenditures. If the system can limit expenditures for each activity, enter those limits.

Establishing schedules for reports and meetings

To be sure you satisfy your information needs and those of your project's audiences, set up a schedule of reports you'll prepare and meetings you'll hold during the project. Planning your communications with your audiences in advance helps ensure that you adequately meet their individual needs and allows them to reserve time on their calendars to attend the meetings.

Meet with project audiences and team members to develop a schedule for regular project meetings and progress reports. Confirm the following details:

- ✔ Reports that will be issued
- ✔ Meetings that will be held and their specific purposes
- ✔ When reports will be issued and when meetings will be held
- ✔ Who will receive the reports and attend the meetings
- ✔ The formats and content of the reports and meetings

See Chapter 13 for a discussion of the reports and meetings you can use to support ongoing project communications.

Setting your project's baseline

The project *baseline* is the version of your project's plan that guides your project activities and provides the comparative basis for your performance assessments. At the beginning of your project, use the plan that was approved at the end of the organizing and preparing stage, modified by any approved changes made during the carrying out the work stage, as your baseline (see Chapter 1 for a discussion of the project life cycle stages). During the project, use the most recent approved version of the project plan as your baseline. (See Chapter 12 for more discussion on setting, updating, and using your project's baseline to control your project.)

Hear Ye, Hear Ye! Announcing Your Project

After you've notified your key project audiences (that is, the drivers and supporters) that your project has been approved and when it'll start, it's time to introduce it to others who may be interested (see Chapter 3 for a discussion of how to identify the observers in your project's audience). Consider one or more of the following approaches to announce your project to all interested parties:

- ✔ An e-mail to selected individuals or departments in your organization
- ✔ An announcement in your organization's newsletter
- ✔ A flyer on a prominent bulletin board
- ✔ A formal kickoff meeting (if your project is large or will have broad organizational impact)
- ✔ A press release (if your project has stakeholders outside your organization)

Regardless of how you announce your project, be sure to mention the purpose and scope of your project, your intended outcomes and results, and the key dates. Tell people how they can get in touch with you if they have questions or would like detailed information.

Setting the Stage for Your Post-Project Evaluation

A *post-project evaluation* (which I describe in detail in Chapter 15) is a meeting in which you

✔ Review the experience you have gained from the project.

✔ Recognize people for their achievements.

✔ Plan to ensure that good practices are repeated on future projects.

✔ Plan to head off problems you encountered on this project on future projects.

Start laying groundwork as soon as your project begins to ensure you capture all relevant information and observations about the project to discuss at the post-project evaluation meeting. You can lay the groundwork for the post-project evaluation by doing the following:

✔ Tell the team you'll hold a post-project review when the project ends.

✔ Encourage team members to keep records of problems, ideas, and suggestions throughout the project. When you prepare the final agenda for the post-project evaluation session, ask people to review these records and notes to find topics to discuss.

✔ Clarify the criteria that define your project's success by reviewing the latest version of your project's objectives with team members.

✔ Describe the details of the situation your project is designed to address before you begin the project work (if the project was designed to change or improve a situation). Doing so enables you to assess the changes in these details when the project ends.

✔ Maintain your own *project log* (a narrative record of project issues and occurrences), and encourage other team members to do the same.

Relating This Chapter to the PMP Exam and PMBOK 4

Table 11-1 notes topics in this chapter that may be addressed on the Project Management Professional (PMP) certification exam and that are also included in *A Guide to the Project Management Body of Knowledge,* 4th Edition (*PMBOK 4*).

Table 11-1	Chapter 11 Topics in Relation to the PMP Exam and *PMBOK 4*	
Topic	*Location in PMBOK 4*	*Comments*
Finalizing team members' project assignments (see the section "Are you in? Confirming your team members' participation")	3.5.3. Acquire Project Team 9.2. Acquire Project Team	The steps discussed in both books are very similar.
Recruiting resources from outside the organization (see the section "Filling in the blanks")	9.2.2.3. Acquisition	Both sources discuss similar approaches for obtaining the personnel required to staff the project team.
Helping the team establish project and personal goals, individual roles, and team processes and relationships (see the section "Developing Your Team")	9.3. Develop Project Team G.2. Team Building G.6. Decision Making	The steps for developing a team presented in both books are similar. This book highlights the individual and project elements that help to create a focused team. *PMBOK 4* presents models for several of the team processes discussed.
Scheduling project meetings and progress reports (see the section "Establishing schedules for reports and meetings")	10.2. Plan Communications	Both books emphasize the need to plan regular project meetings and project-progress reports in advance. This book lists information that should be addressed in these plans; see Chapter 13 for more information on alternative communication approaches.

Part IV

Steering the Ship: Managing Your Project to Success

The 5th Wave   By Rich Tennant

"Your supervisor tells me you're the guy I talk to for fast tracking a project."

In this part . . .

The further ahead you try to plan, the more likely conditions are to change. Thus, successful project management requires that you start off strong, keep moving in the right direction, and make necessary changes to your plan in a timely manner along the way.

In this part, I discuss different information systems you can use to monitor your project's performance and expenditures. I show you ways to track, analyze, and report on project activities, and I discuss techniques to sustain team members' focus and commitment. Finally, I suggest steps to bring your project to a successful close and ways to plan and conduct a post-project evaluation.

Chapter 12

Tracking Progress and Maintaining Control

A sad reality for many projects is that although they're born accompanied by high hopes and expectations, they die amid frustration and disappointment. Your project plans represent visions that you believe will work; however, those plans don't implement themselves automatically, and they can't predict the future with certainty.

Successful projects require continued care and management to ensure that they follow their plans correctly and, in turn, produce the desired results. When unexpected situations occur, you, as the project manager, must react promptly to adjust your efforts and keep your project on track.

This chapter discusses the steps in the project control process and focuses on the systems and techniques you can use to collect, analyze, and report on schedule performance, labor hours, and expenditures, as well as the process for taking corrective actions when needed.

Holding On to the Reins: Project Control

Project control entails the following activities, which you perform throughout your project to ensure that it proceeds according to plan and produces the desired results (see the appendix for a flowchart illustrating the cyclical nature of project control):

- ✓ **Reconfirming the plan:** At the beginning of each performance period, reaffirm with team members the following project responsibilities and commitments they made for the coming period:

  - Activities they agreed to perform

  - Dates they agreed they will start and end these activities

  - Amount of person-effort they agreed they'll need to perform these activities (see Chapter 6 for information on estimating this effort)

- ✓ **Assessing performance:** During the performance period, have team members record information on the following:

  - Completed intermediate and final deliverables

  - Dates they reached milestones

  - Dates they started and ended activities

  - Number of hours they worked on each activity

  - Amount of nonpersonnel resources they used for each activity

  - Expenditures they made for each activity

  Collect this information at the end of the performance period, compare it with the plan, and determine the reasons for any differences.

- ✓ **Taking corrective action:** If necessary, take steps to bring your project's performance back into conformance with your plans, or if doing so isn't possible, change the plans to reflect new expectations.

- ✓ **Keeping people informed:** Share your achievements, problems, and future plans with your project's audiences. (See Chapter 13 for suggestions on how to do so.)

Choose the periods for monitoring your project's performance based on the overall length of the project, the risk of unexpected occurrences, and your proximity to major milestones. Although you may choose to monitor selected project activities on a daily basis in certain situations, plan to assess your project's overall performance at least once a month to identify promptly any unexpected occurrences or performance problems that must be addressed.

Initially, you may be uncomfortable reconfirming commitments people have made for an upcoming performance period because you feel doing so

- ✓ **Suggests that you don't trust the person.** After all, the person has made a commitment to do the specified work; wouldn't she tell you if she were unable to live up to that commitment?

✔ **Increases the likelihood that she'll say she can't live up to the original promise.** You're concerned that raising the topic may actually encourage her to say she can't honor her commitments.

In most cases, however, neither situation proves to be true. Why? Because of the following two reasons:

✔ Raising the issue doesn't suggest a lack of trust; if you didn't trust the person, you wouldn't talk with her at all! Checking in with her reflects your understanding that she may not have had a chance to tell you about new circumstances that make it difficult to honor her commitments.

✔ Raising the issue doesn't increase the chances that she'll opt out of a commitment — it buys you time. If the person can't perform according to her promises, you'll find that out at the end of the performance period anyway — when she hasn't finished the work. So taking time to reconfirm actually provides an entire performance period to develop alternative ways of dealing with her new restrictions.

When a person reaffirms her existing commitments for the upcoming performance period, the chances are greater that she'll perform her assignments successfully, on time, and within budget. If she's unable to honor the commitments she made previously (for example, if she has unexpectedly been assigned to work on another high-priority effort during the same time period), you can work with her to develop new plans for how and when she will complete her assignment for your project.

Establishing Project Management Information Systems

A *project management information system* (PMIS) is a set of procedures, equipment, and other resources for collecting, analyzing, storing, and reporting information that describes project performance. A PMIS contains the following three parts:

✔ **Inputs:** Raw data that describe selected aspects of project performance

✔ **Processes:** Analyses of the data to compare actual performance with planned performance

✔ **Outputs:** Reports presenting the results of the analyses

In addition to requiring that you define the data, designing a PMIS also requires that you specify how to collect the data, who collects it, when they collect it, and how they enter the data into the system. All these factors can affect the timeliness and accuracy of the data and, therefore, of your project performance assessments.

To support your ongoing management and control of the project, you need to collect and maintain information about schedule performance, work effort, and expenditures. The following sections tell you how to collect, analyze, and report on these three parts of your project's performance.

Many information systems have the technical support of computers, scanners, printers, and plotters. But an information system can consist of manual processes and physical storage devices, as well. For example, you can record project activities in your notebook or calendar and keep records of project budgets in your file cabinet. However, you still need to monitor your procedures for collecting, storing, analyzing, and reporting your information; they affect the accuracy and timeliness of your performance assessments.

The clock's ticking: Monitoring schedule performance

Regularly monitoring your project's schedule performance can provide early indications of possible activity-coordination problems, resource conflicts, and cost overruns that may occur in the future. The following sections show you what information you need to monitor schedule performance, how to collect and evaluate it, and how to ensure its accuracy.

Defining the schedule data to collect

As I discuss in further detail in Chapter 4, your project's *Work Breakdown Structure* (WBS) is a deliverable-oriented decomposition of the work required to produce your project's deliverables. The lowest level of detail of each branch of the WBS is a *work package,* and each work package, in turn, is composed of *activities* (pieces of work performed during the project).

You can describe an activity's schedule performance either by noting the dates it began and ended or by describing how much of it has been done.

If you choose to describe your project's schedule performance by noting the status of individual activities, collect either or both of the following data items to support your analyses:

✔ The start and end dates for each activity in your project

✔ The dates when milestones (such as *contract signed, materials received,* or *environmental test completed*) are reached (see Chapter 5 for more information about milestones)

Be careful if you decide to use *percent completed* to indicate an activity's progress, because most often you have no clear way to determine this percentage. For example, saying that your new product design is 30 percent complete is virtually meaningless because you can't determine objectively *how much* of the thinking and creating is actually done. Suggesting that you have completed 30 percent of your design because you have expended 30 of the 100 hours budgeted for the task or because three of the ten days allotted for its performance have passed is equally incorrect. The first indicator is a measure of *resource* use, and the second is a measure of *time* elapsed. Neither measure indicates the amount of substantive *work* completed.

On the other hand, if your activity has clear segments that take roughly the same amount of time and effort, you may be able to determine an accurate measure of percent completed. For example, if you planned to conduct telephone interviews with 20 different people and you have completed 10, you can argue that the activity is 50 percent complete.

Analyzing schedule performance

Assess your project's schedule status by comparing actual activity start/end dates and actual milestone dates to their planned dates. Figures 12-1 and 12-2 present formats that support ready comparisons of this data.

Figure 12-1 depicts a *combined activities and milestones report.* The following information in this report comes from your project plan:

✔ The activity or milestone identification code and name

✔ The person responsible for ensuring the activity or milestone occurs

✔ The dates the activity should start and end or the milestone should occur

Compare this information with the following data to describe performance during the period of the report:

✔ The actual activity start and end dates or the actual milestone date

✔ Relevant comments about the activity or milestone

Figure 12-2 illustrates a *progress Gantt chart.* You shade an appropriate portion of each bar to represent deliverable progress (see Chapter 5 for more information about Gantt charts). This sample chart presents project performance as of the end of week 4 of the project. According to the chart, the design phase is complete, the development phase is one week behind schedule, and the testing phase is one week ahead of schedule.

Activity/Milestone	Person Responsible	Start Date Planned	Start Date Actual	End Date Planned	End Date Actual	Comments
2.1.1. Design of questionnaire	F. Smith	Feb 14	Feb 15	Feb 25	Feb 25	
KE 2.1.1. Questionnaire design approved	F. Smith	-	-	Feb 28	Feb 28	
2.2.2. Questionnaire pilot test	F. Smith	Apr 20	Apr 21	Apr 30	Apr 25	Critical path

Figure 12-1: A combined activities and milestones report.

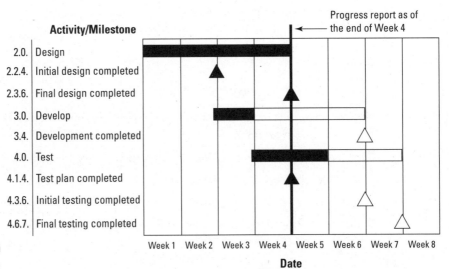

Figure 12-2: A progress Gantt chart.

The shaded portion of the bar stops at the date by which you had originally planned to accomplish the portion of the activity that you have achieved by the date of the progress report.

The most meaningful way to assess progress on a WBS component is to note the component's intermediate deliverables that you've achieved to date. The progress Gantt chart in Figure 12-2 really says that, by the end of week 4, you produced all the intermediate deliverables for Task 3.0 — development — that you had planned to produce by the end of week 3 or that Task 3.0 is one week behind schedule.

Note: You can prepare these project schedule reports with any level of detail you choose, depending on your audiences' interests and needs. This higher-level report presents information for four-week portions of project work, but the detailed data used to determine the status of these four-week portions of work was for activities that were two weeks or less.

Not everyone interprets a progress Gantt chart the same way. I intended the chart to suggest that Task 3.0 is one week behind schedule. However, some people have told me that they interpret the report to mean Task 3.0 is 25 percent complete because one of the four segments for Task 3.0 is shaded. The message is: Be sure you include a legend with your graph that explains clearly how you want people to interpret it.

Collecting schedule performance data

To collect the schedule performance data, develop a standard format and process for recording your work accomplishments. Standard formats and processes improve the accuracy of your information and take less time to complete. I frequently use the combined activities and milestones report format.

Consider the following factors when you schedule your activity monitoring:

- ✔ **Is the activity on a critical path?** Delayed activities on a critical path will delay your overall project schedule (see Chapter 5 for a detailed discussion of critical paths). Therefore, consider monitoring critical-path activities more often to identify potential problems as soon as possible and minimize their effect on the project schedule.

- ✔ **Is the activity on a path that's close to being critical?** Activities on non-critical paths can have some delays before their paths become critical. The maximum delay for noncritical activities is called *slack time* or *float* (see Chapter 5). If an activity's slack time is very short, a small delay can cause the path to become critical. Therefore, consider monitoring activities that have very small slack times more often (again to identify potential problems as soon as possible).

- ✔ **Is the activity risk high?** If you feel that an activity is very likely to encounter problems, consider monitoring it more frequently to identify those problems as soon as they occur. (Flip to Chapter 8 for details on risk and uncertainty.)

- ✔ **Have you already encountered problems with this activity?** Consider monitoring activities more frequently if you've already had problems with them. Past problems often increase the chances of future problems.

- ✔ **Are you approaching the activity's planned completion date?** Consider monitoring activities approaching completion more frequently to ensure all final details are addressed and the schedule is met.

At the beginning of a performance period, I print separate reports for each team member that include their planned activities and milestones for the period. I ask team members to record actual activity start and end dates and actual milestone dates in the appropriate columns, along with any comments they want to share. I ask them to send me a copy of the completed report on the first business day after the performance period.

Recording and reporting on progress this way has several advantages:

- ✔ Recording achievements at the time they occur increases the likelihood that the data are accurate.

- ✔ The agreed-upon submission schedule reduces the chances that I'll surprise people with unexpected requests for progress data.

- ✔ Having people continuously review their proposed schedules and record their accomplishments heightens their awareness of goals and increases the chances that they'll meet their commitments.

- ✔ The purpose of project control is to encourage people to perform according to your plan, not just to collect data. The more aware the team members are of their work in relation to the overall schedule, the greater the likelihood that they'll hit the schedule. If they don't know or care about the target date, they're unlikely to hit it.

I use the combined activities and milestones report format to reaffirm people's commitments at the start of a performance period. When I give them the report detailing their activities and events for the coming period, I ask them to verify the information and reaffirm their commitments. Then we immediately discuss and resolve any issues they identify.

Monitor schedule performance at least once a month. Experience has shown that waiting longer does the following:

- ✔ Allows people to lose focus and commitment to the activity and increases the chances that the activity won't end on schedule

- ✔ Provides more time for small problems to go undetected and, thus, evolve into bigger problems

Improving the accuracy of your schedule performance data

Collecting the right data is the first requirement for effectively controlling your project's schedule. However, your analyses will be meaningless unless the data are correct. Do the following to improve the accuracy of your schedule performance data:

- ✔ **Tell the team members how you plan to use their schedule performance data.** People are always more motivated to perform a task if they understand the reasons for it.

✔ **Provide schedule performance reports to the people who give you the data.** People are even more motivated to perform a task if they get direct benefits from it.

✔ **Publicly acknowledge those people who give you timely and accurate data.** Positive reinforcement of desired behavior confirms to people that they're meeting your expectations; it also emphasizes that desirable behavior to other people.

✔ **Clearly define activities and milestones.** Clear definitions help you confirm when an event or activity does or doesn't occur.

✔ **Use all the data that you collect, and don't collect more data than you'll use.** Collect only the data that you know you'll use to assess schedule performance.

Choosing a vehicle to support your schedule tracking system

Check to see whether your organization uses an enterprise-wide project planning and tracking system. The best places to look for this information are your organization's project management office (PMO), information technology department, and finance department (see Chapter 16 for different types of software used to support project management). If your organization does have such a system, check to see whether you can use it to monitor your project, whether it provides the information you need, and whether its information is timely and accurate.

If your organization doesn't have an existing tracking system you can use, you need to develop your own. You can use either a manual system or a computer-based system; both offer advantages and disadvantages:

✔ **Manual tracking systems:** These systems include day planners, personal calendars, and handwritten project logs. If you use any of these systems to record your activities and achievements, you don't need special computers or software, which may save you money.

However, manual systems have these disadvantages:

- Storing your data requires physical space. The more data you have, the more space you need.

- Comparing and analyzing the data by hand can be time-consuming, and the chances for errors are greater.

- Preparing reports by hand is time-consuming.

✔ **Computer-based tracking systems:** These systems offer the advantages of faster processing, more efficient data storage, and professionally designed reports. The following types of software can support a computer-based tracking system:

- Integrated project-management software, such as Microsoft Project and Microsoft Project Server

• Database software, such as Microsoft Access

• Spreadsheet software, such as Microsoft Excel

• Word processing software, such as Microsoft Word

However, computer-based systems are more difficult to learn to use, more difficult to maintain, and more expensive.

Many manufacturers offer software packages in these categories, but more than 80 percent of the organizations I've worked with use Microsoft software for these functions. Check to see whether this software is available on your organization's local area network (LAN).

All in a day's work: Monitoring work effort

Comparing work effort expended with work effort planned can highlight when people are incorrectly expanding or reducing the scope of an activity, are more or less qualified than you anticipated, are encountering unexpected difficulties performing the work, or are in danger of using up allocated work effort before your project ends.

Monitoring work effort requires that you collect the actual effort spent on each WBS work package or activity. In the following sections, I discuss what data to collect, how to collect it, how to improve its accuracy, and how to analyze it.

Analyzing work effort expended

Evaluate your project's work-effort expenditures by comparing the actual expenditures with those in your plan. Figure 12-3 depicts a typical labor report that describes the work effort by each team member on each work package. The following information comes from your project plan:

✔ The work package identifiers and names

✔ The total hours budgeted for each team member to spend on each work package

✔ The hours budgeted for each team member to spend on each work package every week

You obtain or derive the following information for the labor report from data during the period covered by the report:

✔ The number of hours each team member spent on each work package

✔ The number of hours left for each team member to spend on each work package

✔ The difference between the number of hours in the plan and the number of hours each team member actually spent on each work package

Work Package				Work Effort Expended (Person-hours)					
WBS Code	Description	Employee		Budget	Week 1	Week 2	Week 3	Week 4	...
3.1.2.	Questionnaire design	H. Jones	Planned	130	20	40	30	30	...
			Actual	0	10	30	20	25	...
			Remaining	130	120	90	70	45	...
			Difference	0	+10	+20	+30	+35	...
		F. Smith	Planned	70	0	20	20	15	...
			Actual	0	0	25	10	15	...
			Remaining	70	70	45	35	20	...
			Difference	0	0	-5	+5	+5	...

Figure 12-3: A labor report.

Actual labor expenditures rarely agree 100 percent with the planned amounts. (In fact, if the number of hours for each task each month is identical to the number in your plan for several months, you may wonder whether people are copying the numbers from the plan onto their time sheets! See the next section for more info on time sheets.) Typically, variances of up to 10 percent above or below the expected numbers in any month are normal.

Consider the work-effort expenditures for the two team members in the labor report in Figure 12-3. Smith appears to be working in accordance with the plan. He charged more hours in week 2 than planned, fewer than planned in week 3, and the same as planned in week 4. Jones's situation is very different. Each week, Jones spends less time on the project than planned, and the total shortfall of hours increases steadily. Whether or not this shortfall indicates a problem isn't clear from the report, but the systematic undercharging does point to a situation that needs further investigation.

Collecting work-effort data

Having people fill out time sheets is the most effective way to collect work-effort expenditure data. You need to include the following information on each time sheet (see Figure 12-4 for an example of a typical time sheet):

✔ The number of hours a team member worked on each work package each day

✔ The team member's signature verifying that the information is correct

✔ An approval signature (typically the project manager or someone he designates) verifying that the time charges are valid and appropriate

	Work Package		Sun	Mon	Tue	Wed	Thu	Fri	Sat	Total
Project No.	WBS Code	Name	Apr 3	Apr 4	Apr 5	Apr 6	Apr 7	Apr 8	Apr 9	
Total Hours										

Employee: Name   Signature   From _____ to _____   Approval: Name   Signature

Figure 12-4:
A typical weekly time sheet.

Generally, recording work on activities to the nearest half-hour is sufficient.

Note: Some people may record their time in intervals smaller than half-hours. Lawyers, for example, often allocate their time in six-minute segments. Their clients would have it no other way — given that a lawyer may charge $300 or more per hour!

A *time log* is a form that breaks the day into intervals and enables a team member to record the specific activity he worked on in each interval. For example, to record time in half-hour intervals for a member who begins work at 8:30 a.m., the first interval on the log is 8:30 to 9 a.m., the second is 9 to 9:30 a.m., and so on.

If team members fill out time logs conscientiously, they provide more-accurate data because the log allows them to account for every segment of the day. However, maintaining a time log is far more time-consuming than filling out a time sheet. Normally, recording on a time sheet the total time a person spends working on different activities each day is sufficient.

Improving the accuracy of your work-effort data

Just as with schedule performance data, the more accurate your work-effort expenditure data are, the more meaningful your analyses will be. Take the following steps to increase the accuracy of the work-effort expenditure data you collect:

✓ **Explain to people that you're using their labor-effort expenditures to help you determine when you may need to change aspects of the plan.** When you ask people to detail the hours they spend on specific assignments, they often fear that you'll criticize them for not spending time exactly in accordance with the plan — no matter what the reason — or for not spending enough hours on project work as opposed to other administrative duties. Unfortunately, if they believe these are your motives, they'll allocate their work-hours among activities to reflect what they think you want to see instead of what they're really doing.

✔ **Encourage people to record the actual hours they work instead of making their total hours equal 40 hours per week.** If people must record a total of 40 hours per week and they work overtime, they'll omit hours here and there or try to reduce them proportionately. You want workers to record accurate data.

✔ **Include categories for time on nonproject activities, such as *unallocated, administrative overhead,* and so on.** If you want people to record their time expenditures honestly, you must provide them with appropriate categories.

✔ **Encourage people to fill out their own time sheets.** Some people ask a third person, such as a secretary, to fill out time sheets for them. But people have a hard enough time remembering what they themselves did the past day or the past week; expecting someone else to accurately remember it for them is totally unrealistic.

✔ **Collect time sheets weekly, if possible, or at least once every two weeks.** No matter how often you ask people to fill out their time sheets, many people wait until the sheet is due to complete it. If you collect sheets once a month, those people will be sitting there at the end of the month trying to remember what they did four weeks ago!

✔ **Don't ask people to submit their time sheets before the period is over.** On occasion, managers ask workers to submit time sheets on Thursday for the week ending on Friday. But this practice immediately reduces the accuracy of the data because a worker can't be certain what he'll do tomorrow. More importantly, though, this practice suggests to workers that, if guessing at Friday's allocation is acceptable, maybe they don't have to be too concerned with the accuracy of the rest of the week's data, either.

Choosing a vehicle to support your work-effort tracking system

Before you choose a method for tracking your work effort, check whether your organization has a time-recording system in place that can accurately record data the way you need it. When assessing an existing time-recording system, consider the following:

✔ Time-recording systems typically allocate a person's pay to regular work, vacation time, sick leave, and holiday leave. As such, the system may require exempt employees (that is, employees who aren't paid for overtime) to record no more than 40 hours per week. Additionally, these systems are often unable to track work by detailed WBS categories.

✔ People are often uncomfortable recording the hours they spend on different assignments because they aren't sure how the organization will use the information.

✔ A time-recording system's standard reports may not present information the way you need it to support your work-effort tracking.

If you decide to create your own work-effort recording and storage capability, you have to decide whether to develop a manual or computer-based system. As you decide, consider the following:

✔ Manual systems typically involve having people note in their daily calendars or personal diaries the hours they spent on different activities. Unfortunately, data recorded this way are often incomplete and inaccurate. In addition, you'll have difficulty pulling the data together to perform organized assessments and prepare meaningful reports.

✔ You can support a computer-based system with the following software:

  • Project-management software, such as Microsoft Project

  • Database software, such as Microsoft Access

  • Spreadsheet software, such as Microsoft Excel

See Chapter 16 for a discussion of the potential uses and benefits of software to support project management.

Follow the money: Monitoring expenditures

You monitor your project's expenditures to verify that they're in accordance with the project plan and, if they're not, to address any deviations. You may think that you can determine project funds used to date and funds remaining just by reading the balance in your project's financial account (the project's *checkbook*). However, spending project funds entails several steps before you actually pay for an item. After each step, you have a better sense of whether you'll incur the expenditure and, if you do, its exact amount.

The process leading up to and including the disbursement of funds for goods and services includes the following steps:

1. **You include a rough estimate of the item's cost in your project's budget.**

   You can develop this rough estimate by using your prior experience, by checking with others who have purchased similar items in the past, or by checking with your procurement department. Usually, you don't check with specific vendors or supplies when developing this rough estimate.

2. **You submit a written, approved request for the item to your procurement department.**

   This request specifies the rough estimate of the cost included in your project budget and any upper limit that the actual cost can't exceed. The project manager or his designee approves it, and anyone else who controls the expenditure of project funds (such as the finance department) approves it.

3. **Your procurement department selects a vendor and submits a purchase order.**

   The purchase order formally requests the vendor to furnish you the item and specifies the procurement department's estimate of the price.

4. **The vendor agrees to provide the item you requested.**

   The vendor provides you written confirmation that he will sell you the item, together with the item's price (including applicable taxes and shipping and handling charges) and the projected delivery date.

5. **You receive and accept the item but aren't yet billed for it.**

   You receive the item and verify that it meets the agreed specifications. If you don't accept the item after the vendor makes repeated attempts to fix any problems you have with it, your procurement department cancels the purchase order and you begin looking for a different vendor or a different item that will meet your needs.

6. **You or your finance department receives a bill for the item.**

   This bill details the item's final cost, together with associated discounts, taxes, and shipping and handling charges.

7. **Your finance department disburses funds to pay for the item.**

   The bill for your item is paid with money from your project's funds.

Depending on the size of your purchase and the size and formality of your organization, you may handle some of these stages informally for some purchases. As you proceed from the first step to the last, your estimate of the item's price becomes more accurate, and the likelihood that you'll actually make the purchase increases.

Responsible project monitoring requires that you have a clear idea of available project funds at each stage of the process. To do so, you typically want to monitor purchase requisitions, purchase orders, commitments (that is, purchase orders or contracts that you and the contractor or vendor agreed to), accounts payable, and expenditures.

In the following sections, I discuss how to analyze your project's expenditures, how to get the expenditure data you need for your analyses, and how to improve the accuracy of that data.

Analyzing expenditures

You evaluate your project's financial performance by comparing actual expenditures with those you planned. Figure 12-5 depicts a typical cost report that presents expenditures for the current performance period and from the beginning of the project for different levels of WBS components. The following information in this report comes from your project plan:

- ✔ Identifying codes and names for each WBS component
- ✔ The funds budgeted for each WBS component in the performance period
- ✔ The cumulative funds budgeted to date for each WBS component
- ✔ The total budget for each WBS component

The actual numbers for the period come from the data you obtain during that period. *Actual* in this illustration may mean the value of purchase requisitions, purchase orders, commitments, accounts payable, and/or expenditures. Total remaining funds are the difference between the total budget and the actual amounts expended to date.

Earned Value Management (EVM) is a method of determining — from resource expenditures alone — whether you're over or under budget and whether you're ahead of or behind schedule. On complex projects, EVM is a useful way to identify areas you should investigate for possible current problems or potential future problems. See Chapter 17 for further discussion of EVM.

Cost Report										
WBS Component		**Performance Period**			**To Date**			**Total**		
WBS Code	**Title**	**Budget**	**Actual**	**Budget – Actual**	**Budget**	**Actual**	**Budget – Actual**	**Budget**	**Remaining**	
1.0.	Total	$12,500	$11,200	$1,300	$27,500	$25,500	$2,000	$200,000	$174,000	
1.1.	Requirements	$5,000	$4,400	$600	$12,300	$11,400	$900	$45,000	$33,600	
1.2.	Focus groups	$3,000	$2,900	$100	$7,500	$7,100	$400	$10,000	$2,900	
1.3.	Document reviews	$1,500	$1,200	$300	$4,000	$3,800	$200	$5,000	$1,200	
1.4.	Report of requirements	$500	$300	$200	$800	$500	$300	$4,000	$3,500	
	⋮									

Figure 12-5: A cost report.

Collecting expenditure data and improving its accuracy

Typically, you obtain your expenditure data from purchase requisitions, purchase orders, vendor bills, and written checks. You normally see all purchase requisitions because, as the project manager, you probably have to approve them. The procurement department typically prepares purchase orders, and you may be able to get copies. Vendor bills usually go directly to the accounts payable group in the finance department, and these people pay the checks. You may be able to have the finance department send copies of bills to you to verify the amounts and so forth, and you can request reports of all payments from your project's account if they're tracked by project code.

Do the following to increase the accuracy of your project's expenditure data:

- ✔ Remove purchase orders from your totals after you receive the bill (or verify that payment has been made) to avoid double-counting an expenditure.

- ✔ Be sure to include the correct work package charge code on each purchase requisition and purchase order.

- ✔ Periodically remove voided or canceled purchase requisitions and purchase orders from your lists of outstanding documents.

Choosing a vehicle to support your expenditure tracking system

Before developing your own system to monitor your project's expenditures, first check the nature and capabilities of your organization's financial tracking system. Most organizations have a financial system that maintains records of all expenditures. Often the system also maintains records of accounts payable. Unfortunately, many financial systems categorize expenses by cost center but don't have the capacity to classify expenses by project or WBS component within a project.

If you have to develop your own system for tracking project expenditures, consider using the following types of software:

- ✔ Integrated project-management software, such as Microsoft Project

- ✔ Accounting software, such as QuickBooks

- ✔ Database software, such as Microsoft Access

- ✔ Spreadsheet software, such as Microsoft Excel

See Chapter 16 for more information on the potential uses and benefits of software to support project management.

Even if your organization's financial system can classify expenditures by work package within a project, you'll probably have to develop your own system for tracking purchase requisitions and purchase orders. Consider using a spreadsheet program or database software to support this tracking.

Putting Your Control Process into Action

The first part of this chapter tells you how to set up the systems that provide you the necessary information to guide your project. This section tells you how to use those systems to consistently monitor and guide your project's performance.

Heading off problems before they occur

Great project plans often fall by the wayside when well-intentioned people try to achieve the best-possible results on their own. They may spend more hours than the plan allowed for, hoping the additional work can produce better results. They may ask people who weren't in the original plan to work on the project or spend more money for an item than the budget allowed, believing these choices will result in higher-quality outcomes.

If possible at the start of your project, set up procedures that prevent people from exceeding established budgets without prior approval. For example, if people record the number of hours they spend on each project activity

- Confirm with them the maximum number of hours they may charge to each activity before they start it.
- Arrange for the time-recording system to reject attempts to charge more hours than planned for an activity unless the person has your prior written approval.
- Arrange for the time-recording system to reject any project hours charged by unauthorized people.

For purchases of equipment, materials, supplies, and services

- Confirm anticipated purchases, the upper limits for cost of individual items (if any), and the upper limit on the total expenditures.
- Arrange for the procurement office or financial system to reject attempts to overspend these limits without your prior written approval.

A change to your project's budget may be necessary and desirable. However, you want to make that decision with full awareness of the change's effect on other aspects of the project.

Formalizing your control process

To guide your project throughout its performance, establish procedures to collect and submit required progress data, to assess work and results, to take corrective actions when needed, and to keep audiences informed of your project's status. Follow these procedures throughout your project's life by doing the following:

1. **At the start of a performance period, reconfirm with people their commitments and your expectations.**

   See the earlier section "Holding On to the Reins: Project Control" for more details on how to do so.

2. **During the performance period, have people record schedule performance data, work effort, and any purchase requisitions and purchase orders they issue.**

   See the earlier sections "Collecting schedule performance data," "Collecting work-effort data," and "Collecting expenditure data and improving its accuracy" for more details.

3. **At agreed-upon intervals during or at the end of the performance period, have people submit their activity performance, expenditures, and work-effort data either to all relevant organizational systems or to systems specially maintained for your project.**

4. **At the end of the performance period, enter people's tracking data into the appropriate PMIS, compare actual performance for the period with planned performance, identify any problems, formulate and take corrective actions, and keep people informed.**

   See the later sections "Identifying possible causes of delays and variances," "Identifying possible corrective actions," and "Getting back on track: Rebaselining" for more details.

5. **At the beginning of the next performance period, start these steps again.**

Monitoring project performance doesn't identify problems; it identifies symptoms. When you identify a symptom, you must investigate the situation to determine the nature of any underlying problems, the reasons for the problems, and ways to fix them. But you can't get an accurate picture of where your project stands by monitoring only one or two aspects of your project. You must consider your project's performance in all three of its dimensions — outcomes produced, activity time frames, and resources used — together to determine the reasons for any inconsistencies you identify.

Suppose a member of your project team spent half as much time working on a project activity during the period as you had planned. Does this discrepancy mean you have a problem? You really can't tell. If the person reached all her planned milestones and the quality of her deliverables met the established standards, perhaps you don't have a problem. However, if she didn't reach some milestones or the quality of her deliverables was subpar, a problem may exist. You must consider product quality and schedule achievement together with the discrepancy between planned and actual work-hours to determine whether your project actually has a problem.

Identifying possible causes of delays and variances

After you confirm that a problem exists, you have to understand what caused the problem before you can bring your project back on track. The following circumstances may cause schedule delays:

- ✔ During the performance period, people spend less time on the activity than they agreed to.
- ✔ The activity requires more work effort than you planned.
- ✔ People are expanding the scope of the activity without the necessary reviews and approvals.
- ✔ Completing the activity requires steps you didn't identify in your plan.
- ✔ The people working on the activity have less experience with similar activities than you anticipated.

The following situations may result in people charging more or less time to activities than you planned:

- ✔ The person is more or less productive than you assumed when you developed the plan (see Chapter 6 for a discussion of productivity).
- ✔ You allowed insufficient time for becoming familiar with the activity before starting to work on it.
- ✔ The person is more or less efficient than you considered (see Chapter 6 for a discussion of efficiency).
- ✔ The activity requires more or less work than you anticipated.

You may spend more or less money on your project activities than you planned for the following reasons:

- ✔ You receive the bills for goods or services later than you planned, so they're paid later than you planned.
- ✔ You prepay for certain items to receive special discounts.
- ✔ You don't need certain goods or services that you budgeted for in your plan.
- ✔ You need goods or services that you didn't budget for in your plan.

Identifying possible corrective actions

When your project's performance deviates from your plan, first try to bring your project back in accordance with the existing plan. Then, if necessary, investigate the option of formally changing some of the commitments in the existing plan to create a new plan.

Consider the following approaches for bringing a project back in line with its existing plan:

- ✔ **If the variance results from a one-time occurrence, see whether it will disappear on its own.** Suppose you planned to spend 40 person-hours searching for and buying a piece of equipment, but you actually spent 10 person-hours because you found exactly what you wanted for the price you wanted to pay at the first store. Don't immediately change your plan to reallocate the 30 person-hours you saved on this activity. Most likely, you'll wind up overspending slightly on some future activities, and the work-effort expenditures will even each other out.

- ✔ **If the variance suggests a situation that will lead to similar variances in the future, consider changing your plan to prevent the future variances from occurring.** Suppose a team member requires twice the allotted work effort to finish her assignment because she's less experienced than the plan anticipated. If her lack of experience will cause her to be less productive on future assignments, revise the plan for her to spend more effort on those assignments. (See Chapter 5 for information on how to reduce the time it takes to complete a project and Chapter 6 for a discussion of how to modify personnel assignments.)

Getting back on track: Rebaselining

Your project's *baseline* is the current version of your project plan that guides project performance and provides a standard against which to compare your actual project performance. *Rebaselining* is officially adopting a new project plan to guide activities and serve as the comparative basis for future performance assessments.

If you think adopting a new baseline is necessary, do the following:

- ✔ Consult with key project audiences to explain why the changes are necessary and to solicit the audiences' approval and support.

- ✔ Make sure all key project audiences know about the new baseline.

- ✔ Keep a copy of your original plan and all subsequent modifications to support your final performance assessment when the project is over.

Rebaselining is a last resort when project work isn't going according to plan. Exhaust all possible strategies to get back on track before you attempt to change the plan itself. (Chapter 5 has information about changing the order and duration of activities to make up for unexpected delays; Chapter 6 has details on reallocating work effort to activities.)

Reacting Responsibly When Changes Are Requested

No matter how carefully you plan, occurrences you don't anticipate will most likely happen at one point or another during your project. Perhaps an activity turns out to be more involved than you figured, your client's needs and desires change, or new technology evolves. When these types of situations arise, you may need to modify your project plan to respond to them.

Even though change may be necessary and desirable, it always comes at a price. Furthermore, different people may have different opinions about which changes are important and how to implement them.

This section helps you manage changes in your project. It provides some helpful steps to follow when considering and acting on a change request. It also looks at gradual and unapproved project expansion and steps you can take to avoid it.

Responding to change requests

On large projects, formal change-control systems govern how you can receive, assess, and act on requests for changes. But whether you handle change requests formally or informally, always follow these steps:

1. **When you receive a request for change to some aspect of your project, clarify exactly what the request is asking you to do.**

2. **If possible, ask for the request in writing or confirm your understanding of the request by writing it down yourself.**

   In a formal change-control system, people must submit every request for change on a change-request form.

3. **Assess the change's potential effects on all aspects of your project.**

   Also consider what may happen if you don't make the change.

4. **Decide whether you'll implement the change.**

   If this change affects other people, involve them in the decision, too.

5. **If you decide not to make the change, tell the requester and explain the reason(s).**

6. **If you decide to make the change, write down the necessary steps to implement the change.**

   In a formal change-control system, all aspects of a change are detailed in a written change order.

7. **Update your project's plan to reflect any adjustments in schedules, outcomes, or resource budgets as a result of the change.**

8. **Tell team members and appropriate audiences about the change and the effect you expect it to have on your project.**

Observe the following guidelines to ensure that you can smoothly incorporate changes into your project:

- ✔ **Don't use the possibility of changes as an excuse for not being thorough in your original planning.** Make your project plan as accurate and complete as possible to reduce the need for future changes.

- ✔ **Remember that change always has a cost.** Don't ignore that cost, figuring you have to make the change anyway. Determine the cost of the change so you can plan for it and, if possible, minimize it.

- ✔ **Assess the effect of change on all aspects of your project.** Maintain a broad perspective — a change early in your project may affect your project from beginning to end.

Creeping away from scope creep

Scope creep is the gradual expansion of project work without formal consideration and acceptance of these changes or their associated costs and effects. Scope creep can occur as a result of any of the following:

- ✔ Lack of clarity and detail in the original description of project scope, objectives, and work

- ✔ Willingness to modify a project without formal review and approval

- ✔ Allowing people who don't do the work associated with the changes to decide whether to make changes

- ✔ Feeling that you should never say "No" to a client

- ✔ Personal pride that encourages you to believe you can do anything

Control scope creep by doing the following:

- ✔ Include detailed descriptions of all project objectives in your plan.
- ✔ Always assess the effect of requested changes on project products, schedules, and resources.
- ✔ Share your true feelings about whether you can implement the requested changes.
- ✔ Develop honest and open relationships with your clients so they're more receptive when you raise issues associated with their requested changes.

Relating This Chapter to the PMP Exam and PMBOK 4

Table 12-1 notes topics in this chapter that may be addressed on the Project Management Professional (PMP) certification exam and that are also included in *A Guide to the Project Management Body of Knowledge*, 4th Edition (*PMBOK 4*).

Table 12-1	Chapter 12 Topics in Relation to the PMP Exam and *PMBOK 4*	
Topic	*Location in PMBOK 4*	*Comments*
Steps in project control (see the section "Holding On to the Reins: Project Control")	3.6. Monitoring and Controlling Process Group	*PMBOK 4* notes the importance of having project cost and schedule tracking systems; this book delves into what the systems should contain and how information should be analyzed.
How to collect, analyze, and present information about project schedule, cost, and labor performance (see the section "Establishing Project Management Information Systems")	6.6. Control Schedule 7.3. Control Costs: Tools and Techniques	*PMBOK 4* mentions the schedule and cost data required and different analytical techniques that may be used to analyze project schedule and cost performance. This book also explores how to collect and analyze this information.
Making changes (see the section "Reacting Responsibly When Changes Are Requested")	4.5. Perform Integrated Change Control	The processes presented in both books are very similar.

Chapter 13

Keeping Everyone Informed

. . . .

In This Chapter

▶ Understanding important elements of communication

▶ Choosing how to share the news: Writing or meeting?

▶ Authoring your project-progress report and managing an assortment of meeting styles

▶ Putting together a project communications plan

. . . .

*I*magine standing at one end of a large room filled with assorted sofas, chairs, and tables. You've accepted a challenge to walk to the other end without bumping into any of the furniture. But, as you set off on your excursion, the lights go off, and you now have to complete your trip in total darkness, with only your memory of the room's layout to guide you.

Sounds like a pretty tough assignment, doesn't it? How much easier it would be if the lights went on every few seconds — you could see exactly where you were, where you had to go, and where the furniture got in the way. The walk would still be challenging, but it would be much more successful than in total darkness.

Surprisingly, many projects are just like that walk across the room. People plan how they'll perform the project — who will do what, by when, and for how much — and they share this information with the team members and other people who will support the project. But as soon as the project work begins, people receive no information about their progress, the work remaining, or obstacles that may lie ahead.

Effective communication — sharing the right messages with the right people in a timely manner — is a key to successful projects. Informative communications support the following:

✔ Continued buy in and support from key audiences and team members

✔ Prompt problem identification and decision making

✔ A clear project focus

✔ Ongoing recognition of project achievements

✔ Productive working relationships among team members

Planning your project communications upfront enables you to choose the appropriate media for sharing different messages. This chapter can help you keep everyone in the loop so no one's left wondering what your project's status is.

I Said What I Meant and I Meant What I Said: Successful Communication Basics

Have you ever played the game of telephone with a group of people sitting around a table? The first person at the table has a written message, and the object of the game is for the group to transmit that message accurately to the last person at the table by having each person in turn whisper the contents of the message to the next person in line. The rules are simple — no one other than the first person can see the original written message, and each person must ensure that only the next in line hears the message that's whispered to him or her. Invariably, the message received by the last person bears little, if any, resemblance to the original message because, even in this controlled setting, a myriad of factors influence how well people send and receive messages.

Sadly, sometimes this type of miscommunication can occur in a project-management environment. But don't worry! This section is here to help. It explores important parts of the communication process, distinguishes different types of communication, and offers suggestions to improve the chances that the message a receiver gets is the one the sender intended to give.

Breaking down the communication process

Communication is the transmitting of information from a sender to a receiver. Whenever you communicate, during the life of a project or at any other time, your goal is to ensure that the right person correctly receives your intended message in a timely manner.

The process of transmitting information includes the following components:

- **Message:** The thoughts or ideas being transmitted
- **Sender:** The person transmitting the message
- **Encoded message:** The message translated into a language understandable to others (This language may consist of words, pictures, or actions.)
- **Medium:** The method used to convey the message (I discuss different mediums in detail in the "Choosing the Appropriate Medium for Project Communication" section later in this chapter.)

✔ **Noise:** Anything that hinders successfully transmitting the message (Noise may include preconceived notions, biases, difficulty with the language used, personal feelings, nonverbal cues, and emotions.)

✔ **Receiver:** The person getting the message

✔ **Decoded message:** The message translated back into thoughts or ideas

Depending on the nature of a particular communication, any or all of these elements can affect the chances that a message is received as intended.

Distinguishing one-way and two-way communication

Certain types of communication are more effective for transmitting particular types of information. The two main types are one-way and two-way:

✔ **One-way communication:** Going from the sender to the receiver with no opportunity for clarification or confirmation that the receiver got and correctly understood the intended message. This type of communication can be effective for presenting facts, confirming actions, and sharing messages that have little chance of being misinterpreted.

One-way communications are either:

- **Push:** Proactively distributed to particular people; examples include memos, reports, letters, faxes, and e-mails

- **Pull:** Available to people who must access the communications themselves; examples include Internet and intranet sites, knowledge repositories, and bulletin boards

✔ **Two-way communication:** Going from the sender to the receiver and from the receiver back to the sender to help ensure that the intended audience received and correctly interpreted the intended message. Examples include face-to-face discussions, phone calls, in-person group meetings, interactive teleconferences, and online instant messaging. Two-way communication is effective for ensuring that more complex content is correctly received and for conveying the sender's beliefs and feelings about the message.

Can you hear me? Listening actively

The one skill that most strongly influences the quality of your communications is your ability to listen actively. Although you can assume that the information contained in a message and the format in which it's presented affect how well that message is received, you can find out whether the recipient actually received the message as you intended by listening carefully to the recipient's reactions.

Active listening is exploring and discussing a message that's being sent to help ensure that the message is understood as intended. If you're sending a message, you should encourage your intended recipient to use active listening techniques to help ensure that she correctly understands your message. If you're receiving a message, you should use these techniques to verify to yourself that you have correctly received the intended message.

Because listening to and observing your recipient's response to a message you sent her involves information flowing first from you to the recipient and then from the recipient back to you, active listening is, by definition, a form of two-way communication.

Active listening techniques include the following:

✔ **Visualizing:** Forming a mental picture of the content of a message. Forming this picture gives the receiver the opportunity to identify pieces of the message that may be missing or misunderstood, as well as to seek additional information that may improve the overall understanding of the original message.

Consider that you've been asked to redesign the layout of your group's offices to create a more open environment that will encourage people to feel more relaxed and to engage in more informal working group discussions. To help clarify what's expected, you may try to visualize how the office environment will look and how people will behave after the changes in the layout are made. In particular, you may think about the following:

- Whether you'll have to use the existing furnishings or you'll be able to buy new ones

- Where people might hold informal meetings

- How much soundproofing partitions of differing heights will provide

As you try to visualize these different parts of the new office layout, you realize that the following aspects aren't quite clear to you:

- Will window offices have couches or just chairs?

- How many people should be able to sit comfortably in an office?

- Should "white noise" machines be installed?

As you talk with people to find answers to your questions, you get a better idea of what your boss does and doesn't want.

✔ **Paraphrasing:** Explaining the message and its implications, as the receiver understands them, back to the sender in different words than the original message. To be most effective, the receiver should repeat the message in his or her own words to give the sender the best chance of identifying any misinterpretations.

Consider that your boss asks you to prepare a report of your company's recent sales activity by the end of the week. Many aspects of this request are unclear, such as the time period the report should cover, the specific time by when the report must be finished, the format in which you should prepare the report, and so forth. To clarify these items, you can paraphrase the request back to your boss as follows:

"I'd like to confirm that you're asking me to prepare for you by this coming Friday at 5:00 p.m. a PowerPoint presentation on the company's total gross and net sales of products a, b, and c for the period from January 1 to March 31 of this year."

✔ **Checking inferences:** Clarifying assumptions and interpretations that the receiver makes about the message received.

Consider the previous example in which your boss asks you to redesign the layout of your group's offices. As you start to calculate the numbers of desks and chairs you'll need in the new arrangement, you realize you're assuming that the group will have the same number of people it has now after the move. However, instead of making this assumption, you can check with your boss to find out how many people he would like you to plan for as you design the new layout.

Active listening is particularly useful in emotionally charged situations, situations in which understanding is critical, situations in which consensus and clarity are desired in resolving conflict, and situations in which trust is sought.

Choosing the Appropriate Medium for Project Communication

When deciding how to communicate with your team and your project's audiences, choosing the right medium is as important as deciding what information to share (check out Chapter 3 for a detailed discussion of project audiences). Your choice of medium helps ensure that people get the information they need when they need it.

Project communications come in two forms:

✔ **Formal:** Formal communications are preplanned and conducted in a standard format in accordance with an established schedule. Examples include weekly team meetings and monthly progress reports.

✔ **Informal:** Informal communications occur as people think of information they want to share. These communications occur continuously in the normal course of business. Examples include brief conversations by the water cooler and spur-of-the-moment e-mails you dash off during the day.

Take care not to rely on informal communications to share important information about your project because these interchanges often involve only a small number of the people who should hear what you have to say. To minimize the chances for misunderstandings and hurt feelings among your project's team members and other audiences

- Confirm in writing any important information you share in informal discussions.

- Avoid having an informal discussion with only some of the people who are involved in the topic.

Both formal and informal communications can be either written or oral. The following sections suggest when to use each format and how to make it most effective.

Just the facts: Written reports

Unlike informal oral communication, written reports enable you to present factual data efficiently, choose your words carefully to minimize misunderstandings, provide a historical record of the information you share, and share the same message with a wide audience.

Although written reports have quite a few benefits, they also have some drawbacks that you need to consider:

- ✔ They don't allow your audience to ask questions to clarify the content, meaning, and implication of your message.

- ✔ With written reports, you can't verify that your audience received and interpreted your message as you intended.

- ✔ They don't enable you to pick up nonverbal signals that suggest your audience's reactions to the message, and they don't support interactive discussion and brainstorming about your message.

- ✔ You may never know whether your audience reads the report!

Keep the following pointers in mind to improve the chances that people read and understand your written reports (see the later section "Preparing a Written Project-Progress Report" for specifics on writing this special type of communication):

✔ **Prepare regularly scheduled reports in a standard format.** This consistency helps your audience find specific types of information quickly.

✔ **Stay focused.** Preparing several short reports to address different topics is better than combining several topics into one long report. People are more likely to pick up the important information about each topic.

✔ **Minimize the use of technical jargon and acronyms.** If a person is unfamiliar with the language in your report, she'll miss at least some of your messages.

✔ **Use written reports to share facts, and be sure to identify a person or people to contact for clarification or further discussion of any information in the reports.** Written reports present hard data with a minimum of subjective interpretation, and they provide a useful, permanent reference. A contact person can address any questions a recipient has about the information or the reasons for sharing it.

✔ **Clearly describe any actions you want people to take based on information in the report.** The more specifically you explain what you want people to do, the more likely they are to do it.

✔ **Use novel approaches to emphasize key information.** For example, print key sections in a different color or on colored paper, or mention particularly relevant or important sections in a cover memo. This additional effort increases the chances that your audience will see the report *and* read it.

✔ **After you send your report, discuss one or two key points that you addressed in the report with people who received it.** These follow-up conversations can quickly tell you whether your recipients have read it.

When you come across people who clearly haven't read your report, in addition to following the other suggestions in this section, explain to them the specific parts of the document that are most important for them to review and why. Then tell them that you'd like to set up a follow-up meeting with them to discuss any questions or issues they may have regarding the information contained in those parts of the document.

✔ **Keep your reports to one page, if possible.** If you can't fit your report on one page, include a short summary (one page or less) at the beginning of the report (check out the nearby sidebar "Keep it short — and that means you!").

Keep it short — and that means you!

Be careful of the *"yes, but"* syndrome — in which you think an idea sounds great for others, but your *special* situation requires a different approach. In a training program a number of years ago, I shared my suggestion to keep project reports to one page or less. Most people agreed that doing so made sense, but one participant rejected the notion. He proceeded to explain that his project was so important and so complex that he sent his boss monthly project reports that were a minimum of ten pages in length. "And," he added, "My boss reads every word."

A few weeks after the training session, I had the opportunity to speak with this participant's boss about a totally unrelated matter. In the course of our conversation, he happened to mention his frustration with a person on his staff who felt his project was so important that he had to submit monthly progress reports no fewer than ten pages long. He said that he usually read the first paragraph, but he rarely had time to review the reports thoroughly. He added that he hoped this person had listened carefully when I suggested that reports should be one page or less!

Move it along: Meetings that work

Few words elicit the same reactions of anger and frustration that the word *meeting* can provoke. People consider meetings to be everything from the last vestige of interpersonal contact in an increasingly technical society to the biggest time waster in business today.

You've probably been in meetings where you wanted to bang your head against the wall. Ever been to a meeting that didn't start on time? How about a meeting that didn't have an agenda or didn't stick to the agenda it did have? Or how about a meeting at which people discussed issues you thought were resolved at a previous meeting?

Meetings don't have to be painful experiences. If you plan and manage them well, meetings can be effective forms of communication. They can help you find out about other team members' backgrounds, experiences, and styles; stimulate brainstorming, problem analysis, and decision making; and provide a forum to explore the reasons for and interpretations of a message.

You can improve your meetings by using the suggestions in the following sections. (In addition, be sure to check out the later section "Holding Key Project Meetings" for information on different types of meetings.)

Planning for a successful meeting

To have a good meeting, you need to do some pre-meeting planning. Keep these pointers in mind as you plan:

- ✓ **Clarify the purpose of the meeting.** This step helps you ensure that you invite the right people and allows attendees to prepare for the meeting.

- ✓ **Decide who needs to attend and why.** If you need information, decide who has it, and make sure they attend the meeting. If you want to make decisions at the meeting, decide who has the necessary authority and who needs to be part of the decision making, and make sure they attend.

- ✓ **Give plenty of advance notice of the meeting.** This step increases the chances that the people you want to attend will be able to do so.

- ✓ **Let the people who should attend the meeting know its purpose.** People are more likely to attend a meeting when they understand why their attendance is important.

- ✓ **Prepare a written agenda that includes topics and their allotted discussion times.** This document helps people see why attending the meeting is in their interests. The agenda is also your guideline for running the meeting.

- ✓ **Circulate the written agenda and any background material in advance.** Doing so gives everyone time to suggest changes to the agenda and to prepare for the meeting.

- ✓ **Keep meetings to one hour or less.** You can force people to sit in a room for hours, but you can't force them to keep their minds on the activities and information at hand for that long. If necessary, schedule several meetings of one hour or less to discuss complex issues or multiple topics.

Conducting an efficient meeting

How you conduct the meeting can make or break it. The following tasks are essential for conducting a productive meeting:

- ✓ **Start on time, even if people are absent.** After people see that you wait for latecomers, everyone will come late!

- ✓ **Assign a timekeeper.** This person reminds the group when a topic has exceeded its allotted time for discussion.

- ✓ **Assign a person to take written minutes of who attended, which items you discussed, and what decisions and assignments the group made.** This procedure allows people to review and clarify the information and serves as a reminder of actions to be taken after the meeting.

✔ **Keep a list of action items that need further exploration, and assign one person to be responsible for each entry.** This step helps ensure that when you meet to discuss these issues again, you have the right information and people present to resolve them.

✔ **If you don't have the right information or the right people to resolve an issue, stop your discussion and put it on the list of action items.** Discussing an issue without having the necessary information or the right people present is just wasting everyone's time.

✔ **End on time.** Your meeting attendees may have other commitments that begin when your meeting is supposed to end. Not ending on time causes these people to be late for their next commitments or to leave your meeting before it's over.

Following up with the last details

Your meeting may be over, but your work isn't done. Make sure you complete the following post-meeting tasks to get the greatest benefit from the session:

✔ **Promptly distribute meeting minutes to all attendees.** These minutes allow people to reaffirm the information discussed at the meeting when it's still fresh in their minds, and minutes quickly remind people of their follow-up tasks. Try to distribute the minutes within 24 hours of the meeting, and ask recipients to let you know if they have any corrections or additions.

✔ **Monitor the status of all action items that are performed after the meeting.** Because each action is itself a miniproject, monitoring its progress increases the chances that people successfully complete it.

Don't just talk about these suggestions for making your meetings more effective. Discussing them can't improve your meetings. Act on them!

Preparing a Written Project-Progress Report

The *project-progress report* is a project's most common written communication. The report reviews activities performed during a performance period, describes problems encountered and the corrective actions planned and taken, and previews plans for the next period. (Check out Chapter 12 for some tips on how to choose the length of your project's *performance period* — the length of time between performance assessments.)

This section helps you identify the audience for your project-progress report, provides pointers on what to include in your report, and suggests improvements for that content so it doesn't put your team to sleep.

Making a list (of names) and checking it twice

A project-progress report is a convenient way to keep key audiences involved in your project and informed of their responsibilities. Decide who should get regularly scheduled project-progress reports by answering the following questions:

✔ Who needs to know about your project?

✔ Who wants to know about your project?

✔ Whom do you want to know about your project?

At a minimum, consider providing project-progress reports to your supervisor, upper management, client or customer, project team members, and other people who are helping you on the project, as well as to people who are interested in or who will be affected by the project's results.

Knowing what's hot (and what's not) in your report

Preparing the project-progress report gives you an opportunity to step back and review all aspects of your project so you can recognize accomplishments and identify situations that may require your early intervention. Be sure to include some or all of the following information in your project-progress report for each performance period:

✔ **Performance highlights:** Always begin your report with a summary of project highlights, such as "The planned upper-management review was successfully conducted on schedule" or "Our client Mary Fisher approved our training outline according to schedule." (Just remember to keep it to one page!)

✔ **Performance details:** Describe the activities, outcomes, milestones, labor hours, and resource expenditures in detail.

✔ **Problems and issues:** Highlight special issues or problems that you encountered during the period, and propose any necessary corrective actions.

✔ **Approved changes to the plan:** Report all approved changes to the existing project plan.

✔ **Risk-management status:** Update your project risk assessment by reporting on changes in project assumptions, the likelihood of these updated assumptions occurring, and the effect of those updated assumptions on existing project plans. (Chapter 8 covers the basics of dealing with risk and uncertainty.)

✔ **Plans for the next period:** Summarize major work and accomplishments that you have planned for the next performance period.

Earning a Pulitzer, or at least writing an interesting report

When you write your project-progress report, make sure it's interesting and tells the appropriate people what they need to know. After all, you don't want your report to end up as a birdcage liner. Use the following tips to improve the quality of each of your project-progress reports:

✔ **Tailor your reports to the interests and needs of your audiences.** Provide only the information that your audience wants and needs. If necessary, prepare separate reports for different audiences. (See Chapter 3 for more on defining your project's audiences.)

✔ **If you're preparing different progress reports for different audiences, prepare the most detailed one first and extract information from that report to produce the others.** This approach ensures consistency among the reports and reduces the likelihood that you'll perform the same work more than once.

✔ **Produce a project-progress report at least once a month, no matter what your audience requests.** Monitoring and sharing information about project progress less often than once per month significantly increases the chances of major damage resulting from an unidentified problem.

✔ **Make sure that all product, schedule, and resource information in your report is for the same time period.** Accomplishing this may not be easy if you depend on different organization systems for your raw performance data.

If you track project schedule performance on a system that you maintain yourself, you may be able to produce a status report by the end of the first week after the performance period. However, your organization's financial system, which you use to track project expenditures, may not generate performance reports for the same period until a month later.

Address this issue in your project's start-up phase (see Chapter 11 for suggested start-up activities). Determine your sources for status data, the dates your updated data are available from each source, and the time periods that the data apply to. Then schedule your combined analysis and reporting so that all data describe the same time period.

- ✓ **Always compare actual performance with respect to the performance plan.** Presenting the information in this format highlights issues that you need to address.

- ✓ **Include no surprises.** If an element requires prompt action during the performance period (like a key person unexpectedly leaves the project team), immediately tell all the people involved and work to address the problem. However, be sure to mention the occurrence and any corrective actions in the progress report to provide a written record.

- ✓ **Use your regularly scheduled team meetings to discuss issues and problems that you raise in the project-progress report.** Discuss any questions people have about the information in the project-progress report. (However, don't read verbatim to people from the written report they've already received — and hopefully read!)

Using a project dashboard

To make your written project-progress reports most effective, you want to include the greatest amount of information in the least amount of space. A *project dashboard* is an information display that depicts key indicators of project performance in a format that resembles an instrument panel on a dashboard. This format can convey the project's overall progress and highlight particular problems that require further attention.

When designing a dashboard for your project, take the following steps:

1. **Select the major categories of information.**

2. **Choose specific indicators for each information category.**

3. **Select the format for each indicator.**

Typical information categories that reflect important aspects of project performance include

- ✓ **Results:** Desired products your team has produced to date

- ✓ **Performance to schedule:** Dates that your team achieved milestones and started and completed activities compared to the schedule plan for milestones and activities

- ✓ **Performance to resource budgets:** Labor hours, funds, and other resources your team has used to date compared to their budgeted amounts

- ✓ **Risk management:** Current status of factors that may unexpectedly impede project performance

Choose specific indicators for each category in conjunction with the project's drivers and supporters. As an example, a project that develops an operations manual for a piece of equipment may have the following indicators:

- ✓ **Results:** The number of manual chapters written or the number of people who have approved the final manual

(continued)

(continued)

✔ **Performance to schedule:** The number of milestone dates you've met and the number you've missed

✔ **Performance to resource budgets:** The ratio of actual funds expended to those budgeted for all completed activities

✔ **Risk management:** The number of original risks that may still occur or the number of new risks you've identified during the project

You can display indicators in a table, bar graph, pie chart, or speedometer format. In addition, indicators often have a traffic light format:

✔ **Green light:** The element is proceeding according to plan.

✔ **Yellow light:** One or more minor problems exist.

✔ **Red light:** One or more serious situations require immediate attention.

Determine the specific criteria for green-, yellow-, and red-light status for each indicator in consultation with the project's drivers and supporters.

The following illustrations depict the types of displays in a project dashboard.

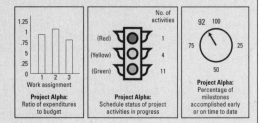

Project Alpha: Ratio of expenditures to budget

Project Alpha: Schedule status of project activities in progress

Project Alpha: Percentage of milestones accomplished early or on time to date

When creating a dashboard for your project, be sure to

✔ Work with the intended audiences of a report to select the categories, indicators, and their display formats.

✔ Always present *actual* indicator values alongside *planned* values.

✔ Keep the project dashboard report to one page or less.

Holding Key Project Meetings

Active, ongoing support from all major project audiences gives you the greatest chance for achieving project success. To gain that support, continually reinforce your project's vision and your progress toward it, and help your project's audiences understand when and how they can most effectively support your efforts. This section looks more closely at the three types of meetings you may hold during your project.

Regularly scheduled team meetings

Regularly scheduled team meetings give members an opportunity to share progress and issues and to sustain productive and trusting interpersonal relationships. These meetings also provide an opportunity to reaffirm the project's focus and to keep team members abreast of activities within and outside the project that affect their work and the project's ultimate success. Recognizing that most people work on several projects at the same time, these meetings can reinforce the team's identity and working relationships.

Consult with team members to develop a meeting schedule that's convenient for as many people as possible. If some people can't attend in person, try to have them participate in a conference call. (See Chapter 16 for more about how you can use technology to support your project.)

In addition to following the suggestions for productive meetings in the "Move it along: Meetings that work" section earlier in this chapter, observe the following guidelines when planning and conducting regular team meetings:

- ✔ Even though your team meetings are held regularly, before each meeting, prepare a specific agenda, distribute it beforehand, and solicit comments and suggestions.

- ✔ Before the meeting, distribute the project-progress report for the most recent performance period (take a look at the earlier section "Preparing a Written Project-Progress Report" for details on this report).

- ✔ Distribute any other background information related to topics on the agenda before the meeting.

- ✔ Limit discussions that require more in-depth consideration; deal with them in other forums.

- ✔ Start on time and end on time (there, I said it again!).

- ✔ Prepare and distribute brief minutes of the meeting within 24 hours after its end.

Ad hoc team meetings

Hold ad hoc team meetings to address specific issues that arise during your project. An ad hoc meeting may involve some or all of your team's members, depending on the topic. Because issues often arise unexpectedly, do the following as you plan an ad hoc meeting:

- ✔ Clarify the issue and what you hope to achieve at your meeting.

- ✔ Identify and invite all people who may be interested in, affected by, or working on the issue.

- ✔ Clearly explain the meeting's purpose to all meeting invitees.

✔ Carefully document all action items that the attendees develop at the meeting, and assign responsibility for their completion.

✔ Be sure to share the results of an ad hoc meeting with all team members who may be affected by the results, who have an interest in them, and/ or whose support you need to implement them.

Upper-management progress reviews

An *upper-management progress review* is usually presided over by a senior manager, run by a project manager, and attended by team members and representatives of all functional areas. This review gives you the chance to tell upper management about your project's status, its major accomplishments, and any issues that require their help. The review is also an opportunity for you to note ways to keep the project in line with major organization initiatives.

Take every opportunity to help upper management remember why your project is important to them. They may have approved your project only months ago, but chances are your project's now just one of many activities in your busy organization.

Make your upper-management progress review effective by observing the following tips:

✔ Identify the interests of your audience, and explain how your project is meeting those interests.

✔ Keep your presentation short; choose a few key messages and emphasize them.

✔ Highlight your key information, but be prepared to go into more detail on issues if anyone asks you to do so.

✔ Use both text and graphics to convey important information.

✔ Allow time for questions.

✔ Present updated information on project risks, and explain how you're addressing them.

✔ Distribute a brief handout at the meeting that summarizes the key points of your presentation.

✔ After the meeting, distribute notes that highlight issues raised and actions that you agreed on during the review.

Preparing a Project Communications Management Plan

With the diversity of audiences that will be looking for information about your project and the array of data that you will be collecting, it's essential that you prepare a project Communications Management Plan to avoid duplication of effort and to ensure that nothing and no one falls through the cracks.

A project *Communications Management Plan* is a document that specifies all project communications generated throughout the project, their target audiences, their information content, and their frequency. Prepare an initial version of your project Communications Management Plan in the starting the project stage of your project, and update it as needed in the carrying out the work stage. (Flip to Chapter 1 for details on the distinct stages of a project.)

At a minimum, your plan should specify the following for all project communications:

- ✓ **Target audience:** The people whose information needs are addressed through the project communication (Check out Chapter 3 for a discussion of how to identify and classify project audiences.)

- ✓ **Information needs:** The information that the target audience wants and/ or needs

- ✓ **Information-sharing activity:** The specific type of information-sharing activity to be used to transmit information to the target audience (written reports, presentations, and meetings, for example) (Check out the section "Choosing the Appropriate Medium for Project Communication" earlier in this chapter for more on when different types of information-sharing activities should be used.)

- ✓ **Content:** The specific data to be shared in the project communication

- ✓ **Frequency:** When the information-sharing activity occurs (can be either regularly scheduled or ad hoc)

- ✓ **Data collection:** How and when the data for the report are collected

Relating This Chapter to the PMP Exam and PMBOK 4

Pay special attention to Table 13-1, which notes topics in this chapter that may be addressed on the Project Management Professional (PMP) certification exam and that are included in *A Guide to the Project Management Body of Knowledge*, 4th Edition (*PMBOK 4*).

Table 13-1	Chapter 13 Topics in Relation to the PMP Exam and *PMBOK 4*	
Topic	*Location in PMBOK 4*	*Comments*
Components of the communication process and different types of communication (see the section "I Said What I Meant and I Meant What I Said: Successful Communication Basics")	10.2.2. Plan Communications: Tools and Techniques 10.3. Distribute Information G.4. Communication	Both books identify similar components of the communication process. *PMBOK 4* mentions a number of techniques, while this book gives more descriptive information and illustrations.
Form and content of written project reports (see the section "Preparing a Written Project-Progress Report")	10.3. Distribute Information 10.5. Report Performance	*PMBOK 4* identifies issues to consider when preparing reports, while this book goes into more depth describing different techniques and explaining how to apply them.
What to include in a plan to meet audience information needs (see the section "Preparing a Project Communications Management Plan")	10.2.3.1. Communications Management Plan	*PMBOK 4* provides an extensive list of information concerning the preparation of reports, as well as administrative requirements that can influence report generation and distribution, that can be included in a Communications Management Plan. This book focuses more on the types of information required to guide the preparation and distribution of reports.

Chapter 14

Encouraging Peak Performance by Providing Effective Leadership

• •

In This Chapter

▶ Clarifying the difference between leadership and management

▶ Tapping into different sources of power

▶ Developing and maintaining motivation on your team

• •

*B*ecause of the rapid changes that are occurring in every facet of business and personal life today, leadership is one of the most important issues facing organizations. As a result, a large body of literature has emerged to explore how to guide people to achieve common goals in a wide variety of settings.

When working in a matrix environment, your project's success depends on your ability to organize, coordinate, and support a diverse team that's working toward a common goal (see Chapter 9 for more specifics about the matrix structure). Often the people on your team come from different areas of your organization, have different operating styles, and don't report to you administratively. Successfully guiding such a group of people requires both vision and structure.

This chapter discusses tips for aligning, focusing, and motivating the people supporting your project to maximize the chances for your project's success.

Comparing Leadership and Management

Leadership and management are two related but distinct sets of behaviors for guiding and supporting people through a project. Here are the differences:

✔ Leadership emphasizes defining a vision and encouraging other people to help make that vision a reality; management focuses on creating plans and assessing performance.

- ✔ Leadership focuses on people; management focuses on systems, procedures, and information.

- ✔ Leadership facilitates change; management creates order and predictability.

As you plan your project, explore the *why* of the project (a leadership issue) to help elicit people's buy in and commitment. Also explore the *what, when,* and *how* (management issues) to develop a feasible approach for successfully achieving the project's goals. As you organize your project, clarify who will support the different project activities (a management task) and help them get excited about doing so (a leadership task).

Throughout the project, continually let people know how the project is progressing, and deal with any problems you encounter along the way (management tasks). Remind people of the project's benefits, and acknowledge their contributions to the project's success (leadership tasks). Table 14-1 illustrates leadership and management approaches to support the key activities in a project.

Table 14-1	Comparison of Leadership and Management Approaches to Project Activities	
Activity	*Leadership Approach*	*Management Approach*
Planning	Create and share visions and strategies.	Specify objectives, schedules, and budgets.
Organizing	Elicit commitments from members.	Assign people to the team, and define their roles.
Performing	Motivate team members.	Monitor and report on progress, and deal with problems.

Developing Personal Power and Influence

Power is the ability to influence the actions of others. Establishing effective bases of power enhances your ability to coordinate your team and other key audiences. In this section, I explain how to develop your personal power bases and how to use the power you can derive from those bases to energize and motivate people throughout the life of your project.

Understanding why people do what you ask

Because personal power is the ability to influence and guide the actions of others, the first step in developing this power is understanding why people choose to do what you ask in the first place. People respond to your requests and directions for many reasons, including the following:

- ✓ **Rewards:** People do what you ask because they want the benefits you can give them. Examples of rewards include raises and recognition.

- ✓ **Punishments:** People do what you ask because they *don't* want what you can give them. Examples of punishments include poor performance appraisals and undesirable job assignments.

- ✓ **Your position:** People take your requests more seriously because they feel the project manager should direct team members. You can lose this power if you behave inappropriately, but you have it initially.

- ✓ **What you stand for:** People do what you ask because they agree with your goals. They know that your requests and actions are attempts to achieve the same results they want to achieve.

- ✓ **Who you are:** People listen to you because they appreciate and respect who you are, as reflected by your sensitivity, your loyalty to others, your sense of humor, or other positive characteristics of your attitudes and behaviors.

- ✓ **Your expertise:** People listen to you because they respect the skills and knowledge that you bring to your job. They listen to you because they believe you're probably right.

You don't have to be the technical expert on your project to command the respect of your team members and effectively lead your project. But you do have to be an expert in the skills and knowledge that your job demands on the project. Because you're the project manager, these skills and knowledge include your abilities to plan and control the project, encourage effective communication, encourage a positive and productive work environment, and understand the political environment in your overall organization.

Of course, your technical expertise can be a significant asset if you use it correctly. Your praise for a job well done means a lot more to your team members than praise from someone who's less qualified to assess the work.

Take note that being both the technical expert and the project manager on your project can work against you. If you're not careful, you can discourage others from accepting responsibilities and performing their work independently for one or more of the following reasons:

✔ They feel that their work can never be as good as yours.

✔ You keep the more challenging and important assignments for yourself because you like the work and think you can do it best.

✔ You resist approaches that differ from the ones you normally take.

✔ You tend to micromanage people to ensure that they're performing assignments just as you would.

Although many factors can contribute to your ability to influence people, your power over your team members is generally one of the following:

✔ **Ascribed:** Someone gives you authority to reward and punish others.

✔ **Achieved:** You earn the respect and allegiance of other people.

Achieved power is far more effective and longer-lasting than ascribed power. People who act in response to your ascribed power usually do the least amount of work necessary to get the rewards they want or to avoid the consequences they fear. On the other hand, people motivated by your achieved power work to accomplish the highest possible quality of results because they've decided that doing so is in their best interests (and yours).

Whether or not you recognize and acknowledge it, you have considerable opportunity to develop and use achieved power. You can *choose* how you want to influence people's behavior, or you can *inadvertently* influence their behavior. Either way, your actions influence other people's behavior.

Establishing the bases of your power

You can get a sense of the power you have over someone by taking note of the willingness with which she agrees to do and then does what you request. If you already get all the cooperation from others that you need, just keep doing what you're doing. However, if you feel frustrated by people's resistance and lack of cooperation when you ask for their help, take steps to improve the power you have over them.

Successfully influencing the behavior of others requires, first, that you understand the different types of power you have over them and, second, that you effectively use that power. Your ascribed power over people depends, in part, on their perceptions of the specific authority you and others whom you can influence have over them. Your achieved power is based on people's perceptions of what you know, who you are, and what you stand for. (I introduce ascribed and achieved power in the preceding section.)

Take the following steps to improve your ability to influence your team members and other people in your project environment:

- ✔ **Determine the authority you have over the people you want to influence.** Common types of authority include the ability to give salary increases and promotions, complete performance appraisals, and assign people to future jobs.

- ✔ **Find out who else has authority over the people you want to influence.** If you don't make the decision about whether and how much to increase a person's salary but you can influence the individual who does, the person will react to you as if you, too, have some measure of ascribed power over her.

- ✔ **Clarify for yourself how and why the project's successful completion benefits your organization, and share those benefits with the people you want to influence.** Knowing all the benefits your project is designed to yield puts you in a better position to help others see why helping you complete your project is in their best interests.

- ✔ **Get to know the people you want to influence; understand, appreciate, and acknowledge their special talents and strengths.** Getting to know other people helps you understand the types of rewards and recognition they appreciate most. It also tells them you care for them as people, not just as technical resources for your project.

- ✔ **Let the people you want to influence get to know your good side.** Your achieved power over others is based on their perceptions of your character and abilities.

- ✔ **Don't condemn or complain, but do give feedback when necessary.** *Condemning* is making negative judgments about others; *complaining* is criticizing people or things without doing anything to improve them. Both behaviors entail sharing negative opinions rather than facts, which demoralizes and demotivates people while doing little to achieve high-quality results. *Constructive feedback,* on the other hand, entails sharing factual information to improve people's performance. People respect others whom they feel are interested in helping them succeed.

- ✔ **Become proficient in the tasks you have to perform.** People listen to you more seriously when they believe you know what you're talking about.

You must reestablish your bases of power for each new project you perform because you may be dealing with different people on each project and because your power bases depend heavily on the specific details of the project itself. Further, even on the same project, your bases of power can diminish over time if you don't consistently reinforce them. Meeting with team members at the start of your project can help them appreciate your style and recognize that everyone wants to accomplish similar goals. However, if you don't have any more contact with your team members for six months, their initial positive impressions can fade — right along with your ability to influence their commitment and performance.

You Can Do It! Creating and Sustaining Team Member Motivation

Efficient processes and smooth relationships create the opportunity for successful projects. And having team members personally commit to your project's success gives you the greatest chance of achieving it. Therefore, your major task as a project manager is to encourage every team member to be motivated and committed to your project's success.

Motivation is a personal choice — the only person you can motivate directly is yourself. You can create the *opportunity* for other people to become motivated, but you can't make the decision for them. The following factors encourage a person to become and remain motivated to achieve a goal:

- ✔ **Desirability:** The value of achieving the goal
- ✔ **Feasibility:** The likelihood that you can achieve the goal
- ✔ **Progress:** Your accomplishments as you work to reach your goal
- ✔ **Reward:** The payoff when you reach the goal

When your project meets people's professional and personal needs in each of these four areas, you strengthen their commitment to the project's success. In this section, I show you specific ways to meet these needs.

Increasing commitment by clarifying your project's benefits

Although some people commit to completing an assignment because someone tells them to do so, you get a much more serious commitment when a person recognizes and appreciates a project's benefits. When discussing your project's benefits with your team, consider those benefits that are most important to your organization, its employees, and its clients, such as

- ✔ Improved products and services
- ✔ Improved internal processes and procedures
- ✔ Increased sales
- ✔ Improved productivity
- ✔ Better work environment

Also consider potential benefits to each team member, such as

✔ Acquiring new skills and knowledge

✔ Working in an enjoyable environment

✔ Expanding business contacts

✔ Enhancing career potential

When you help people realize the personal benefits they can get from participating in your project, you increase their commitment to the project and, therefore, the chances that the project will succeed.

Occasionally, someone reminds me that his team members receive salaries for doing their jobs. In other words, this person is suggesting that he doesn't have to worry about whether his team members realize personal benefits from doing their assigned tasks. As far as he's concerned, people will perform their assignments because they want to receive their paychecks. Unfortunately, however, this type of reward power encourages people to do the least work necessary to ensure they receive their next paychecks rather than to work toward the highest-quality results.

I'm not suggesting your main concerns on a project are your team members' personal benefits. However, people are more committed if they feel they can accomplish their personal goals while helping their organization achieve its goals.

Do the following to help your team understand and appreciate the benefits your project can achieve for the organization:

✔ Identify the situation that led to your project.

✔ Identify your project's key drivers, and clarify their hopes for the project (see Chapter 3 for more about project drivers).

✔ Encourage team members to discuss the expected benefits and the value of those benefits.

Do the following to encourage your team members to identify the personal benefits they may realize from participating in your project:

✔ Discuss their personal interests and career goals, and relate those interests and goals to aspects of the project.

✔ Discuss past projects they've enjoyed and the reasons they've enjoyed them.

✔ Discuss some of the benefits that you and other people hope to realize by working on this project.

Encouraging persistence by demonstrating project feasibility

A project is *feasible* if it's possible to accomplish. No matter how desirable you may feel a project is, if you're convinced that nothing you do can lead to its success, you'll give up more easily when you encounter the slightest of difficulties (and so will your team members). You don't need a guarantee of success, but you must believe that you have a reasonable chance at it.

Feasibility is a subjective assessment. What seems impossible to one person can appear feasible to another. Further, your assessment of feasibility can become a self-fulfilling prophecy. If you think an assignment is feasible, you work hard to complete it; if you encounter problems, you try to work them out. However, if you really believe you have no chance of succeeding, you give up at the first sign of difficulty. Any problems you encounter just confirm what you already knew — the project was doomed from the start. Of course, as soon as you give up, you have no chance of succeeding, so you've confirmed your initial belief that the project wasn't feasible!

Help people believe a project is feasible by working with them to define what the team will produce, when, and how. Specifically, do the following:

✔ Involve team members in the planning process.

✔ Encourage them to identify potential concerns so you can address them.

✔ Explain why you feel that your targets and plans are feasible.

✔ Develop responsive risk-management plans (see Chapter 8).

Letting people know how they're doing

Getting your team members to appreciate your project's value and feasibility helps you motivate them initially. However, if the project lasts longer than a couple of weeks, the team's initial motivation can die out without continual reinforcement from you. In general, people working on a particular task need to know how they're doing over time for three reasons:

✔ Achieving intermediate milestones provides personal satisfaction.

✔ Recognizing their successes confirms they're on the right track.

✔ Successfully completing intermediate steps reinforces their belief that they can accomplish the final goals.

Have you ever seen a 12-month project in which all the major milestones occurred in months 11 and 12? When do you think people got serious about this project? Months 10, 11, and 12 (if they were still around by then)! Obviously, you want your team members to stay interested and motivated throughout the life of your project, not just at its climax. Do the following to help keep people on track and excited about your project:

- ✔ Establish meaningful and frequent intermediate milestones.

- ✔ Continually assess how people are doing.

- ✔ Frequently share information with people about their performance.

- ✔ Continually reinforce the project's potential benefits.

See Chapter 13 for ways to inform people of your project's progress.

Providing rewards for work well done

Rewarding people at a project's conclusion for their effort and accomplishments confirms to them that they accomplished the desired results and met the audience's needs. It also reassures them that team members and managers recognize and appreciate their contributions. This recognition, in turn, makes it more likely that they'll welcome the opportunity to participate in future projects.

Post-project rewards can take several forms, including the following:

- ✔ You talk with the person and express your appreciation for her help.

- ✔ You express your appreciation in a written note or e-mail to the person.

- ✔ You express your appreciation in writing to the person's supervisor.

- ✔ You formally submit input to the person's performance appraisal.

- ✔ You nominate the person for a future assignment she particularly wants.

- ✔ You nominate the person for a cash award.

- ✔ You issue the person a certificate of appreciation.

- ✔ You take the person out to lunch.

Rather than guessing which form of reward your team members will appreciate most, ask each of them directly.

To make the rewards you offer the most effective, do the following:

✔ Be sure your acknowledgment and appreciation is honest and sincere.

✔ Note the specific contribution the reward recognizes.

✔ Respect the person's personal style and preferences when giving the reward:

• Some people enjoy receiving acknowledgements in front of their coworkers, while others prefer receiving them in private.

• Some people appreciate receiving an individual award; others appreciate receiving an award presented to the entire team.

Relating This Chapter to the PMP Exam and PMBOK 4

Table 14-2 notes topics in this chapter that may be addressed on the Project Management Professional (PMP) certification exam and that are also included in *A Guide to the Project Management Body of Knowledge,* 4th Edition (*PMBOK 4*).

Table 14-2	Chapter 14 Topics in Relation to the PMP Exam and *PMBOK 4*	
Topic	*Location in PMBOK 4*	*Comments*
Distinctions between leading and managing (see the section "Comparing Leadership and Management")	9.4.2.5. Interpersonal Skills G.1. Leadership	The discussion of leadership and management in *PMBOK 4* is very brief and limited to noting the names of different leadership and management skills and techniques.
Power, influence, and motivation (see the sections "Developing Personal Power and Influence" and "You Can Do It! Creating and Sustaining Team Member Motivation")	G.1. Leadership	The discussion of interpersonal skills in *PMBOK 4* is also very brief and limited to noting the names of different interpersonal skills and techniques.

Chapter 15

Bringing Your Project to Closure

. . . .

. . . .

*O*ne characteristic that distinguishes a project from other work assignments is its distinct end — the point at which all work is complete and the results are achieved. However, with intense demands pulling you to your next assignment, you may be compelled to let your completed projects languish and eventually fade away instead of clearly ending them with an announcement, recognition of the results, and a thank-you to all the people who made them possible.

Unfortunately, not bringing your projects to full closure hurts both the organization and the people who performed the work. When you don't assess the extent to which your project achieved the desired outcomes, you can't determine whether you conceived, planned, and performed the project well. Furthermore, team members don't have the chance to experience closure, achievement, and a job well done.

This chapter shows you how to close your project successfully by finishing all substantive work, performing the final administrative tasks, and helping team members complete their association with your project and move on. In addition, this chapter helps you announce your project's end and conduct a post-project evaluation.

 As discussed in Chapter 1, very large projects are often subdivided into phases and each phase is treated as a separate miniproject. The discussions in this chapter apply to closing project phases, as well as to closing the entire project.

Staying the Course to Completion

Following your project all the way through to completion helps ensure that everyone gets the maximum benefits from your project's results. It also allows you to determine all these benefits and compare them with the costs incurred, confirm the company's return on investment, and validate its process for selecting projects.

Bringing a project to an end typically entails wrapping up a multitude of small details and open issues. Dealing with these numerous assignments can be frustrating under the best of circumstances. However, the following situations can make the end of a project even more difficult:

✔ You don't have a detailed, written list of all the activities you must perform during closeout.

✔ Some team members transferred to new assignments during your project's course, forcing the remaining members to assume new responsibilities in addition to their original ones.

✔ The project staff loses motivation as general interest in the project wanes and people look forward to new assignments.

✔ The project staff wants the project to continue because they don't want to end the personal and professional relationships they've developed or they're not excited about their next assignments.

✔ Your customers (internal and/or external) aren't overly interested in completing the final details of the project.

Reduce the impact of difficult situations like these and increase the chances for your project's success by planning for closure at the outset of your project, identifying and attending to all closure details and tasks, and refocusing your team. This section shows you how to do so (and more).

Planning ahead for your project's closure

If you wait until the end of your project to start thinking in detail about its closure, it may be too late to gather all the necessary information and resources. Instead, start planning for your project's completion at the same time that you prepare your initial project plan by doing the following (see Chapter 1 for information on what goes into the project plan):

✔ **Describe your project objectives completely and clearly, and identify all relevant objective measures and specifications.** If one of the project objectives is to change an existing situation, describe that situation before you begin your project so you have a comparative basis for assessment at the end of your project.

✔ **Prepare a checklist of everything you must do before you can officially close your project.** Here are some examples of closure items to include on your checklist:

- Complete any unfinished project activities.

- Complete all required deliverables.

- Obtain all necessary acceptances and approvals of project results, including those of the client(s).

- Assess the extent to which project results met expectations.

- Perform all required administrative tasks.

- Terminate all related contracts for goods and services.

- Transition team members to their new assignments.

- Ensure that all project documentation and deliverables are archived in the appropriate storage locations.

For each item on the project-closure checklist, specify who will perform it, when it will be done, and what resources will be required.

✔ **Include closure activities in your project plan.** In your project's Work Breakdown Structure (WBS), specify all activities you'll have to perform to close out your project, and then plan for sufficient time and resources to perform them (see Chapter 4 for more on this tool).

Updating your initial closure plans when you're ready to wind down the project

Encourage your team members to consider the closing the project stage of your project to be a separate assignment with its own objectives, tasks, and resource requirements (see Chapter 1 for more on the closing the project stage of your project). As you complete the main project's work, review and update the preliminary closure plans you developed in your initial project plan (see the preceding section for details on these preliminary plans).

Charging up your team for the sprint to the finish line

As team members work hard to fulfill project obligations, their focus often shifts from accomplishing the project's overall objectives to completing their individual assignments. In addition, other audiences who were initially very interested in the project's results may become involved with other priorities and activities as the project continues (which means they likely lose interest and enthusiasm for your project). Yet, successful project completion requires a coordinated effort by all key participants.

To reinforce your team's focus and interest, do the following:

✔ **Remind people of the value and importance of the project's final results.** Frequently discuss the benefits the organization will realize from your project's final results as well as the individual benefits your team members will gain. People are more likely to work hard to successfully complete a project when they realize the benefits they'll achieve by doing so.

✔ **Call your team together, and reaffirm your mutual commitment to bring the project to successful completion.** Discuss why you feel the project is important, and describe your personal commitment to completing it successfully. Encourage other people to make similar commitments. People overcome obstacles and perform difficult assignments more effectively when they're committed to succeed.

✔ **Monitor final activities closely, and give frequent feedback on performance to each team member.** Set up frequent milestones and progress-reporting times with team members. Staying in close touch with team members provides you and them up-to-date info on how close you are to final closure; it also provides the opportunity to identify and deal with any issues and problems that may arise throughout the course of your project.

✔ **Be accessible to all team members.** Make yourself available when team members want to confer with you. Consider having lunch periodically with them and letting them see you around their office area. Being accessible affirms your interest in and the importance of their work.

Handling Administrative Issues

Just as you must have authorization for people to legally spend time, effort, and resources to perform work on your project, you must rescind this authorization when you close the project to ensure that people won't continue to spend time, effort, or resources on it in the future. You can officially terminate this authorization by doing the following:

✔ **Obtain all required approvals.** Obtain written approval that your project has passed all performance tests and adhered to applicable standards and certifications. In addition, be sure you've obtained customer or client acceptances. This step confirms that no additional work is necessary on the project.

✔ **Reconcile any outstanding transactions.** If you've made project purchases from outside sources, resolve any disputes with vendors and suppliers, pay all outstanding bills, and make sure the contracts are officially closed. Make sure you adjust any project work effort or expenditures that were posted to incorrect accounts.

✔ **Close out all charge categories.** Get official confirmation that no future labor or financial charges can be made to your project accounts.

Providing a Good Transition for Team Members

As part of successfully finishing your own project, you need to help project team members complete their project responsibilities and move on to their next assignments. Handling this transition in an orderly and agreed-upon fashion allows people to focus their energies on completing their tasks on your project instead of wondering where and when their next assignments will be. In particular, do the following:

✔ **Acknowledge and document team members' contributions.** Express your appreciation to people for their assistance on your project, and share with them your assessment of their performance. Take a moment to thank their supervisors for making them available to your project, and provide the supervisors with an assessment of their performance.

As a general rule, share positive feedback in public; share constructive criticisms and suggestions for improvement in private. In both cases, be sure to share your comments with team members personally and follow up your conversation in writing.

✔ **Help people plan for their transition to new assignments.** If appropriate, help people find their next project assignments. Help them develop a schedule for winding down their involvement with your project while making sure they fulfill all their remaining obligations. Consider holding a final project meeting or lunch to provide your team members closure on their work and project relationships.

✔ **Announce to the organization that your project is complete.** You can make this announcement in an e-mail, in an announcement on the company intranet, in a meeting, or through an organization-wide publication, such as a newsletter. You need to make this announcement for the following three reasons:

- To alert people in your organization that the planned outcomes of your project are now available

- To confirm to people who supported your project that their efforts led to a successful result

- To let people know they can no longer charge time or resources to your project

✔ **Take a moment to let team members and others who supported your project know the true results of the time and work they invested.** Nothing can give your team members stronger motivation to jump into the next assignment and provide continued high-quality support than telling them about the positive results of their previous work.

See the sidebar "Using a novel approach to announce your project's closure" to see one person's unusual way to let people know his project was over.

Using a novel approach to announce your project's closure

If your project was small, chances are all the participants already know it's over and are aware of its results. But if the project took a long time (six months or more) and involved many groups in your organization, people who participated early may never see the actual results of their efforts.

A while back, a client of mine had just completed a one-year project that entailed the design, development, production, and introduction of a small piece of equipment for an aircraft cockpit. At the official end of his project, he reflected on the many different people from all areas of his organization who had played some role in the project. In addition to the engineers who completed the final installation and testing of the equipment, contract officers, procurement specialists, financial managers, human resources specialists, test lab personnel, logisticians, and others had all helped make the project a success.

He realized that, if past experience was any indicator, the vast majority of these support people would never see the final result of their efforts. So he decided to do something that his organization had never done; he put together a small display in his workplace that illustrated the birth, evolution, and fruition of his project. He included everything from the signed contract document and purchase orders to the initial design model and engineering drawings to pictures of the device in an airplane, a pilot who would use it, as well as the maintenance people who would support it. He then sent messages to all the people who had worked on the project, announcing the display and inviting them to come by his workplace to visit.

The response was overwhelming. He estimated that more than 100 people came by to look at the display. He overheard comments by people throughout the organization about how they'd performed individual tasks large and small that contributed to the success of this equipment — equipment that they now could see would affect people's lives. The most poignant comment he received was from a technician who worked in the test laboratory. The technician told him this was the first time in his 11 years with the organization that he'd ever seen the final results of an item he'd tested.

My client estimated that he spent several hours assembling the display. But the positive results he and his organization received from this sharing were immeasurable.

Surveying the Results: The Post-Project Evaluation

Lay the groundwork for repeating on future projects what worked on past ones (and avoiding what didn't) by conducting a post-project evaluation.

A *post-project evaluation* (also called a *post-project review* or *lessons learned*) is an assessment of project results, activities, and processes that allows you to

- ✔ Recognize project achievements and acknowledge people's work.
- ✔ Identify techniques and approaches that worked, and devise steps to ensure they're used in the future.
- ✔ Identify techniques and approaches that didn't work, and devise steps to ensure they aren't used again in the future.

A *project postmortem* is another term for post-project evaluation. I avoid using this term, however, because it conjures up the image of an autopsy to determine the cause of death! I prefer to leave people with a more positive memory of their experience with a project.

This section helps you plan for, conduct, and follow up on a post-project evaluation.

Preparing for the evaluation throughout the project

Take steps in each stage of your project's evolution (starting the project, organizing and preparing, carrying out the work, and closing the project) to lay the groundwork for your post-project evaluation (see Chapter 1 for more on the four states of a project):

- ✔ **Starting the project:**
  - Determine the benefits your project's *drivers* wanted to realize when they authorized your project. (See Chapter 3 for a discussion of drivers and the other types of project audiences.)
  - If your project is designed to change an existing situation, take *before* measures to describe the existing situation so that you have something to compare to the *after* measures you take when the project is completed.

✔ **Organizing and preparing:**

- Identify additional project drivers you may have overlooked in the first stage of your project. Your project drivers' expectations serve as the criteria for defining your project's success, so you want to know who they all are before you begin your project's work.

- Develop clear and detailed descriptions of all project objectives.

- Include the activity *Conduct a post-project evaluation* in your Work Breakdown Structure (WBS), and allow time and resources to perform it. (See Chapter 4 for a discussion of the WBS.)

✔ **Carrying out the work:**

- Tell team members that the project will have a post-project evaluation.

- Encourage team members to record issues, problems, and successes throughout their project involvement in a handwritten or computerized project log. Review the log when proposing topics for discussion at the post-project evaluation meeting.

- Maintain files of cost, labor-hour charges, and schedule performance reports throughout the project. (See Chapter 12 for details on how to track and report this information.)

✔ **Closing the project:**

- If changing an existing situation was a project objective, take *after* measures of that situation's key characteristics to see whether you successfully met that objective.

- Obtain final cost, labor-hour, and schedule performance reports for the project.

- Survey key stakeholders to determine how well they feel the project addressed their needs and their assessments of project team and project manager performance.

Setting the stage for the evaluation meeting

A post-project evaluation is only as good as the results, expenditures, and performance information it's based on. The information must be complete, detailed, and accurate. Prepare for your post-project evaluation meeting by collecting information on the following:

✔ Project results

✔ Schedule performance

- Resource expenditures
- Problems that arose during the project
- Changes during the project in objectives, schedules, and budgets
- Unanticipated occurrences or changes in the environment during the project
- Customers' satisfaction with the project results
- Management's satisfaction with the project results
- Effectiveness of the project-management processes
- Lessons learned

You can collect this information from the following sources:

- Progress reports
- Project logs
- Cost reports
- Schedule reports
- Project memos, correspondence, and meeting minutes
- Interviews and surveys of customers, managers, and team members

Prepare a detailed agenda for the post-project evaluation meeting that specifies the times when topic discussions will start and end. Consider including the following topics on your agenda:

- Statement of the meeting's purpose
- Specific meeting outcomes to be accomplished
- Highlights of project performance, including the following:
    - Results, schedules, and resources
    - Approaches to project planning
    - Project-tracking systems and procedures
    - Project communications
    - Project team practices and effectiveness
- Recognition and discussion of special achievements
- Review of customer and management reactions to the project
- Discussion of problems and issues
- Discussion of how to reflect experiences from this project in future efforts

Circulate a draft agenda, related background materials, and a list of attendees to all expected attendees at least one week before the meeting. This advance notice gives people time to suggest additions, deletions, and changes to the agenda. Revise the agenda to address these suggestions, and distribute the final agenda to all meeting participants at least one day before the meeting.

Conducting the evaluation meeting

A successful post-project evaluation meeting (which you can hold in person, via video conference, or through most other meeting methods) requires that you address the right topics and that people share their project thoughts and experiences openly and honestly.

At the post-project evaluation meeting, explore the following issues:

✔ Did you accomplish all the project objectives?

✔ Did you meet the project schedule?

✔ Did you complete the project within budget?

✔ With regard to problems during the project

- Could you have anticipated and planned for them in advance? If so, how?

- Did you handle them effectively and efficiently when they arose?

✔ Did you use the organization's project-management systems and procedures effectively?

To ensure you get the most accurate information and the best recommendations for future actions, do the following before and during your post-project evaluation meeting:

✔ **Invite the right people.** Invite all the people who participated in your project at all points throughout its life. If the list of potential invitees is too long, consider meeting separately with select subgroups and then holding a general session at which everyone reviews the results of the smaller meetings and you solicit final comments and suggestions.

✔ **Declare at the beginning of the meeting that it's supposed to be a learning experience rather than a finger-pointing session.** As the project manager, you run the post-project evaluation meeting. At its outset, you need to declare that the session is a time for self-examination and suggestions for ensuring the success of future projects. If people start to attack or criticize other participants, you can immediately bring the discussion back on track by asking the participants the following questions:

- What can you do in the future to deal more effectively with such situations?

- What can you do in the future to head off such situations?

If people resist your attempts to redirect their conversations, you can mention actions that you, as project manager, can take in the future to head off or deal with similar situations more effectively and then ask people to share additional ideas.

✔ **Encourage people to**

- Identify what other people did well.

- Examine their own performance and see how they could've handled situations differently.

✔ **Consider holding the session away from your office.** People often feel more comfortable critiquing existing practices and discussing new approaches when they're away from their normal work environments.

Be sure to assign a person to take notes during the post-project evaluation meeting. In addition to a list of attendees and highlights of information, the notes should list all the agreed-on activities to implement the lessons learned from the meeting and the people responsible for those activities.

Following up on the evaluation

Often your busy schedule pulls you to new projects before you've had a chance to analyze and benefit from previous ones. However, even when people do take a few moments to review previous project experiences, they seldom incorporate the lessons learned in their future operating practices.

As soon as possible after your post-project evaluation meeting, you, as project manager, need to prepare and distribute a report that's based on the meeting minutes and that addresses the following topics:

✔ Practices to incorporate in future projects

✔ Steps to take to encourage these practices

✔ Practices to avoid in future projects

✔ Steps to take to discourage these practices

Consider this wrap-up report as you plan future projects to make sure you apply the lessons you learned.

Relating This Chapter to the PMP Exam and PMBOK 4

Table 15-1 notes topics in this chapter that may be addressed on the Project Management Professional (PMP) certification exam and that are also included in *A Guide to the Project Management Body of Knowledge,* 4th Edition (*PMBOK 4*).

Table 15-1	Chapter 15 Topics in Relation to the PMP Exam and *PMBOK 4*	
Topic	*Location in PMBOK 4*	*Comments*
Activities performed when closing a project (see the sections "Staying the Course to Completion" and "Handling Administrative Issues")	3.7. Closing Process Group 4.6. Close Project or Phase	Both sources identify similar activities.
Issues addressed in a post-project evaluation (see the section "Surveying the Results: The Post-Project Evaluation")	4.6.3.2. Organizational Process Assets Updates 8.3.3.4. Organizational Process Assets Updates 10.3.3.1. Organizational Process Assets Updates 12.4.3.2. Organizational Process Assets Updates	Both sources identify similar issues.
Providing a transition for your team (see the section "Providing a Good Transition for Team Members")	9.1.3.1. Human Resources Plan	*PMBOK 4* states the importance of planning for a smooth release of project team members.

Part V

Taking Your Project Management to the Next Level

"For a more aggressive approach, we have our 'Or Else' series of motivational posters."

In this part . . .

You become a truly skilled project manager by continuing to increase your knowledge and refine your practices and by effectively using tools and resources from start to finish. Lucky for you, this part is here to help you do just that.

In this part, I suggest ways to use new technologies and, just as important, ways to avoid some of their pitfalls. I also walk you through an advanced method for assessing project schedule and cost performances that can provide early warning signs of potential problems on larger projects.

Chapter 16

Using Technology to Up Your Game

In This Chapter

▶ Recognizing software's role in project planning and control

▶ Sizing up the benefits and limitations of e-mail

▶ Using technology to support virtual teams

A major part of project management is information — getting it, storing it, analyzing it, and sharing it. But the key to successful project management is using this information to guide and encourage people's performance.

Today's technology provides easier and more affordable ways to handle information. For example, computer software allows you to enter, store, and analyze information and then present the results in professional formats. E-mail allows written communication with people in remote locations at all hours of the day (and night!).

Even with all these advances, however, technology alone can't ensure focused and committed team performance. In fact, excessive reliance on today's technology can actually result in poor morale, confused and disorganized team members, and lower overall performance.

In this chapter, I suggest how you can use technology in jobs that work well with it. For the jobs that aren't so well-suited for technology, I discuss other, more appropriate means for handling people's information needs.

Using Computer Software Effectively

Today's software for special analyses and reporting looks so good that you may be tempted to believe it's all you need to ensure your project's success. However, even though the software works effectively and efficiently, it *can't* perform the following essential tasks:

✔ **Ensure that information is appropriately defined, timely, and accurate.** In most instances, people record information to support project planning and control, and then they enter the info into a computer. You can program the software to check for correctness of format or internal consistency, but the software can't ensure the quality and integrity of the data.

Suppose you use a computer program to maintain records of labor hours that team members charge to your project. You can program the computer to reject hours that are inadvertently charged with an invalid project code. However, you can't program the computer to recognize hours charged to the wrong project with a valid code.

✔ **Make decisions.** Software can help you objectively determine the results of several possible courses of action. However, software can't effectively take into account all the objective and subjective considerations that you must weigh before making a final decision.

✔ **Create and sustain dynamic interpersonal relationships.** Despite people's fascination with chat rooms, e-mail, and other types of computer-aided communication, computers don't foster close, trusting relationships between people. If anything, technology makes relationships more difficult to develop because it removes your ability to see facial expressions and body language.

So how *can* computer software help you during the life of a project? This section looks at what different types of software are available, how software can help you manage your project, and how to introduce software into your work environment.

Looking at your software options

When your project is sufficiently complex, you can use software for a wide variety of tasks, including storing and retrieving important information, analyzing and updating that information, and preparing presentations and reports that describe the information and results of the analyses.

The available software falls into two categories: stand-alone specialty software and integrated project-management software. Each type has benefits and drawbacks, as I discuss in the following sections.

Stand-alone specialty software

Stand-alone specialty software consists of separate packages that perform one or two functions very well. The following types of specialized software can support your project planning and performance:

✔ **Word processing:** Useful for preparing the narrative portions of project plans, maintaining a project log, creating progress reports, and preparing written project communications (Microsoft Office Word, for example)

✔ **Business graphics and presentation:** Useful for preparing overheads and slide shows for project presentations and developing charts and artwork for written reports and publications (Microsoft Office PowerPoint, for example)

✔ **Spreadsheet:** Useful for storing moderate amounts of data, performing repetitive calculations, running statistical analyses, and presenting information in chart formats (Microsoft Office Excel, for example)

✔ **Database:** Useful for storing and retrieving large amounts of data for analysis and presentation (Microsoft Office Access, for example)

✔ **Accounting:** Useful for keeping records of project income and expenses and producing a variety of descriptive and comparative reports (Intuit QuickBooks, for example)

✔ **Time and information management:** Useful for scheduling your calendar, maintaining a to-do list, keeping your address book, and managing your e-mail activities (Microsoft Office Outlook, for example)

Note: Many manufacturers offer software packages in the preceding categories. However, because so many of the organizations I've worked with use Microsoft software, I've noted examples of Microsoft software packages in the different categories. You may have heard of them before, and, if you don't have them already, you can easily install them on your computer.

Initially, specialty packages performed one or two functions very well. As they've evolved, however, they've expanded to include capabilities that support their primary functions. For example,

✔ Word-processing packages now possess some spreadsheet, business-graphics, and database capabilities.

✔ Spreadsheet packages now have some business-graphics and word-processing capabilities.

✔ Database packages now have some spreadsheet and word-processing capabilities.

In general, specialty packages offer the following benefits:

✔ **They offer powerful capabilities in their areas of specialty.** For example, a business-graphics-and-presentation package makes it relatively easy to prepare professional-quality presentations that effectively share information and stimulate your audience's interest.

✔ **You most likely have several packages already on your computer.** Having these packages already available means you can use them immediately for no additional cost.

✔ **People probably know how to use many of the common specialty packages.** As a result, people are more apt to use them and use them correctly. Also, you save time and money because people don't require special training to use them.

Keep in mind that these packages have the following potential drawbacks:

✔ **They're likely to encourage piecemeal approaches to project planning and control, which may omit certain key steps.** You can use a business-graphics package to draw a Gantt chart (see Chapter 5). However, ensuring that your schedule is feasible requires you to consider the effect of activity interdependencies when you prepare it. A business-graphics package can't perform that function for you.

✔ **They don't integrate easily.** For example, you can depict your project's schedule in a Gantt chart in a graphics package and display personnel hours over the duration of each task in a spreadsheet. However, if a team member is unexpectedly out for a week, you have to make separate changes by revising the person's hours in the spreadsheet and then changing the Gantt chart in the graphics package to reflect new activity start and end dates. Even though some programs can share data directly with other programs, this process is often cumbersome.

Integrated project-management software

Integrated project-management software combines database, spreadsheet, graphics, and word-processing capabilities to support many of the activities normally associated with planning and performing your project. An example of an integrated package is Microsoft Office Project, although hundreds of such packages of all shapes and sizes are on the market today.

A typical integrated project-management package allows you to

✔ Create a hierarchical list of activities and their components.

✔ Define and store key information about your project, activities, and resources.

✔ Define activity interdependencies (see Chapter 5 for more information on activity interdependencies).

✔ Develop schedules by considering activity durations, activity interdependencies, and resource requirements and availability.

✔ Display your plan for performing project activities in a network diagram (see Chapter 5).

✔ Display a schedule in Gantt-chart and table formats (see Chapter 5).

✔ Assign people to work on project activities for specific levels of effort at certain times.

✔ Schedule other resources for project activities at specified times.

✔ Determine your overall project budget (see Chapter 7 for how to prepare project budgets).

✔ Determine the effect of changes on the project's schedule and resources.

✔ Monitor activity start and end dates and milestone dates.

✔ Monitor person-hours and resource costs.

✔ Present planning and tracking information in a wide array of graphs and tables.

As you may have guessed, integrated project-management packages offer benefits as well as drawbacks. The benefits include the following:

✔ **The package's functions are linked.** For example, if you enter personnel requirements one time, the program considers them when developing schedule and resource budgets and when reporting project progress.

✔ **Packages typically have a variety of predesigned report templates.** Having predesigned report templates allows you to use formats that are proven to be effective. It also saves you time and money when preparing and distributing your reports.

Integrated project-management packages also have their drawbacks:

✔ **The package may not be immediately available.** If it isn't currently available, you have to devote time and money to buy and install the software before you can use it to support project planning and control.

✔ **Most people require training to become comfortable with the package.** Training takes additional time and money.

✔ **Having a wide range of capabilities in a software package doesn't guarantee that you'll use them correctly.** Remember the old adage: Garbage in, garbage out. Even the most advanced software package can't help your project if people don't submit accurate and timely data.

If you decide to use an integrated project-management package, consider the following factors when choosing your program:

✔ **Types and formats of reports:** Choose a package that supports your reports and means of reporting with minimum customization.

✔ **Your team members' general comfort and familiarity with computers and software:** Will they take the time and effort to learn and then use the package? Having a package with state-of-the-art analysis and reporting capabilities is no help if people don't know how to use it.

✔ **Your organization's present software:** If several software packages are equal in most aspects, choose a package that's already available and in use because team members most likely have experience with it.

✔ **Your organization's existing systems to record labor hours and expenses:** If your organization has such systems, consider a package that can easily interface with them. If the organization doesn't have these systems, consider a package that can store the information you need.

✔ **The project environment in your organization:** What's the size of the human-resource pool for projects, the number and typical size of projects, and so on? Choose a package that has the necessary capacity and speed.

✔ **Software used by clients and companies you work with:** Choosing a package that allows you to communicate and coordinate easily with your customers' and collaborators' software saves you time and money.

Check out *Microsoft Office Project 2007 For Dummies* by Nancy C. Muir (Wiley) for more information on effectively using this software's capability.

Helping your software perform at its best

No matter which type of project-management software you choose (either stand-alone specialty software or integrated project-management software), your project's success depends on how well you coordinate and support your project planning and control activities. Table 16-1 illustrates the activities that software can support, the types of software that can provide the support, and how you can ensure that the activity is performed correctly.

Project-Portfolio Management software: Raising the bar on project management

Most integrated project-management software packages support the planning, tracking, and reporting of an individual project. Project-Portfolio Management software, however, is special because it also

✔ Supports the assigning and tracking of people to activities on more than one project

✔ Takes into account interproject activity dependencies when determining different schedule possibilities

✔ Tracks and reports the progress and accomplishments of numerous projects simultaneously

✔ Supports communication throughout the organization regarding the planning and performance of different projects

Consider using Project-Portfolio Management software to support project planning and control when your organization meets these criteria:

✔ It has several large, cross-departmental projects underway.

✔ It staffs these projects from a common resource pool.

✔ It has well-established project-management and data-collection practices and procedures.

Table 16-1		Helping Your Software Support You
Software Capability	*Software to Use**	*Your Responsibilities*
Document project objectives (see Chapter 2)	WP, IPMS	Ensure all project objectives have measures and performance targets; ensure key people approve the objectives.
Keep a record of project audiences (see Chapter 3)	WP, IPMS, S, TIM	Identify the audiences.
Store and display the project Work Breakdown Structure (see Chapter 4)	WP, S, BG, DB, IPMS	Identify all required activities.
Display team roles and responsibilities (see Chapter 10)	WP, S, BG, IPMS	Have people agree and commit to their roles and responsibilities.
Develop possible schedules (see Chapter 5)	IPMS	Ensure duration estimates are accurate; determine all interdependencies; ensure that project drivers and supporters buy into the schedules.
Display schedule possibilities	WP, S, BG, IPMS, TIM	Choose actual schedule dates from among the possibilities.
Display the personnel needed and their required levels of effort (see Chapter 6)	WP, S, BG, IPMS	Determine personnel needs; estimate people's required levels of effort.
Display planned personnel allocations over time	S, BG, IPMS	Choose when people will spend their hours (over time) on task assignments; decide how to deal with resource conflicts.
Display funds and other nonpersonnel budgets (see Chapter 7)	S, BG, IPMS	Determine budgets; explain budgets to project team members.
Keep records of actual activity and milestone dates	S, IPMS, TIM	Develop procedures for collecting and submitting schedule-performance data (see Chapter 12); ensure people submit data on time.

(continued)

Table 16-1 *(continued)*

Software Capability	Software to Use*	Your Responsibilities
Keep records of work-hours charged to the project	S, IPMS, TIM	Create charge codes; develop procedures for recording and submitting work-hour data; ensure work-hours are charged to the correct accounts; ensure data are submitted and entered on time.
Keep records of funds, commitments, and expenditures	S, DB, A, IPMS	Create the charge codes; ensure expenditures are charged to the correct accounts; ensure data are submitted and entered on time.
Prepare reports of schedule and resource performance (see Chapter 13)	WP, A, S, IPMS	Define report formats and timetables; select people to receive reports; interpret the reports; ensure that people read the reports they receive; develop necessary corrective actions.
Prepare presentations of project progress	WP, S, BG, IPMS	Choose information to be included; select people to receive reports or attend the presentations.

The following abbreviations represent the different types of packages available: A: Accounting; BG: Business graphics; DB: Database; IPMS: Integrated project-management software; S: Spreadsheet; TIM: Time and information management; WP: Word processing.

Introducing project-management software into your operations

Before you rush out and buy any project-management software, plan how to maximize its capabilities and avoid associated pitfalls. Do the following to help you select and install your software:

- ✔ Be sure you have a firm grasp of project planning and control approaches before you consider any software.

- ✔ See what software other groups in your organization are using or have used; find out what they like, what they don't like, and why.

- ✔ If possible, ask someone who already has a copy of the software whether you can spend a few minutes exploring its operation.

- ✔ After the package is on your computer, load a simple project or a small part of a larger project to practice with (that is, enter the activities, durations, interdependencies, resources, and so on).

> ✔ Use only a few of the program's capabilities at first (determine the effect of small changes on your schedule, print out some simple reports, and so on); use more capabilities as you get more comfortable with the software and feel the need for them.
>
> ✔ Consider attending a formal training program after you've become comfortable accessing the software's different capabilities.

After you've undertaken these steps, you can effectively use software to support your project planning and control activities. On an ongoing basis, ensure that you obtain all updates and changes to the software, and consider purchasing software upgrades that introduce significant new capabilities.

Making Use of E-Mail

Before the advent of e-mail, people consistently told me that the two most common frustrations in their daily routine were unproductive meetings and playing telephone tag. Is it any wonder that people embraced e-mail as soon as it hit the workplace?

Because e-mail is so common, I don't devote too much time to it in this book. However, this section briefly looks at its pros and cons, its appropriate uses with your project team, and ways to use it to your advantage.

Distinguishing the pros and cons of e-mail

E-mail is a fast and convenient means of one-way, written communication. It has many desirable qualities when it comes to project management:

> ✔ **The sender and receiver don't have to be present at the time of communication.** You can write an e-mail message whenever you want, and your recipient can read it at his convenience.
>
> ✔ **The sender and receiver don't have to be in the same place.** You can send your message anywhere from Iowa to Tibet.
>
> ✔ **Your message is delivered quickly.** Relaying your message doesn't depend on delivery schedules, work-hours, or weather conditions.
>
> ✔ **E-mail serves as written documentation.** The receiver can read your message several times to clarify its meaning, and it serves as a reminder that you have shared the information.
>
> ✔ **You can store e-mail on computer hard disks, Zip disks, USB flash drives, CDs, or DVDs rather than in hard copy.** This capability saves you space and money and makes retrieval easier.

Reading between the lines of your e-mails

An old adage claims "It's not *what* you say — it's *how* you say it that counts." In face-to-face communication, people often pay more attention to the speaker's tone of voice, facial expressions, and body language than to his words. Because e-mail can't transmit nonverbal cues, people have developed a new vocabulary to share their nonverbal messages with their e-mail recipients. Unfortunately, incorrect use of this vocabulary can send the wrong message, creating misunderstandings and hard feelings.

A client once told me of a time he sent an e-mail to a coworker. To emphasize a particular message, he typed it in bold characters. But the recipient never responded and actually appeared to ignore him when they passed in the hallways. After several days, my client sought the person out and asked whether there was a problem. The coworker said he was upset and insulted that my client had yelled at him in his e-mail. My client expressed complete surprise and confusion and asked how an e-mail could suggest a person was yelling. Apparently, some people equate boldface typing to yelling. Fortunately, my client was able to discover the misunderstanding and correct it. But it makes you wonder how often such misunderstandings go unnoticed and unaddressed!

Unfortunately, e-mail also has the following drawbacks:

✔ **People may not read it.** I often meet people who receive 50 to 100 e-mails each day! They readily admit to scanning the first few lines to decide whether a message is worth reading. Some people just read the sender's name to decide whether to read any further.

✔ **The medium doesn't provide real-time interaction between sender and receiver.** The receiver may have difficulty correctly interpreting the message because she can't quickly ask questions, check inferences, or ask you to paraphrase the message. You can try to clarify any issues through subsequent e-mails, but people often lose interest in the process.

✔ **Communication is limited to the exchange of words.** The sender's nonverbal cues (such as facial expressions, body language, and tone of voice) are lost.

✔ **Readers can often misinterpret the content or intent.** E-mail has a growing dictionary of meanings associated with different modes of expression. (For an example, check out the nearby sidebar, "Reading between the lines of your e-mails.") Unfortunately, when people's e-mail recipients pick up these meanings informally, the e-mails may convey the wrong messages.

Using e-mail appropriately

E-mail can be an effective component of a comprehensive communication system for your project team. For example, you can use e-mail to confirm oral discussions and agreements. In these instances, you want a written message to stand on its own with no interactive discussion or explanation. If a recipient needs to ask questions, the written message hasn't documented the information clearly and accurately.

You can also use e-mail to share factual information that requires little or no clarification. Write simple messages using straightforward language. Tell recipients how they can reach you if they have any questions.

Take note that e-mail *can't* be the exclusive means of communication to do any of the following tasks:

✔ **Brainstorm to analyze problems and develop new ideas.** Use e-mail to announce the brainstorming session, invite people to attend, identify the topic(s) you'll explore, and provide relevant background material for people to review before the session. Use e-mail to share a summary of the results and future actions. But conduct the actual interchange of ideas in a face-to-face session.

✔ **Build and sustain team members' trust and commitment.** Even though you use e-mail to inform team members of each other's background and experience, commitments, and accomplishments, be sure you provide sufficient opportunities for face-to-face meetings so team members become familiar and comfortable with each other.

✔ **Share an important message.** Perhaps you can share the message initially through e-mail, but follow up with phone calls and in-person meetings to emphasize its importance and ensure that your recipients have correctly understood its content.

Getting the most out of your e-mail

When used correctly, e-mail can be a valuable tool for clear, timely, convenient, and inexpensive communications. Do the following to get the most from your team e-mail communications:

✔ **Be concise.** Use clear, measurable words, and avoid technical jargon and acronyms when possible.

✔ **Read your e-mail before you send it.** People's impressions of you, your ideas, and your attitude are strongly affected by what you say and how you say it. Take a moment to proof your e-mail message before you hit *Send.* Make sure you've made no typos.

✔ **Anticipate miscommunications.** Put yourself in your audience's shoes. How might they misinterpret your message? What additional information might they want to have? Have you been clear about how you want them to respond to your message? In other words, minimize the need for extra e-mails back and forth to raise questions and clarify points by writing one, well-thought-out e-mail.

✔ **Be sure people have received it.** If possible, program your system to let you know automatically when your audience has opened your e-mail. Otherwise, ask the receiver to verify that he's received the message via a return e-mail, a phone call, or a quick face-to-face conversation.

✔ **Keep a copy of important e-mails.** Maintain a file of important messages you've sent. I keep computerized records of all sent e-mails on an external hard drive, and I keep paper copies of especially important e-mails. These copies confirm the information, date, and recipients. (Chapter 13 has more on communicating with your project audience.)

Supporting Virtual Teams with Communication Technology

The globalization of today's businesses creates a greater need for people around the world to work together on projects. This lack of proximity creates unique challenges for encouraging successful team performance. Lucky for you and me, today's technology can support the communication needs of these virtual teams.

A *virtual project team* is a group of people who work together across geographic, time, and organizational boundaries to accomplish a common set of goals and objectives. Although the needs of a virtual project team are the same as those of more conventional teams, many processes and resources used by conventional teams aren't available to the virtual team. Only through creative use of the communication technology available can virtual teams perform at peak capacity.

High-performance team members on both virtual and conventional teams must successfully accomplish the following tasks:

✔ Share project and team-related information in a timely and accurate manner.

✔ Create and sustain trusting and productive interpersonal relationships.

✔ Effectively collaborate to perform project work.

Each of these tasks requires effective and timely communication. But, as virtual teams approach these activities, they face these unique challenges:

- **Members may never meet each other in person.** Becoming familiar with and trusting each other is more difficult; the use of nonverbal signals and body language when communicating is severely limited.

- **Members may have different primary languages.** This challenge increases the chances that people may incorrectly interpret a message.

- **Members may come from different organizational and cultural environments.** People's work styles and communication practices may differ.

- **Members may be in different time zones.** People may not be available to interact with each other during certain time periods.

Today's communication technology can help you and your virtual team address these challenges (see Table 16-2 for specific ways that today's technology can support communications on a virtual team).

Table 16-2	Using Communication Technology to Support Virtual Teams	
Communication Need	**Approach**	**Application**
Share project-related information	E-mail	Sharing factual information; confirming and recording discussions and agreements
	Company intranet	Storing plans; entering, storing, and reporting on progress data; storing project-management forms and procedures
	Videoconferencing	Discussing and clarifying issues
Support interpersonal relationships	Videoconferencing	Introducing new team members; acknowledging team and individual accomplishments
Collaborate on project activities	Interactive Web conferencing	Discussing technical topics; brainstorming
	Videoconferencing	Discussing technical topics; brainstorming
	E-mail	Sharing data and reports

Available communication technology can address a wide range of the virtual team's routine communication needs. When possible, however, people should meet in person to periodically reinforce their relationships and the team's focus and identity.

Relating This Chapter to the PMP Exam and PMBOK 4

Table 16-3 notes topics in this chapter that may be addressed on the Project Management Professional (PMP) certification exam and that are included in *A Guide to the Project Management Body of Knowledge,* 4th Edition (*PMBOK 4*).

Table 16-3	Chapter 16 Topics in Relation to the PMP Exam and *PMBOK 4*	
Topic	*Location in PMBOK 4*	*Comments*
How different types of software can support your project (see the section "Using Computer Software Effectively")	6.3.2.5. Project Management Software	None.
How new resources can support virtual teams (see the section "Supporting Virtual Teams with Communication Technology")	9.2.2.4. Virtual Teams	None.

Chapter 17

Monitoring Project Performance with Earned Value Management

*B*ecause you're reading this chapter, I assume you're looking for a way to assess your ongoing project performance. *Earned Value Management* (EVM), formerly called *Earned Value Analysis* (EVA), is a technique that helps determine your project's schedule status and cost status from your resource expenditures alone. EVM is particularly useful for identifying potential problems on larger projects.

To get the most from this chapter, you need to have some prior experience or knowledge in project management. This chapter helps you better understand EVM by defining it, discussing how to determine and interpret variances, and showing you how to use it in your project.

Defining Earned Value Management

Monitoring your project's performance involves determining whether you're on, ahead of, or behind schedule and on, under, or over budget. But just comparing your actual expenditures with your budget can't tell you whether you're on, under, or over budget — which is where EVM comes in. In this section, I explain the basics of EVM and the steps involved in conducting an EVM analysis to determine your project's schedule and cost performance.

Understanding EVM terms and formulas

Suppose you're three months into your project and you've spent $50,000. According to your plan, you shouldn't have spent $50,000 until the end of the fourth month of your project. You appear to be over budget at this point, but you can't tell for sure. Either of the following situations may have produced these results:

✔ You may have performed all the scheduled work but paid more than you expected to for it — which means you're on schedule but over budget (not a good situation).

✔ You may have performed more work than you scheduled but paid exactly what you expected to for it — which means you're on budget and ahead of schedule (a good situation).

In fact, many other situations may also have produced these same results, but you probably don't have the time or the motivation to go through each possible situation to figure out which one matches yours. That's where EVM comes in handy. Evaluating your project's performance using EVM can tell you how much of the difference between planned and actual expenditures is the result of under- or overspending and how much is the result of performing the project work faster or slower than planned. In the following sections, I describe some terms and formulas you need to know to use EVM.

Spelling out some important terms

The basic premise of EVM is that the *value* of a piece of work is equal to the amount of funds budgeted to complete it. As part of EVM, you use the following information to assess your schedule and cost performance throughout your project (see Figure 17-1 for an example):

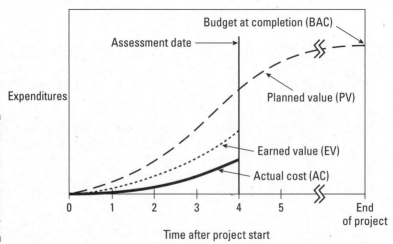

Figure 17-1: Monitoring planned value, earned value, and actual cost.

> ✓ **Planned value (PV):** The approved budget for the work scheduled to be completed by a specified date; also referred to as the *budgeted cost of work scheduled* (BCWS). The total PV of a task is equal to the task's *budget at completion* (BAC) — the total amount budgeted for the task.
>
> ✓ **Earned value (EV):** The approved budget for the work actually completed by the specified date; also referred to as the *budgeted cost of work performed* (BCWP).
>
> ✓ **Actual cost (AC):** The costs actually incurred for the work completed by the specified date; also referred to as the *actual cost of work performed* (ACWP).

To describe your project's schedule and cost performance with EVM, you use the following indicators:

> ✓ **Schedule variance (SV):** The difference between the amounts budgeted for the work you actually did and for the work you planned to do. The SV shows whether and by how much your work is ahead of or behind your approved schedule.
>
> ✓ **Cost variance (CV):** The difference between the amount budgeted and the amount actually spent for the work performed. The CV shows whether and by how much you're under or over your approved budget.
>
> ✓ **Schedule performance index (SPI):** The ratio of the approved budget for the work performed to the approved budget for the work planned. The SPI reflects the relative amount the project is ahead of or behind schedule, sometimes referred to as the project's *schedule efficiency.* You can use the SPI to date to project the schedule performance for the remainder of the task.
>
> ✓ **Cost performance index (CPI):** The ratio of the approved budget for work performed to what you actually spent for the work. The CPI reflects the relative value of work done compared to the amount paid for it, sometimes referred to as the project's *cost efficiency.* You can use the CPI to date to project the cost performance for the remainder of the task.

Figure 17-2 shows the key information in an EVM analysis. In this figure, the difference between *planned* and *actual* expenditures up to the date of the report is the result of both a schedule delay and cost savings. You can approximate the amount of time you're behind or ahead of the approved schedule by drawing a line from the intersection of the EV and assessment date lines parallel to the *x*-axis to the PV line. Doing so in Figure 17-2 suggests that the project being described by the graph is about one month behind schedule.

Defining the formulas of EVM performance descriptors

Schedule and cost variances and performance indicators are defined mathematically as follows:

Schedule variance (SV) = Earned value (EV) – Planned value (PV)

Cost variance (CV) = Earned value (EV) – Actual cost (AC)

Schedule performance index (SPI) = Earned value (EV) ÷ Planned value (PV)

Cost performance index (CPI) = Earned value (EV) ÷ Actual cost (AC)

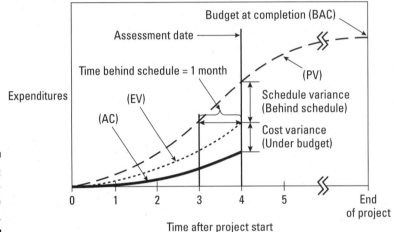

Figure 17-2:
EVM performance indicators.

Tables 17-1 and 17-2 illustrate that a positive variance, or a performance indicator greater than 1.0, indicates something desirable (that is, you're either under budget or ahead of schedule) and a negative variance, or a performance indicator less than 1.0, indicates something undesirable (you're either over budget or behind schedule).

Table 17-1	Interpretations of Cost and Schedule Variances		
Variance	**Negative**	**Zero**	**Positive**
Schedule	Behind schedule	On schedule	Ahead of schedule
Cost	Over budget	On budget	Under budget

Table 17-2	Interpretations of Cost and Schedule Performance Indicators		
Index	**Less than 1.0**	**1.0**	**Greater than 1.0**
Schedule	Behind schedule	On schedule	Ahead of schedule
Cost	Over budget	On budget	Under budget

Last but not least: Projecting total expenditures at completion

The final step when assessing task performance to date is to update what you expect your total expenditures will be upon task completion. Specifically, you want to determine the following:

- ✔ **Estimate at completion (EAC)**: Your estimate today of the total cost of the task
- ✔ **Estimate to complete (ETC):** Your estimate of the amount of funds required to complete all work still remaining to be done on the task

You can use the following two approaches to calculate the EAC:

- ✔ **Method 1: Assume that the cost performance for the remainder of the task will revert to what was originally budgeted.**

  EAC = Approved budget for the entire task – Cost variance for the work done to date on the task

  = Budget at completion (BAC) + Actual cost (AC) – Earned value (EV)

- ✔ **Method 2: Assume that the cost performance for the remainder of the task will be the same as what it has been for the work done to date.**

  EAC = Budget at completion (BAC) ÷ Cumulative cost performance index (CPI)

Whether you use Method 1 or Method 2 to calculate EAC, ETC is determined as follows:

ETC = Budget at completion (BAC) – Actual costs to date (AC)

Looking at a simple example

The terms and definitions associated with EVM (see the preceding section) are easier to understand when you consider an example. Suppose you're planning to conduct a series of telephone interviews. Your interview guide is ready, and each phone interview is independent of the others. You state the following in your project plan:

- ✔ Your project will last ten months.
- ✔ You will conduct 100 interviews each month.
- ✔ You will spend $300 to conduct each interview.
- ✔ Your total project budget is $300,000.

During your first month, you do the following:

- ✔ Conduct 75 interviews
- ✔ Spend a total of $15,000

Because you planned to conduct 100 interviews in the first month and you only conducted 75, you're behind schedule. But, because you planned to spend $300 per interview and you spent only $200 ($15,000 ÷ 75 interviews = $200 per interview), you're under budget. To calculate and then interpret the EVM information associated with this example, follow these steps:

1. **Determine the planned value (PV), earned value (EV), and actual costs (AC) for the month as follows:**

   PV = Amount budgeted for the 100 interviews you planned to conduct in the first month

   = 100 interviews × $300 per interview = $30,000

   EV = Amount budgeted for the 75 interviews you actually conducted in the first month

   = 75 interviews × $300 per interview = $22,500

   AC = Actual costs for the first month = $15,000

2. **Determine your schedule variance (SV), cost variance (CV), schedule performance index (SPI), and cost performance index (CPI) for the month as follows:**

   SV = EV − PV = $22,500 − $30,000 = −$7,500

   CV = EV − AC = $22,500 − $15,000 = $7,500

   SPI = EV ÷ PV = $22,500 ÷ $30,000 = 0.75

   CPI = EV ÷ AC = $22,500 ÷ $15,000 = 1.50

   The SPI and CPI make sense when you look at the actual numbers for the month. You originally planned to conduct 100 interviews in the first month, but you finished only 75, which means you accomplished 0.75 of the work scheduled for the month, just as the SPI indicates.

   You originally planned to spend $300 per interview, but in the first month you spent only $200 per interview ($15,000 in actual costs ÷ 75 interviews conducted). So, for the interviews conducted in the first month, you received a benefit equal to 1.50 times the money you spent, just as the CPI indicates.

Finally, you calculate your revised estimate at completion (EAC), as follows:

- ✔ **Method 1: Assume that the remaining work is performed at the originally budgeted rate.**

   EAC = BAC + AC − EV = $300,000 + $15,000 − $22,500 = $292,500

If you keep the $7,500 cost savings from the 75 interviews performed in the first month and do the remaining 925 interviews for the $300 per interview originally budgeted, you'll spend $292,500 to do the 1,000 interviews.

✔ **Method 2: Assume that the remaining work is performed at the same CPI as the work performed to date.**

EAC = BAC ÷ Cumulative CPI = $300,000 ÷ 1.50 = $200,000

In other words, if you continue to perform your interviews for $200 each rather than the planned $300 each, you'll spend two-thirds of your total planned budget to complete all 1,000 interviews.

Although you don't need a formal EVM analysis on a project this simple, in a project with 50 to 100 activities or more, an EVM analysis can help identify general trends in your project's cost and schedule performances. The earlier you identify such trends, the more easily you can address them when necessary.

Determining the reasons for observed variances

Positive or negative cost or schedule variances indicate that your project performance isn't going exactly as you planned. After you determine that a variance exists, you need to figure out what's causing it so you can take corrective actions (if the variance is negative) or continue what you've been doing (if the variance is positive).

Possible reasons for positive or negative cost variances include the following:

✔ Your project requires more or less work to complete a task than you originally planned.

✔ Work outside the approved scope was performed.

✔ The people performing the work are more or less productive than planned.

✔ The actual unit costs of labor or materials are more or less than planned.

✔ Resources used on other projects were incorrectly recorded to your project, or resources from your project were incorrectly recorded to other projects.

✔ Actual organization indirect rates are higher or lower than you originally planned. (See Chapter 7 for a discussion of indirect rates and how they can affect your project expenditures.)

Possible reasons for positive or negative schedule variances include the following:

✔ Work is running ahead of or behind schedule.

✔ The project requires more or less work than you originally planned.

✔ People performing the work are more or less productive than planned.

The How-To: Applying Earned Value Management to Your Project

If your project is fairly complex, you may consider using EVM to help control performance. By providing cost and schedule performance assessments of both the total project and its major parts, EVM allows you to identify the likely problem areas so you can take the most effective corrective actions.

The following example presents a more realistic illustration of how EVM can support insightful analysis of your project's performance.

Suppose the Acme Company has awarded a contract for the production of two specialized and complex corporate brochures to Copies 'R' Us. The contract calls for Copies 'R' Us to produce 500 copies of Brochure A and 1,000 copies of Brochure B. It further states that Copies 'R' Us will produce Brochure A at the rate of 100 per month and Brochure B at the rate of 250 per month. Production of Brochure A is to start on January 1, and production of Brochure B is to start on February 1.

Table 17-3 depicts the project plan.

Table 17-3	Plan for Copies 'R' Us to Produce Brochures A and B				
Activity	**Start**	**End**	**Elapsed Time**	**Number of Copies**	**Total Cost**
Brochure A	Jan 1	May 31	5 months	500	$100,000
Brochure B	Feb 1	May 31	4 months	1,000	$100,000
Total					$200,000

A quick glance reveals that you budgeted $200 a copy for Brochure A ($100,000 ÷ 500 copies) and $100 a copy for Brochure B ($100,000 ÷ 1,000 copies).

Suppose it's the end of March, and you're three months into the project. Table 17-4 presents what has happened as of March 31.

Table 17-4		Project Status as of March 31		
Activity	*Start*	*Elapsed Time*	*Number of Copies Produced*	*Total Cost*
Brochure A	Jan 1	3 months	150	$45,000
Brochure B	Feb 1	2 months	600	$30,000
Total				$75,000

Your job is to figure out your schedule and cost performances to date and to update your forecast of the total amount you'll spend for both brochures. Follow these steps:

1. **Determine the planned value (PV), earned value (EV), and actual cost (AC) for Brochure A through March 31 as follows:**

   PV = $200 per brochure × 100 brochures per month × 3 months = $60,000

   EV = $200 per brochure × 150 brochures = $30,000

   AC = $45,000

2. **Determine the schedule variance (SV), cost variance (CV), schedule performance index (SPI), and cost performance index (CPI) for the production of Brochure A through March 31 as follows:**

   SV = EV – PV = $30,000 – $60,000 = –$30,000

   CV = EV – AC = $30,000 – $45,000 = –$15,000

   SPI = EV ÷ PV = $30,000 ÷ $60,000 = 0.50

   CPI = EV ÷ AC = $30,000 ÷ $45,000 = 0.67

   Your analysis reveals that you produced only half of the copies of Brochure A you thought you would and that each brochure cost you 1.5 times the amount you had planned to spend (1 ÷ CPI = 1 ÷ 0.67 = 1.5; also, actual cost per brochure ÷ planned cost per brochure = [$45,000 expended ÷ 150 brochures produced] ÷ $200 per brochure = 300 ÷ 200 = 1.5).

3. **Determine the planned value (PV), earned value (EV), and actual cost (AC) for Brochure B through March 31 as follows:**

   PV = $100 per brochure × 250 brochures per month × 2 months = $50,000

   EV = $100 per brochure × 600 brochures = $60,000

   AC = $30,000

4. **Determine the schedule variance (SV), cost variance (CV), schedule performance index (SPI), and cost performance index (CPI) for the production of Brochure B through March 31 as follows:**

SV $= \text{EV} - \text{PV} = \$60{,}000 - \$50{,}000 = \$10{,}000$

CV $= \text{EV} - \text{AC} = \$60{,}000 - \$30{,}000 = \$30{,}000$

SPI $= \text{EV} \div \text{PV} = \$60{,}000 \div \$50{,}000 = 1.20$

CPI $= \text{EV} \div \text{AC} = \$60{,}000 \div \$30{,}000 = 2.00$

Your analysis reveals that production of Brochure B is 20 percent ahead of schedule and 50 percent under budget ($1 \div \text{CPI} = 1 \div 2 = 0.5$; also, [$\$30{,}000$ expended $\div 600$ brochures produced] $\div \$100$ per brochure $= 50 \div 100 = 0.5$).

5. **Forecast the estimate at completion (EAC) for Brochure A.**

   Method 1: Assume the remaining work is performed at the originally budgeted rate.

   EAC $= \text{BAC} + \text{AC} - \text{EV} = \$100{,}000 + \$45{,}000 - \$30{,}000 = \$115{,}000$

   Method 2: Assume the remaining work is performed at the same CPI as the work performed to date.

   EAC $= \text{BAC} \div \text{Cumulative CPI} = \$100{,}000 \div 0.67 = \$150{,}000$

   In other words, if the remaining 350 copies of Brochure A are produced for the originally planned cost of $200 per copy, the total cost to produce the entire 500 copies will be $115,000. If the remaining 350 copies of Brochure A are produced for the same $300 per copy cost as the first 150, the total cost to produce the entire 600 will be $150,000.

6. **Forecast the estimate at completion (EAC) for Brochure B.**

   Method 1: Assume the remaining work is performed at the originally budgeted rate.

   EAC $= \text{BAC} + \text{AC} - \text{EV} = \$100{,}000 + \$30{,}000 - \$60{,}000 = \$70{,}000$

   Method 2: Assume the remaining work is performed at the same CPI as the work performed to date.

   EAC $= \text{BAC} \div \text{Cumulative CPI} = \$100{,}000 \div 2.00 = \$50{,}000$

   In other words, if the remaining 400 copies of Brochure B are produced for the originally planned cost of $100 per copy, the total cost to produce the entire 1,000 copies will be $70,000. If the remaining 400 copies of Brochure B are produced for the same $50 per copy cost as the first 150, the total cost to produce the entire 1,000 will be $50,000.

7. **Determine the overall status of your project by adding together the schedule variances (SV), the cost variances (CV), and the updated estimates at completion (EAC) for Brochures A and B.**

Project SV = –$30,000 + $10,000 = –$20,000

Project CV = –$15,000 + $30,000 = $15,000

Method 1: Assume the remaining work is performed at the originally budgeted rate.

EAC = $115,000 + $70,000 = $185,000

Method 2: Assume the remaining work is performed at the same CPI as the work performed to date.

EAC for the project = $150,000 + $50,000 = $200,000

Table 17-5 summarizes this information.

Table 17-5	Performance Analysis Summary		
	Brochure A	*Brochure B*	*Combined*
PV	$60,000	$50,000	N/A
EV	$30,000	$60,000	N/A
AC	$45,000	$30,000	$75,000
SV	–$30,000	$10,000	–$20,000
CV	–$15,000	$30,000	$15,000
SPI	0.50	1.20	N/A
CPI	0.67	2.00	N/A
EAC*	$115,000	$70,000	$185,000
EAC**	$150,000	$50,000	$200,000

*Method 1: Remaining work performed at originally budgeted rate
**Method 2: Remaining work performed at same CPI as work performed to date

If project production rates and costs remain the same until all the required brochures are produced (this is the Method 2 used to develop the EACs):

✔ **You'll finish on budget.** Table 17-5 shows that EAC for the project will be $200,000, the amount originally budgeted for the whole project.

✔ **You'll finish five months late.** Because Brochure A is being produced at only half the anticipated rate, finishing all of them will take twice the time of five months that was originally planned.

Determining a Task's Earned Value

The key to a meaningful EVM analysis lies in the accuracy of your estimates of EV. To determine EV, you must estimate

✔ How much of a task you've completed to date

✔ How much of the task's total budget you planned to spend for the amount of work you've performed

If you assume that the amount of a task's total budget that should be spent to complete a portion of the task is directly proportional to the amount of the task completed, you should spend 60 percent of the total task budget to complete 60 percent of the task.

For tasks with separate components, like printing brochures or conducting telephone surveys, determining how much of a task you've completed is straightforward. However, if your task entails an integrated work or thought process with no easily divisible parts (such as designing the brochure), the best you can do is make an educated guess.

To estimate the EV in your project, you can use one of the three following approaches (Figure 17-3 illustrates these commonly used approaches in different situations):

✔ **Percent-complete method:** EV is the product of the fraction representing the amount of an activity that has been completed and the total budget for the activity.

This method is potentially the most accurate if you correctly determine the fraction of the activity you have completed. However, because that estimate depends on your subjective judgment, this approach is also most vulnerable to errors or purposeful manipulation.

✔ **Milestone method:** EV is zero until you complete the activity, and it's 100 percent of the total activity budget after you complete it.

The milestone method is the most conservative and the least accurate. You expect to spend some money while you're working on the task. However, this method doesn't allow you to declare EV greater than $0 until you've completed the entire activity. Therefore, you'll always appear over budget while you perform the activity.

✔ **50/50 method:** EV is zero before you start the activity, 50 percent of the total activity budget after you start it, and 100 percent of the activity budget after you finish the activity.

The 50/50 method is a closer approximation to reality than the milestone method because you can declare an EV greater than $0 while you perform the task. However, this approximation can inadvertently mask overspending.

For example, suppose you've spent $4,000 to complete 30 percent of a task with a $10,000 budget. Arguably, you should've spent about 30 percent of the total task budget, or $3,000, to complete 30 percent of the work on the task, which means you're $1,000 *over* budget. However, using the 50/50 method, you estimate the EV to be $5,000 (50 percent of the total budget for the task), which makes it appear that you're $1,000 *under* budget.

As you can see, the milestone method and 50/50 method allow you to approximate EV without estimating the portion of a task that you've completed. Choosing which of the three methods to use for your project requires that you weigh the potential for accuracy against the possibility of subjective data resulting in misleading conclusions.

	Activity				Earned Value		
Work Breakdown Structure Code	**Budgeted Cost at Completion**				**% Complete**	**50/50**	**Milestone**
1.2.1	$10,000				$10,000	$10,000	$10,000
1.2.2	$20,000		75% done		$15,000	$10,000	$0
1.2.3	$30,000		20% done		$6,000	$15,000	$0
					$31,000	$35,000	$10,000

Months after project start

Figure 17-3: Three ways to define earned value.

Figure 17-3 compares the accuracy of the three different methods for a simple example. Task 1.2 has three subtasks: 1.2.1, 1.2.2, and 1.2.3. For this illustration, assume the status of each subtask is as follows:

- Subtask 1.2.1 is complete.
- Subtask 1.2.2 is 75 percent complete.
- Subtask 1.2.3 is 20 percent complete.

The EV of Task 1.2 is the sum of the EVs for each of the three subtasks that comprise Task 1.2. According to the percent-complete method, the actual EV should be $31,000. (Remember, you can use this method only if you can *accurately* estimate the percentage of the entire task that you've completed.) According to the milestone method, the actual EV is $10,000, and, according to the 50/50 method, it's $35,000.

When you use either the 50/50 method or the milestone method, improve the accuracy of your EV estimates by defining your lowest-level activities to be relatively short, usually completed in two weeks or less (see Chapter 4 on Work Breakdown Structures). When you determine activity status for your progress assessments, most activities will not have started or will be finished, thereby increasing the accuracy of your EV estimates.

Relating This Chapter to the PMP Exam and PMBOK 4

Table 17-6 notes topics in this chapter that may be addressed on the Project Management Professional (PMP) certification exam and that are also included in *A Guide to the Project Management Body of Knowledge,* 4th Edition (*PMBOK 4*).

Table 17-6	Chapter 17 Topics in Relation to the PMP Exam and *PMBOK 4*	
Topic	**Location in PMBOK 4**	**Comments**
Definitions of EVM concepts and schedule and cost performance indicators (see the section "Understanding EVM terms and formulas")	7.3.2.1. Earned Value Management	The terms and definitions in this book are the same as those used in *PMBOK 4*.
Updating forecasts of total task expenditures (see the section "Understanding EVM terms and formulas")	7.3.2.2. Forecasting	The terms and approaches in this book are the same as those used in *PMBOK 4*.

Part VI
The Part of Tens

The 5th Wave   By Rich Tennant

In this part . . .

*H*aving hundreds of pages of detailed information to guide you through your project's ups and downs is nice. However, when a crisis hits, you may want to reference a few handy tips to head off a potential disaster.

Just like every *For Dummies* book, this part gives you tidbits of interesting information that you can access as needed. I share ten tips for how to plan a project and ten tips for how to be a better project manager.

And don't stop there! This part also includes a helpful appendix. In it, I present the usual order for the planning and control activities that I discuss throughout this book.

Chapter 18

Ten Questions to Ask Yourself as You Plan Your Project

When you begin a project, you always feel the pressure to jump in and start working immediately to meet the aggressive time schedules. Although you're not exactly sure of where to start, you know you have the greatest chance of success if you plan out your project before you start the actual work. Answer the ten questions in this chapter to be sure you've completely identified all the work your project will require.

What's the Purpose of Your Project?

An accurate appreciation of your project's purpose can lead to better plans, a greater sense of team member commitment, and improved performance. As soon as you're assigned to your project, get a clear and complete picture of its significance. You can do so by determining the following:

- ✔ What situation(s) led to your project?
- ✔ Who had the original idea?
- ✔ Who else hopes to benefit from it?
- ✔ What would happen if your project weren't done?

See Chapters 2 and 3 for more details about clarifying a project's purpose.

Whom Do You Need to Involve?

Knowing early whom you need to involve allows you to plan for their participation at the appropriate stages in your project. Involving these people in a timely manner ensures that their input will be available when it's needed and lets them know you value and respect their contributions.

As you determine who may play a role in your project's success, categorize them as follows:

- **Drivers:** People looking for your project's results
- **Supporters:** People who can help your project succeed
- **Observers:** People interested in your project

After you have this comprehensive list, decide whom you need to involve and when and how you want to involve them. (See Chapters 3, 9, and 10 for more information on identifying project audiences.)

What Results Will You Produce?

Specify all the results you expect your project to achieve. Be sure that you clearly describe each product, service, or impact; make the outcomes measurable and include performance targets. Confirm that your project's drivers believe these outcomes meet their needs and expectations (see Chapter 3 for more about project drivers). See Chapter 2 for more discussion about framing your project objectives.

What Constraints Must You Satisfy?

Identify all information, processes, and guidelines that may restrict your project activities and your performance. When you know your constraints, you can plan to minimize their effects on your project. Distinguish between the following:

- **Limitations:** Restrictions that people outside your project team set
- **Needs:** Restrictions that you and your project's team members establish

Chapter 2 has more about project constraints and ways to overcome them.

What Assumptions Are You Making?

As soon as you begin thinking about your project, document all assumptions you make about it — after all, each of those assumptions can lead to one or more project risks that you may choose to plan for in advance. Continue adding to your list of assumptions as you develop the different parts of your project plan. Update your plans whenever an assumption changes or you find out its actual value. See Chapter 2 for further details about project assumptions and Chapter 8 for a lot more information about project risks.

What Work Has to Be Done?

Identify all the activities required to produce your project's deliverables so that you can assign responsibilities for them, develop schedules, estimate resource needs, give specific tasks to team members, and monitor your project's performance. For each activity, specify the following:

- **The work to be done:** The processes and steps that each activity entails

- **Inputs:** All people, facilities, equipment, supplies, raw materials, funds, and information necessary to perform each activity

- **Results you expect:** Products, services, situations, or other deliverables that you expect each activity to produce

- **Interdependencies and relationships:** Activities that you must complete before you can start the next one; activities you can start after you've completed the current one

- **Durations:** The number of work periods required to perform each activity

See Chapter 4 for information on describing project work.

When Does Each Activity Start and End?

Develop a detailed schedule with clearly defined activities and frequent intermediate milestones. Having this information on hand allows you to give team members precise guidance on when to perform their assignments. This information also supports your ongoing monitoring and control of work in progress. Take the following into account when you create your schedule:

- **Duration:** The number of work periods required to perform each individual activity

- **Interdependencies:** What you must finish before you can begin your activity

- **Resource availability:** When you need particular resources and when they're available

See Chapter 5 for more information on how to develop a project schedule.

Who Will Perform the Project Work?

Knowing who will perform each task and how much effort they'll have to devote allows you to plan for their availability and more accurately estimate the overall project budget. Specify the following information for all people who need to work on your project:

- Their names, position descriptions or titles, and the skills and knowledge they need to do the assignment

- The specific roles each person will have on an activity when more than one person will work on the same activity, as well as how they can coordinate their efforts

- The level of effort each person has to invest

- The exact time when people will do their work if they will work less than full time on an activity

Consult with the people who'll perform the project tasks to develop this information. See Chapter 6 for help with estimating personnel requirements.

What Other Resources Do You Need?

Identify all equipment, facilities, services, supplies, and funds that you need to perform your project work. Specify how much of each resource you need and when. Chapter 7 has more on how to identify nonpersonnel resources.

What Can Go Wrong?

Identify those parts of your project that may not go according to plan. Decide which risks pose the greatest dangers to your project's success, and develop plans to minimize their negative effects. See Chapter 8 for information on how to address project risks.

Chapter 19

Ten Tips for Being a Better Project Manager

. . . .

In This Chapter

▶ Being proactive and looking at the big picture

▶ Encouraging others and treating them with respect

▶ Communicating effectively and acknowledging other people's accomplishments

. . . .

Successful project management depends not only on what you do, but also on how you do it. Your attitudes and behaviors toward people affect how they respond to you. If I could, I'd place a large *Tip* icon on this entire chapter because it offers ten tips that can help you successfully win people's support. So why not give it a little of your attention?

Be a "Why" Person

Look for the reasons behind requests and actions. Understanding *why* helps you make sure you respond appropriately to team members, upper managers, and all other project audiences (which, in turn, increases people's motivation and buy in). First, look to understand the reasons behind other people's requests and actions; then share your findings with other people. (Check out Chapter 2 to find out more about how you can be a "why" person.)

Be a "Can Do" Person

Look at all problems as challenges, and do everything you can to find ways to overcome them. Be creative, flexible, and tenacious. Keep working at the problem until you solve it. (Flip to Chapters 2, 4, 5, and 12 for more on how to be a tenacious problem solver.)

Think about the Big Picture

Keep events in perspective. Understand where you want to go and how your plan will get you there. Recognize the effect your actions have on current and future efforts. Share your vision with other people. (Flip to Chapters 2 and 14 for more on how you can keep your project elements in perspective.)

Think in Detail

Be thorough. If you don't think through your project's issues, who will? The more clearly you describe your intended results, the more easily people can recognize the benefits associated with your project. And the more clearly you define your intended work, the more often people will ask important and insightful questions — *and* believe that they can perform the work success-fully. Clarity leads to increased personal motivation and reduced chances of mistakes. (Check out Chapters 2 and 4 for tips on thinking in detail.)

Assume Cautiously

Take the time to find out the facts; use assumptions only as a last resort. With every assumption comes a risk that you're wrong. The fewer assumptions you make, the more confidence you can have in your plan. (Check out Chapter 2 for more information on assumptions and Chapter 8 for info on how to deal with risks and uncertainty.)

View People as Allies, Not Adversaries

Focus on common goals, not individual agendas. Making people feel comfortable encourages brainstorming, creative thinking, and the willingness to try new ideas — all of which are essential to managing a successful project. But viewing and treating people as adversaries can put them on the defensive and encourage them to become enemies. (Refer to Chapters 3 and 14, where I tell you how to get people on your side.)

Say What You Mean, and Mean What You Say

Communicate clearly. Be specific by letting people know exactly what you mean. Tell them what you want them to know, what you want them to do, and what you'll do for them. Don't leave these details up to their imaginations. You may think that being vague gives you more leeway, but, in reality, being vague just increases the chances for misunderstandings and mistakes. (Check out Chapter 13 for ways to communicate more clearly.)

Respect Other People

Focus on people's strengths rather than their weaknesses. In each person on your team, find a quality that you can respect. People work harder and enjoy their work more when they're around others who appreciate them and their efforts. (See Chapter 14 for more helpful tidbits on respecting and encouraging other people.)

Acknowledge Good Performance

Take a moment to acknowledge good performance. When someone does something good, tell the person, tell the person's boss, tell other team members, and tell the person's peers that you appreciate the effort and its results. Recognizing good performance confirms to a person the accuracy and value of his work; your praise tells a person that you appreciate his efforts, which motivates him to work with you and other team members on future projects.

When acknowledging a person's performance, mention the quality of the results he accomplished as well as the effort he invested. Be specific — tell the person exactly what he did or produced that you appreciate. Be sure to provide your feedback promptly — don't wait weeks or months before recognizing someone for his hard work. (See Chapter 14 for more about acknowledging good performance.)

Be a Manager and a Leader

Attend to people as well as to information, processes, and systems. Create and share your vision and excitement with your team members, but don't forget to share a sense of order and efficiency, too. Encourage people to strive for outstanding results, and provide the guidance and support to help them achieve those results. (See Chapter 14 for more information about management and leadership.)

Appendix

Combining the Techniques into Smooth-Flowing Processes

You'll use the tools and techniques in this book many times during any given project — as you hammer out your initial plan, monitor work in progress and its results, and continue to tweak the details as necessary. Even though you can't avoid surprises or changes as your project unfolds, you can provide logical order for your project's planning and its control activities. This sense of order discourages bad surprises (and their faithful companions — change and redirection). I illustrate this order in this appendix.

Preparing Your Project Plan

Figure A-1 depicts the steps in project planning and the parts of the plan that you produce along the way.

When you receive a project assignment, take the following steps to develop a plan for your project:

1. **Clarify the reasons for the project and the desired results.**

   To complete this step, you need to do the following two important activities:

   - Identify the audiences who will have a say in your project.

   - Get info from all the audiences and written sources about expectations.

   See Chapter 2 for more on how to identify your project's audiences and the sources you need to check to find out about the reasons and expectations for your project.

   Perform these two activities interactively. In other words, use the initial statement of your assignment to suggest additional audiences and consult with those audiences to identify more issues to address.

The outcomes from these activities are your Scope Statement and your audience list. (See Chapter 2 for more on preparing a Scope Statement and Chapter 3 for putting together an audience list.)

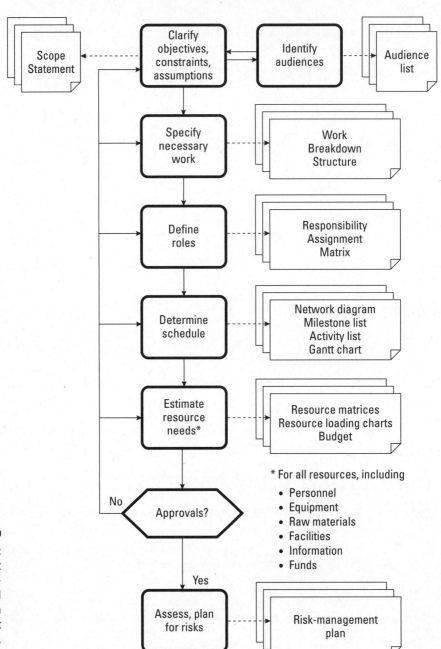

Figure A-1: Flowchart of the activities and information in a project plan.

2. **After you know all the results and deliverables your project is supposed to produce, identify the work required to accomplish them.**

   Record this information in a Work Breakdown Structure (WBS). (See Chapter 4 for information on how to prepare a WBS.)

3. **Consider the WBS and the audience list together to decide on each audience's roles and responsibilities for each project activity.**

   Display this information in a Responsibility Assignment Matrix, also known as a RAM. (See Chapter 10 for a discussion on preparing this matrix.)

4. **Create and analyze a network diagram of the activities from the WBS to develop a schedule that meets your project drivers' requirements and that your project supporters believe is possible.**

   Display your final schedule in a milestone list, an activity list, or a Gantt chart. (See Chapter 5 for how to prepare and display a project schedule.)

5. **Estimate your resource needs, and display them in one or more Resources Matrices and Resources Loading Charts and in your project budget.** After you specify the particular resources you need and when you need them and identify people who may meet those needs, revise your network diagram and schedule to reflect any differences between the capabilities and availability of the people you requested and those being offered to you. Negotiate for different people, if necessary, and modify your schedule accordingly until you have a schedule and a list of resource assignments that you believe will meet your project's needs. See Chapters 6 and 7 for preparing and displaying project resource needs.

6. **Identify, analyze, and plan for any significant project risks.** See Chapter 8 for suggestions on dealing with project risks.

Continue working on each step in this initial process until all project drivers and supporters agree with and support your results.

Controlling Your Project during Performance

Figure A-2 illustrates the steps you routinely perform to monitor and control your project throughout its performance.

To monitor and control your project throughout its life cycle, follow these steps:

1. **At the start of each performance period, reconfirm that the necessary people and resources are available and scheduled in accordance with your current project plan (see Chapter 12 for details).**

2. **At the end of each performance period, do the following:**

   • **Gather activity start and end dates, milestone dates, resource expenditures, and the results of quality assessments.**

   • **Compare the actual results with the planned results, identify any issues or problems, and take any necessary corrective actions.**

3. **Report your progress for the period to your project audiences.**

   See Chapters 12 and 13 for information on tracking, assessing, and reporting project performance.

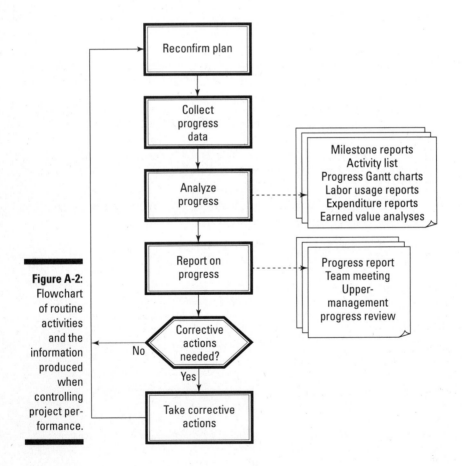

Figure A-2:
Flowchart of routine activities and the information produced when controlling project per-formance.

Index

● ●

• *E* •

• *S* •

Business/Accounting & Bookkeeping

Bookkeeping For Dummies
978-0-7645-9848-7

eBay Business
All-in-One For Dummies,
2nd Edition
978-0-470-38536-4

Job Interviews
For Dummies,
3rd Edition
978-0-470-17748-8

Resumes For Dummies,
5th Edition
978-0-470-08037-5

Stock Investing
For Dummies,
3rd Edition
978-0-470-40114-9

Successful Time
Management
For Dummies
978-0-470-29034-7

Computer Hardware

BlackBerry For Dummies,
3rd Edition
978-0-470-45762-7

Computers For Seniors
For Dummies
978-0-470-24055-7

iPhone For Dummies,
2nd Edition
978-0-470-42342-4

Laptops For Dummies,
3rd Edition
978-0-470-27759-1

Macs For Dummies,
10th Edition
978-0-470-27817-8

Cooking & Entertaining

Cooking Basics
For Dummies,
3rd Edition
978-0-7645-7206-7

Wine For Dummies,
4th Edition
978-0-470-04579-4

Diet & Nutrition

Dieting For Dummies,
2nd Edition
978-0-7645-4149-0

Nutrition For Dummies,
4th Edition
978-0-471-79868-2

Weight Training
For Dummies,
3rd Edition
978-0-471-76845-6

Digital Photography

Digital Photography
For Dummies,
6th Edition
978-0-470-25074-7

Photoshop Elements 7
For Dummies
978-0-470-39700-8

Gardening

Gardening Basics
For Dummies
978-0-470-03749-2

Organic Gardening
For Dummies,
2nd Edition
978-0-470-43067-5

Green/Sustainable

Green Building
& Remodeling
For Dummies
978-0-470-17559-0

Green Cleaning
For Dummies
978-0-470-39106-8

Green IT For Dummies
978-0-470-38688-0

Health

Diabetes For Dummies,
3rd Edition
978-0-470-27086-8

Food Allergies
For Dummies
978-0-470-09584-3

Living Gluten-Free
For Dummies
978-0-471-77383-2

Hobbies/General

Chess For Dummies,
2nd Edition
978-0-7645-8404-6

Drawing For Dummies
978-0-7645-5476-6

Knitting For Dummies,
2nd Edition
978-0-470-28747-7

Organizing For Dummies
978-0-7645-5300-4

SuDoku For Dummies
978-0-470-01892-7

Home Improvement

Energy Efficient Homes
For Dummies
978-0-470-37602-7

Home Theater
For Dummies,
3rd Edition
978-0-470-41189-6

Living the Country Lifestyle
All-in-One For Dummies
978-0-470-43061-3

Solar Power Your Home
For Dummies
978-0-470-17569-9

Internet
Blogging For Dummies,
2nd Edition
978-0-470-23017-6

eBay For Dummies,
6th Edition
978-0-470-49741-8

Facebook For Dummies
978-0-470-26273-3

Google Blogger
For Dummies
978-0-470-40742-4

Web Marketing
For Dummies,
2nd Edition
978-0-470-37181-7

WordPress For Dummies,
2nd Edition
978-0-470-40296-2

Language & Foreign Language
French For Dummies
978-0-7645-5193-2

Italian Phrases
For Dummies
978-0-7645-7203-6

Spanish For Dummies
978-0-7645-5194-9

Spanish For Dummies,
Audio Set
978-0-470-09585-0

Macintosh
Mac OS X Snow Leopard
For Dummies
978-0-470-43543-4

Math & Science
Algebra I For Dummies,
2nd Edition
978-0-470-55964-2

Biology For Dummies
978-0-7645-5326-4

Calculus For Dummies
978-0-7645-2498-1

Chemistry For Dummies
978-0-7645-5430-8

Microsoft Office
Excel 2007 For Dummies
978-0-470-03737-9

Office 2007 All-in-One
Desk Reference
For Dummies
978-0-471-78279-7

Music
Guitar For Dummies,
2nd Edition
978-0-7645-9904-0

iPod & iTunes
For Dummies,
6th Edition
978-0-470-39062-7

Piano Exercises
For Dummies
978-0-470-38765-8

Parenting & Education
Parenting For Dummies,
2nd Edition
978-0-7645-5418-6

Type 1 Diabetes
For Dummies
978-0-470-17811-9

Pets
Cats For Dummies,
2nd Edition
978-0-7645-5275-5

Dog Training For Dummies,
2nd Edition
978-0-7645-8418-3

Puppies For Dummies,
2nd Edition
978-0-470-03717-1

Religion & Inspiration
The Bible For Dummies
978-0-7645-5296-0

Catholicism For Dummies
978-0-7645-5391-2

Women in the Bible
For Dummies
978-0-7645-8475-6

Self-Help & Relationship
Anger Management
For Dummies
978-0-470-03715-7

Overcoming Anxiety
For Dummies
978-0-7645-5447-6

Sports
Baseball For Dummies,
3rd Edition
978-0-7645-7537-2

Basketball For Dummies,
2nd Edition
978-0-7645-5248-9

Golf For Dummies,
3rd Edition
978-0-471-76871-5

Web Development
Web Design All-in-One
For Dummies
978-0-470-41796-6

Windows Vista
Windows Vista
For Dummies
978-0-471-75421-3

DUMMIES.COM®

How-to?
How Easy.

From hooking up a modem to cooking up a casserole, knitting a scarf to navigating an iPod, you can trust Dummies.com to show you how to get things done the easy way.

Visit us at Dummies.com

Go to www.Dummies.com

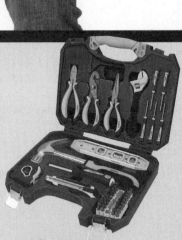